RESEARCH METHODS FOR MANAGERS:
A Skill-building Approach

Wiley Series in Management

RESEARCH METHODS FOR MANAGERS:
A Skill-building Approach

Uma Sekaran

JOHN WILEY & SONS

New York   Chichester   Brisbane   Toronto   Singapore

Library of Congress Cataloging in Publication Data:

Sekaran, Uma.
　Research methods for managers.

　(Wiley series in management, ISSN 0271-6046)
　Includes indexes.
　1. Management research.　2. Organizational research.
3. Research, Industrial—Management.　I. Title.
II. Series

HD30.4.S44　1984　　658.5'6　　83-6916
ISBN 0-471-87099-4

Printed in the United States of America

10 9 8 7

To Kiren R. Sekar
with love

PREFACE

The word research seems to evoke different ideas, thoughts, and feelings in different people. To some it connotes creativity and innovation, to others it means simple problem solving and knowledge gathering, and to yet others it is much ado about something we cannot do perfectly in the organizational world. Whichever view we take, we still find ourselves conducting research, utilizing the information generated by research, or critiquing the process of research in our professional lives. Most of the people who do research seem fascinated by the challenges it offers and are inescapably drawn to it because of the sheer joy of discovery that it provides. The intrinsic and extrinsic rewards derived from finding something or solving a complex problem seem to be worth all the effort and frustrations that people sometimes go through in the process of doing research.

As organizations become more complex, managers find they are more often forced to resort to research efforts that enable them to solve the tough problems they encounter from time to time. Hence, the managers of today definitely need to know about research and how it is done. Although the manager need not necessarily become an expert researcher, he has to acquire reasonable knowledge about research and some practical experience in how to do it, in order to understand more fully many of the day-to-day problems on the job, and to comprehend research reports submitted to the organization and utilize them intelligently. Knowledge of research also helps the manager assimilate the information in academic and practitioner-oriented journals more easily and with discrimination. This ability to discriminate and judiciously consider the applicability of published research findings to one's own work setting is probably one of the most important skills that the manager needs to acquire if she is interested in implementing changes in the organizational system with a view to solving problems, and making the system more efficient or effective or both. The need for effectiveness, efficiency, and problem solving is pervasive regardless of whether one happens to be a manager in charge of human resources, marketing, finance, accounting, or any other functional area.

This book sets out to educate prospective and practicing managers in "managing" research in organizations—a function that is increasingly becoming a part of the professional manager's role today. By reading and understanding the contents of this book, organized in eight manageable, practically oriented units, and doing the recommended exercises and projects, one can be reasonably sure of gaining competency in understanding and assimilating research and how to distinguish good from bad research work. The exercises at the end of Units 3 and 5 and Points to Ponder at the end of each unit should provide stimulation and generate healthy class discussions.

The class discussions are also likely to include several examples and exercises covering various aspects of business as suggested in the manual for instructors.

The book was written to serve the needs of students who seek a sense of competence in being able to carry out small research projects in organizations where they are already working or will be working as future managers. The book not only discusses managerial situations where research would be needed, but illustrates through computer outputs how data can be analyzed and interpreted to answer several types of research questions. An example of a student research report is included in Unit 8. The book's uniqueness is that it offers the students both the requisite theoretical knowledge and basic practical skills to do research. Students who have taken the course represented here have frequently expressed their satisfaction even in terms of its utility in helping them to write logical and scholarly papers for other management courses. For the benefit of students who want to acquire more knowledge in specific topic areas, a supplemental list of readings, arranged topically, is given at the end of each unit.

This book has been shaped by the many inputs from the students, by ideas from Dr. Sarah Andrew and Dr. Diane Graham—who read the very first draft of the eight units—and from the final reviewers, Professors Marla Scafe and James G. Hunt. Dr. Donald R. Cooper's useful comments on the first three units of the book are also acknowledged. I owe a debt of gratitude to Professor James C. Taylor, who guided me through the research process steps while I was his student. I also thank the staff of John Wiley and Sons for their help, and my special recognition and thanks go to the editor, Mr. Rick Leyh, for his perennial enthusiasm and pleasantness.

I wish you as much enjoyment in reading the book as I had in writing it.

Uma Sekaran

CONTENTS

UNIT 1
INTRODUCTION TO RESEARCH

ISSUES DISCUSSED

Definition of Research

Applied and Basic Research

Scientific Investigation and the Hallmarks of Science
- Purposiveness and Rigor
- Testability
- Replicability
- Accuracy and Precision
- Objectivity
- Generalizability
- Parsimony

Limitations to Scientific Research in Management

The Building Blocks of Science and the Hypothetico-Deductive Method of Research

The Seven Steps of the Hypothetico-Deductive Method
- Observation
- Preliminary Information Gathering
- Theory Formulation
- Hypothesizing
- Further Scientific Data Collection
- Data Analysis
- Deduction

Managers and Research
- Why Managers Should Know about Research
- The Manager-Researcher Relationship
- Internal versus External Researchers and Consultants

UNIT OBJECTIVES

After completing Unit 1 you should be able to:

1. Describe what research is and how it is defined.
2. Distinguish between applied and basic research, giving examples and discussing why they would fall into one of the categories.
3. Explain what is meant by scientific investigation, giving examples of

nonscientific and scientific investigations, and fully explain the six hallmarks of science.

4. Briefly explain why research in the organizational behavior and management areas cannot be completely scientific.

5. Briefly explain the building blocks of science.

6. Discuss the seven steps in the hypothetico-deductive method, using an example of your own.

7. Explain why managers should know about research.

8. Explain what managers should and should not do in order to interact most effectively with researchers.

9. Identify and fully discuss specific situations in which a manager would be better off using an internal research team, and when an external research team would be more advisable, giving reasons for the decisions.

10. Discuss what research means to you after reading Unit 1, and how you might use the research knowledge as a manager.

The twenty-five-story building housing the Gigantic Multipurpose Company, overlooking the banks of the Ganges River, is bristling with activity. Let us take a look at the events occurring in four specific offices of the building on the fifth, eleventh, sixteenth, and twenty-fifth floors.

The fifth-floor manager in charge of one of the departments seems puzzled, vexed, and somewhat angry. He had been to a management seminar in Los Angeles a year ago, where an "expert" told the attendees that one way of ensuring employee involvement and commitment is by enriching their work. With all good intentions, the manager redesigned the jobs, introducing more variety, challenge, feedback, and "whole" jobs rather than fragmented pieces of work, and within three months of the changes, employee absenteeism has increased tenfold!

In the eleventh-floor office of Ms. Sandy Raj, the purchasing manager, the women managers are holding a caucus. The discussion is about a news item in the morning's paper that women at all levels were being paid at least 40 percent less than males for performing identical jobs and having the same abilities and skills.

The monthly meeting sponsored by the company for executives' wives is in progress in the conference room on the sixteenth floor. Several housewives who are attending the meeting are smiling bemusedly when they hear the speaker mention that members of dual-career families have to rethink their priorities and plan their lives better, because the divorce rate in dual-career families is on the increase. Several of the attendee housewives have been contemplating divorce and seeing marriage counselors.

The president of Gigantic, on the twenty-fifth floor, is vehemently refuting the statement made by the organizational consultant that the organizations of today are to blame for the increasing number of alcoholics in our society.

What is your reaction to the four events just described? If the fifth-floor manager was told by an expert that job enrichment would increase employee involvement and commitment, why is absenteeism on the increase? Is it true that women are actually paid at least 40 percent less than men for equal jobs when they have equal skills and abilities? Is the divorce rate really greater in dual-career families than in single-career families? Are today's organizations really responsible for the increase in alcoholism in the country?

How do we answer these questions? We really cannot do so until and unless we probe more deeply into these issues, obtain more concrete facts, and analyze the relevant data to see what they tell us about the problem situations and their rectification. In other words, if absenteeism, unjust reward systems, divorce, and alcoholism are problems of concern to us, we need to research these issues in order to find viable answers to the problems.

This book discusses research and how it can be conducted to obtain valid information that would help in solving management problems in organizational settings. We begin by describing and defining research.

WHAT IS RESEARCH?

Research can be described as a systematic and organized effort to investigate a specific problem that needs a solution. It is a series of steps designed and followed, with the goal of finding answers to the issues that are of concern to us in the work environment. This means that the first step in research is to know where the problem areas are in the organization, and to identify as clearly and specifically as possible the problems that need to be rectified. Once the problem or problems that need attention are clearly defined, then steps can be taken to gather information, analyze the data, and delineate the factors that are associated with the problem. By taking the necessary corrective action, the problem could be solved.

This entire process by which we attempt to solve problems is called research. Thus, research involves a series of well-thought-out and carefully executed activities that will enable us to know how organizational problems can be solved or at least minimized.

We can now define research as an organized, systematic, data-based, critical, scientific inquiry or investigation into a specific problem, undertaken with the objective of finding answers or solutions to it.

TYPES OF RESEARCH

Research can be undertaken for two different purposes. One is to solve a currently existing problem in the work setting; the other is to add or contribute to the general body of knowledge in a particular area of interest to the researcher. Where research is done with the intention of applying the results of its findings to solving specific problems currently being experienced in the organization, it is called **applied research.** However, when research is being done chiefly to improve our understanding of certain problems that commonly occur in organizational settings, and how to solve them, the research is called **basic** or **fundamental research.** It is also known as **pure research.** The findings from such research contribute to the building of knowledge in the various management areas.

Applied Research

Most organizations are interested in applied research and would pay researchers and consultants to study a problem of concern to them in order to find solutions that can be implemented to rectify the problem situation. For example, the production department in a manufacturing organization may be concerned about the high rate of absenteeism and turnover of their production personnel in the last six months. Management might want to know why this is happening and how they could rectify the situation. To get answers to these questions, they might hire a team of researchers who would attempt to study the problem in an organized and systematic manner. Once the answers have been found, feasible solutions suggested by the research findings would be implemented so that there is no recurrence of absenteeism and turnover, or at least not to the extent of the existing alarming rate.

A second example may be applied to the classroom environment. An instructor might be concerned about students perpetually walking in late to the eight o'clock morning class that he is teaching this semester. This may be of concern because every time someone walks in, the entire class is distracted. The instructor might want to ascertain the reasons for the tardiness of some members in the class, as well as how and to what extent this can be prevented for the rest of the semester. If the instructor then sets out to gather information from the students as to why they arrive late, analyzes this information, and thus finds out the reasons for the tardiness, he can try to solve the problem by addressing some of the existing causes of tardiness. This might help students to be in class on time in the future.

Basic or Fundamental Research

Most research and development departments in various industries, as well as many professors in colleges and universities, do basic or fundamental research, so that more knowledge is generated in particular areas of interest to the industries, organizations, and researchers. The aim here is not to apply the findings to solve an immediate problem at hand, but rather to understand more about certain phenomena and problems that occur in several organizations and industries, and how they can be solved. Such investigations lend themselves to being designed such that the solutions generated for a particular type of problem—say turnover—could be applied not only to one organization such as a specific manufacturing company, but to several types of organizations such as hospitals, financial institutions, or restaurants.

The main purpose of conducting basic research is to generate more knowledge and understanding of the phenomena that occur, and to build theories based on the research results. Such theories are then used in subsequent research by researchers as a foundation for further study of the phenomena. This process of building upon existing knowledge is the genesis for theory building in the management area.

An example of basic research is a university professor's effort to understand and generate more knowledge on how to increase the productivity of white-collar clerical employees in service industries. In order to accomplish this, the professor would go to various service organizations and study the employees' productivity and factors relating to it, so as to add to the existing body of knowledge.

Another example relevant to the classroom would be the research conducted by a professor to determine how instructional methods can be improved so that university students in general could become *actively involved* in the learning process rather than *passively absorbing* the lectures given by the instructors.

As illustrated, the main distinction between applied and basic research is that the former is specifically aimed at solving a current problem, whereas the latter has the more general objective of generating knowledge and understanding of phenomena and problems that occur in various organizational settings. Despite this distinction, both types of research follow the same steps of systematic inquiry to arrive at solutions to problems. As current or prospective practicing managers in organizations, most of us would probably be directly or indirectly engaged in applied research. We would also want to keep abreast of new basic knowledge generated in the management area by reading the published research in management journals, some of which may be relevant and applicable to our own organization.

SCIENTIFIC INVESTIGATION

Earlier we defined research as an organized, systematic, data-based, critical, scientific inquiry into a specific problem that needs a solution. It is necessary to understand what the term *scientific* means. Scientific research has the focused goal of problem solving and pursues a step-by-step logical, organized, and rigorous method to identify problems, gather data, analyze the data, and draw valid conclusions therefrom. Thus, scientific research is not based on hunches, experience, and intuition alone, but is purposive and rigorous. Because of the rigorous way in which it is done, scientific research enables others interested in researching and knowing about similar issues to do research in similar situations and come up with comparable findings. Scientific research also helps researchers to state their findings more accurately and precisely, and to make their solutions applicable to various other organizational settings experiencing similar problems. Furthermore, scientific investigation tends to be more objective than subjective, and it helps managers to highlight the most critical factors in the workplace that need specific attention so as to avoid, minimize, or solve problems.

The Hallmarks of Scientific Research

The hallmarks or main distinguishing characteristics of scientific research can be listed as follows:

1. Purposiveness and rigor.
2. Testability.
3. Replicability.
4. Accuracy and precision.
5. Objectivity.
6. Generalizability.
7. Parsimony.

Each of these characteristics can be explained in the context of a concrete example. Let us consider the case of a researcher who is interested in investigating how employees' commitment to the organization can be increased. We can examine how the seven hallmarks of science apply to this investigation so that it can be called scientific.

Purposiveness and Rigor

The researcher has started with a definite aim or purpose for the research. The focus is on increasing the commitment of employees to the organization, which will help the organization in many ways. An increase in employee commitment will mean less turnover, less absenteeism, and probably increased performance levels, all of which would definitely benefit the organization. The research thus has a purposive focus.

A good theoretical base and a sound methodological design would add rigor to this purposive study. Rigor connotes carefulness, scrupulousness, and the degree of exactitude in research investigations. In our example case, let us say the researcher asks a few employees in the organization—say ten to twelve people—to outline what would increase their commitment to the organization. If, on the basis of these people's responses alone, the researcher reaches several conclusions on how employee commitment can be increased, the whole approach to the investigation would be unscientific. It would lack rigor because, to mention just a few reasons, (1) the conclusion will be incorrectly drawn because they would be based on the thoughts of a few employees whose opinions may not be representative of those of the entire workforce; (2) the way in which the questions were framed and asked could have introduced a lot of bias in the responses; and (3) there may be many other important influences on organizational commitment that this small sample of respondents did not or could not verbalize during the interviews, and the researcher would have failed to include them. Therefore, conclusions drawn from an investigation that lacks a good theoretical foundation, as evidenced by reason (3), and methodological sophistication, as evident from (1) and (2), would be unscientific. Rigorous research involves a good theory base and a carefully thought out methodology. These factors enable the researcher to collect the right kinds of information from an appropriate sample with the minimum amount of bias, and they facilitate appropriate data analysis once the data have been gathered. The rest of the book addresses these theoretical and methodological issues. Rigor in research design also makes possible the achievement of the other six hallmarks of science that will now be discussed.

Testability

If, after talking to a random selection of employees in the organization, and reading about the previous research done in the area of organizational commitment, the researcher develops certain hypotheses on how employee commitment to the organization can be enhanced, then these hypotheses can be tested by applying certain statistical tests to the data collected for the purpose. For instance, the researcher might hypothesize that those employees who perceive greater opportunities for participation in decision making would be more committed to the organization. This is a hypothesis that can be tested when the data are collected. The test would indicate whether the hypothesis is substantiated or not.

Scientific research thus lends itself to testing logically developed hypotheses to see whether or not the data support the educated conjectures or hypotheses that are developed after a careful study of the problem situation. Testability thus becomes another hallmark of scientific research.

Replicability

Let us suppose that our researcher concludes that participation in decision making is one of the most important factors that influences the commitment of employees to the organization. If the same kinds of findings emerge when data are collected from employees in other organizations, we would have more faith in the findings. In other words, the results of the tests of hypotheses should be supported again and again when the research is repeated in other similar circumstances. To the extent that this does happen (i.e., the results are replicated or repeated), we will have confidence in our research being scientific. In other words, our hypothesis would not have been supported merely by chance.

Accuracy and Precision

In management research we seldom have the luxury of being able to interpret and state our findings as "definitive." For instance, if the researcher found that the correlation between participation in decision making and organizational commitment was .63, and on this basis suggested that this single factor alone accounted for almost 40 percent of the variance in organizational commitment ($.63^2$), we cannot expect that in every single situation, participation in decision making would account for exactly 40 percent of the variance in organizational commitment. In some organizations it might account for 35 percent, and in others, 45 percent. Thus, at best, the researcher can state that 99 percent of the time, or 95 percent of the time, participation in decision making would explain anywhere between 35 and 45 percent of the variance in the organizational commitment of the employees. As you can see, we are now talking about the confidence level (accuracy) and the confidence interval (precision) that one studies in statistics.

The more accurate we are (i.e., the greater the level of confidence we have in our research results), and the narrower the gap within which we can estimate the range of our predictions (i.e., the narrower the confidence interval), the more useful and scientific the research becomes. For example, the research study designed such that the researcher can say that 95 times out of 100 we can be sure that participation in decision making would increase organizational commitment and account for 35 to 45 percent of its variance, is much more useful than the study in which the researcher is unsure whether it would work even 50 percent of the time, or whether or not there would be any increase at all in the organizational commitment if opportunities are increased for employee participation! Thus, accuracy and precision are important aspects of research and these can be obtained only by appropriate, scientific sampling design. The more accuracy and precision we aim for in our research, the more scientific the investigation, and the more useful the results.

Objectivity

The conclusions drawn from interpreting the results of our data analysis should be objective ones based on the facts resulting from the actual data and not on our own subjective or emotional values. For instance, if the hypothesis that greater participation in decision making will increase organizational commitment was *not* supported in our example, then there is no point in the researcher continuing to argue that increasing the opportunities for employee participation would still help! Such an argument would be based, not on the factual, data-based research findings, but on the subjective opinion of the researcher. If this was the researcher's belief all along, then there was no need to do the research in the first place!

Much damage can be done in organizations by the implementation of non-data-based or misleading conclusions drawn from research. For example, if the hypothesis relating to organizational commitment in our example was not supported, considerable time and effort would be wasted in finding ways to create opportunities for employee participation in decision making, only to find later that employees still keep quitting, remain absent, and do not commit themselves to the organization. Likewise, if research shows that increasing the pay of the employees is not going to increase their job satisfaction, then implementing a revised increased pay system is only going to cost the company more money without attaining the end result that is hoped for. Such an exercise, then, becomes one of nonscientific interpretation and implementation of the research results.

The more objective the interpretation of the data, the more scientific the research investigation becomes. Researchers might well start with some initial subjective values, but their interpretation of the data should be stripped of personal values and biases. Objectivity is thus another hallmark of scientific investigation.

Generalizability

Generalizability refers to the scope of applicability of the research findings in one organizational setting to other settings. Obviously, the wider the range of applicability of the solutions generated by research, the more useful the research is to the users of such research knowledge. For instance, if our researcher's findings that participation in decision making enhances organizational commitment and accounts for its variance anywhere between 35 and 45 percent, are found to be true in a variety of manufacturing, industrial, and service organizations, and not merely in the one organization studied by the researcher, then the generalizability of the findings to other organizational settings is widened. The more generalizable the research is, the more valuable the research findings and the greater their scientific value.

Of course not many research findings can be generalized to all other settings, situations, or organizations. For wider generalizability, the research sampling design has to be logically developed and a number of other meticulous details in the data-collection methods need to be followed. However, a more elaborate sampling design, though it would increase the generalizability of the results, would also increase our research costs. Hence most applied research is generally confined to research within the particular area where the problem arises, and the results are not often generalizable beyond the particular setting. However, the more generalizable the results, the greater their value to other organizations.

Parsimony

Simplicity in explaining the phenomena or problems that occur, and in the application of solutions to problems, is always preferred to complex research frameworks that consider an unmanageable number of factors. For instance, if the researcher can identify for the manager two or three specific variables in the work situation that, when changed, would raise the organizational commitment of the employees by 45 percent, that would be more useful and valuable to the manager than the researcher telling the manager that the organizational commitment could be increased by 48 percent by changing ten different variables in the organization. Such an unmanageable number of variables might well be totally beyond the manager's control. Therefore, the achievement of a meaningful and parsimonious, rather than an elaborate and cumbersome model for our problem solution, becomes a critical issue in research.

Economy in research models is achieved when we can build into our research framework a lesser number of variables that would explain the variance far more efficiently than a complex set of variables that would only marginally, additionally, explain or add to the variance explained. Parsimony can be introduced with a good understanding of the problem and the important factors that influence it. Such a good conceptual theoretical model can be realized through unstructured and structured interviews with people in the situation, and a thorough literature review of the previous research work in the particular problem area.

In sum, scientific research encompasses the seven criteria just discussed. These criteria are discussed in more detail later in the book.

Some Obstacles to Conducting Scientific Research in the Management Area

In the management and behavioral areas it is not possible to conduct investigations that are 100 percent scientific. This is primarily because of problems we are likely to encounter in the measurement and collection of data in the subjective areas of feelings, emotions, attitudes, and perceptions. These problems crop up whenever we attempt to quantify human behavior. We might also encounter difficulties in obtaining a representative sample, which would restrict the generalizability of the findings. Thus it is not always possible to meet all the hallmarks of science completely. Comparability, consistency, and wide generalizability are often difficult to obtain in research. Still, to the extent that we can design our research to ensure purposiveness and rigor and the maximum possible testability, replicability, generalizability, objectivity, parsimony, and accuracy and precision, we will have endeavored to engage in scientific investigation. Several other possible limitations in research studies are discussed later in Unit 8.

THE BUILDING BLOCKS OF SCIENCE IN HYPOTHETICO-DEDUCTIVE RESEARCH

One way of conducting scientific research in management is by following the hypothetico-deductive method. This method involves a seven-step process starting with the observation of certain phenomena in the work setting. The seven-step process is outlined and discussed later in this unit. The foundation on which the hypothetico-deductive method of scientific research rests could be called the building blocks of scientific inquiry. These building blocks are depicted in Figure 1.1. The significance of these building blocks can be illustrated through an example.

A manager might *observe* that the present performance level of the employees is not as high as it used to be. The manager may not yet know to what extent the performance has fallen, or even that it is a problem. There

Figure 1.1
The building blocks of science.

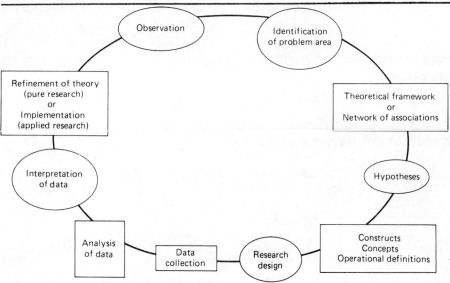

may be only a vague idea that something is changing in the workplace (i.e., a probable fall in the performance levels). This process of culling some information and drawing initial inferences on the basis of **observation** and sensing of the phenomena around us is what initiates most research endeavors—whether applied or basic research. The next step for the manager is to determine if there is a real problem, and if so, what exactly it is. This **problem identification** consists of gathering preliminary data. That is, the manager who sensed lower performance levels of the employees might now talk to several of the workers and discover that the falling performance level may not be a problem in itself, but merely a symptom of the primary problem of low motivation among the workers. The informal and formal interviewing process might thus be useful in integrating all the information gathered from the employees and formulating a basic theory about what is happening in the situation and why the motivation among employees is not as high as it should be. For instance, on the basis of the preliminary information, it may be theorized that low pay, inadequate tools, and poor working conditions might be the reasons for the lack of enthusiasm among the workers.

A logical and meaningful integration of all the information gathered is called the **theoretical framework.** From this theoretical framework, which is a conceptual model for the research, several **hypotheses** can be generated and tested to determine if the data support the hypotheses. Concepts are then **operationally defined** so that they can be measured. A **research design** is set up to decide on, among other issues, how to **collect, analyze,** and **interpret the data,** and, finally, to provide an answer to the problem. The process of drawing from logical analysis an inference that purports to be conclusive is called **deduction.** Thus, the building blocks of science provide the genesis for the hypothetico-deductive method of scientific research that is discussed in the following paragraphs.

THE HYPOTHETICO-DEDUCTIVE METHOD

The Seven-Step Process in the Hypothetico-Deductive Method

The seven steps involved in the hypothetico-deductive method of research are as follows:

1. Observation.
2. Preliminary information gathering.
3. Theory formulation.

4. Hypothesizing.
5. Further scientific data collection.
6. Data analysis.
7. Deduction.

Observation

Observation is the first stage, in which one senses that certain changes are occurring, or that some new behaviors, attitudes, and feelings are vaguely surfacing in the workplace. When the phenomena that are being observed are considered to be potentially important to the organization, one would proceed to the next step.

Preliminary Information Gathering

Preliminary information gathering involves the seeking of information to know more about what one had observed. This could be done by talking informally to several people in the work setting and thus gathering information on what is happening and why. Through these unstructured interviews, one gets an idea or a "feel" for what is happening in the situation. Once the researcher increases her level of awareness of what is happening, she would then focus on the problem and the associated factors through further structured, formal interviews with the employees. Additionally, by doing library research, the investigator would identify how such issues have been tackled in other situations. This information would give additional insights of possible factors operating in this particular situation that had not surfaced in previous interviews.

A mass of information would have been collected through the interviews and the library search. The next step is to make sense of the factors that have been identified in the information-gathering stage by piecing them together in some meaningful fashion.

Theory Formulation

Theory formulation, the next step, is an attempt to integrate the information logically so that the reason for the problem may be conceptualized. In this step the critical variables are examined as to their contribution or influence in explaining why the problem occurs and how it can be solved. The network of associations identified among the variables would then be theoretically woven together with justification as to why they might influence the problem. This process of theory formulation is illustrated in greater detail in Unit 3.

Hypothesizing

Hypothesizing is the next logical step after theory formulation. From the network of associations drawn among the variables, certain testable hypotheses or educated conjectures can be generated. For instance, at this point, one might hypothesize that if noise in the work environment is reduced, then the productivity of the workers will increase. This is a hypothesis that can be tested to determine if the statement would be supported.

Further Scientific
Data Collection

After the development of the hypotheses, data with respect to each variable in the hypotheses need to be obtained. In other words, further scientific data collection is needed to test the hypotheses that are generated in the study. For instance, to test the "noise-versus-productivity" hypothesis mentioned earlier, one needs to collect data on the noise levels at different times (i.e., when they are high, medium, and low), and also to measure the productivity of the workers at these corresponding times. Data would be collected on every variable that is in the theoretical framework from which the hypotheses are generated. These data then form the basis for further data analyses.

Data Analysis

In the data analysis step, the data gathered are statistically analyzed to see if the hypotheses that were generated have been supported. For instance, to see if noise levels relate to the productivity of the workers, one might want to do a correlational analysis and determine the relationship between noise level and productivity. Similarly, other hypotheses could be tested through appropriate statistical analysis. Analyses of both quantitative and qualitative data can be done to determine if certain conjectures are substantiated. Qualitative data refer to information that can, at best, be grouped in some fashion without any underlying quantitative dimensions. Examples of these would be the categorization of employees as to their sex or their citizenship. Various types of nonparametric and other tests can be done with such qualitative data to test hypotheses. Data analysis is discussed in great detail in Unit 7.

Deduction

Deduction is the process of arriving at conclusions by interpreting the meaning of the results of the data analysis. For instance, if it was found from the data analysis that increasing the noise levels had a correlation of

$-.5$ with productivity, one would then conclude or deduce that there is a significant effect of noise on productivity and that the higher the noise level, the lower the productivity of the workers. In other words, if productivity has to be increased, noise has to be kept down. Another inference from this data analysis is that noise levels explain or account for 25 percent of the variance in productivity ($-.5^2$).

Based on these deductions, the researcher would make recommendations on how the "low productivity" problem could be solved in this setting by installing such aids as specially insulated walls or carpeting.

In summary, there are seven steps involved in identifying and resolving a research issue. To make sure that the seven steps of the hypothetico-deductive method are properly understood, let us briefly review an example in an organizational setting and the activities that will be performed in the seven steps.

An Example of the Application of the Hypothetico-Deductive Method in Organizations

Observation

A manager senses that something is wrong in his department. The employees seem to look bored, watch the clock constantly, and make a lot of mistakes in their work. That is, the manager observes various phenomena at the workplace and senses a problem.

Information Gathering Through Informal Interviews

The manager chats with a few of the employees and informally finds out that they find the temperature in their work room to be very hot, that they experience their jobs as somewhat dull and repetitive, and that they are aware of the fact that they are making a lot of errors. That is, the manager has collected some information or data through informal or unstructured interviews with the employees.

Gathering More Information Through Literature Survey

The manager is interested in reading about how other organizations with performance problems in somewhat similar settings had solved the problem. After obtaining a list of the important publications on the subject, the manager surveys the literature, listing the factors that the survey has identified as contributing to poor performance.

Formulating Theory About What Is Happening

Piecing together the information obtained from the interviews and the literature, the manager develops a theory of possible factors that may be influencing the poor performance of the employees in his department. That is, he is developing a theoretical framework of the factors that could account for the low performance.

Hypothesizing

From his theory, the manager is conjecturing the relationships that account for low performance. For example, he hypothesizes that room temperature over 89°F will influence employees' poor performance. (High temperature will enervate employees, resulting in their not being able to concentrate on work. This lack of concentration would result in more mistakes being made on the job.)

Data Collection

In this phase the manager counts the mistakes made by employees on every single day and also records the temperature of the room on each of these days during the summer.

Data Analysis

Then the manager analyzes the data to see if, in fact, there is a correlation between excessive heat and errors made (i.e., he tests his hypothesis). He indeed finds a high correlation.

Deduction

On the basis of the results just discussed, the manager concludes (or deduces) that temperatures over 89°F are uncomfortable and hence more errors do occur. Incidentally, to solve the poor-performance problem, he may think of air-conditioning the work area.

Review of the Hypothetico-Deductive Method

In summary, the hypothetico-deductive method involves the seven steps of observation, preliminary data gathering, theory formulation, hypothesizing, scientific data collection, data analysis, and deduction. Other units in this book will be concerned with how scientific hypothetico-deductive research might be conducted in organizations. This information will be helpful to managers in solving problems while managing people and situations.

MANAGERS AND RESEARCH

Why Should Managers Know About Research?

A question you might be asking at this stage is why you need to be learning about research methods in management, because you probably will bring in researchers to solve any management problems that you might have. The reasons for studying research are fairly clear when one starts to think about it. With the increasing complexity of modern organizations, and the uncertainty of the environment they face, managing organizational systems has become a job ridden with sporadic problems in the work setting. It would help if managers could sense, spot, and deal with problems *before* they become serious. Knowing about research and problem-solving processes helps managers to identify the problems and to find out more about the situation before the problems get out of control. Initial information gathering and analyses of the situation would solve most of the minor problems. However, if they do become serious enough to warrant hiring outside researchers or consultants, then the manager needs to know about the research processes, design, and interpretation of data so as to be an intelligent and knowledgeable consumer of the research findings presented, because they may or may not be appropriate for implementation.

Another reason the professional managers of today need to know about research methods in management is that they can thus become more discriminating consumers of the information contained in the journals they read. Some journal articles are more scientific and objective than others. Even among the scientific articles, some are more appropriate for adaptation to particular organizations and situations than others. This is a function of the sampling design, the types of organizations studied, and other factors reported in the journal studies. Unless the manager is able to comprehend fully what the published empirical research really means, she is likely to err in incorporating some of the suggestions made in such work. Moreover, researchers may have discovered a way to solve a problem presently faced by a manager. The manager who knows about this can implement it, probably with considerable cost savings.

There are several other reasons professional managers should be knowledgeable about research and research methods in management. First, it enhances the sensitivity of the managers to the myriad of variables operating in a situation and reminds them frequently of the multicausality and multifinality of phenomena, thus avoiding inappropriate simplistic notions of one variable "causing" another. Second, when managers understand the research reports on their organizations that are given to them by other professionals, they will be in a position to take intelligent, educated, calculated risks with known probabilities attached to the success or failure of their decisions. Research then becomes a useful decision-making tool rather than a mass of incomprehensible statistical information. Third, because managers become knowledgeable about scientific investigations, vested interests inside or outside the organization will not be allowed to prevail. For instance, an internal research group within the organization will not be able to distort information or to twist the findings if managers are aware of the biases that could creep into research and know how data are analyzed and interpreted. Fourth, knowledge about research helps the manager to relate to, and share pertinent information with, the researcher or consultant hired for problem solving.

In sum, being knowledgeable about research and research methods helps professional managers to

1. Identify and solve small problems in the work setting.
2. Know how to discriminate good from bad research.
3. Appreciate and constantly remember the multiple influences and multiple effects of factors impinging on a situation.
4. Take calculated risks in decision making, knowing fully well the probabilities attached to the different possible outcomes.
5. Prevent possible vested interests from operating in a situation.
6. Relate to hired researchers and consultants more effectively.

The Manager-Researcher Relationship

It often becomes necessary for managers to deal with researchers or consultants during the course of their career. Many academicians and research students engage in basic research, and modern organizations usually allow access to these researchers, asking only that a copy of the research project be made available to the organization. If the research has been done scientifically, then the results of the study would be beneficial to the manager, who would have obtained useful information without paying a cent in consulting fees. By being able to articulate the variables of concern to the researchers who come to do basic work, and by giving them useful insights, the manager thus stands to benefit a great deal. When the manager is knowledgeable about research, then the interactions between the manager and the researcher become more meaningful, purposeful, and beneficial to the organization and the researcher alike.

Quite frequently, organizations also hire outside research agencies to identify and solve problems for them. In such a case, the manager must not only interact effectively with the research team, but also must explicitly delineate the roles for the researchers and the management. He has to inform the researchers of the types of information that can be made available to them, and more importantly, what types of company records *cannot* be made accessible. Such records might include the personnel files of the employees, or certain trade secrets. Making these facts explicit at the very beginning could save a lot of frustration for both parties. Managers who are more knowledgeable about research can more easily decipher the types of information the researchers might require, and if certain documents cannot be made available, they can inform the research team at the outset. It is inefficient for the researchers to discover at a late stage that the company will not let them have certain information. If they know the constraints right from the beginning, the researchers might be able to identify alternate ways of tackling the problems and to formulate other testable hypotheses.

Beyond specifying the roles and constraints, the manager should also make sure that there is a congruence in the value systems of management and the consultants. For example, the organizational philosophy of an institution may be not to fire personnel who are rendering good service. However, one of the ways that the research team might systematically operate is to cut costs by reducing the workforce and instituting better and more efficient work systems. This may give rise to value conflicts. Hence, any management philosophy that is likely to have a bearing on the research design and focus needs to be explicitly stated to the researchers before the negotiation is concluded. Again, research knowledge would help managers to identify and explicitly state the areas where value differences may arise. Clarification of such issues allows the research team the opportunity either to accept the assignment or to regret its inability to undertake the project with these value differences in mind. Either way, it would be a decision that would benefit the organization and prevent a lot of frustration for both sides.

Such exchange of information in a straightforward and forthright manner also helps to increase the rapport and trust levels between the two parties, which in turn motivates the two sides to interact effectively. Under these conditions, the researchers feel free to approach the management to seek assistance in making the research more purposeful. For instance, the research team is likely to request that management inform the employees of the purpose of the research and thus allay any fears they might have about the research.

To summarize, the manager should make sure while hiring researchers or consultants that

1. The roles and expectations of both parties are made explicit.
2. Relevant philosophies and value systems of the organization are made explicit and any special constraints are made known.
3. There is good rapport established with the researchers, and between the researchers and the employees in the organization, so that the latter will cooperate with the researchers.

Internal versus External Consultants and Researchers

Some organizations have their own consulting or research department, which might be called the management services department, the organization and methods department, the research and development department, or some other name. The people in this unit serve as internal consultants to subunits of the organization that face certain problems and seek help. Such a unit within the organization, if it exists, would be useful in several ways, and enlisting its help might be advantageous under some circumstances, but not in others. The manager often has to decide whether to use internal or external researchers or consultants. To make such a decision, the manager should become aware of the strengths and weaknesses of both, in order to weigh the advantages and disadvantages of using either, and thus come to a decision based on the needs of the situation. Some of the advantages and disadvantages of both the internal and external teams are now discussed.

Internal Consultants and Researchers

Advantages The main advantage of the internal team is that they would have a higher probability of being accepted more easily and quickly by the employees in the organization where research needs to be done.

A second advantage is that the internal team would require much less time to understand the structure, the philosophy and climate, and the functioning and work systems of the organization.

A third advantage would be their availability for implementing their recommendations after the research findings are accepted. This is very important because any "bugs" in the implementation of the recommendations could be removed with their help. They would also be available for evaluating the effectiveness of the changes, and for considering further changes when necessary.

A fourth advantage is that the internal team might cost considerably less than an external team for the unit enlisting help in problem solving because they will need less time to grasp and understand the system.

Disadvantages There are also certain disadvantages to engaging internal research teams for purposes of problem solving. The three most critical ones are listed here.

1. Having been with the organization for a long time as internal consultants, the internal team may quite possibly fall into a stereotypical way of looking at the organization and its problems. This would inhibit any fresh ideas and perspectives that might be brought to the problem situation.

2. There is scope for certain powerful coalitions in the organization to influence the internal team to conceal, distort, or falsely report certain facts. In other words, certain vested interests could prevail, especially where the issue is one of allocation of scarce resources.

3. As with the notion that no man is a hero to his valet, there is a possibility that even the most highly qualified internal research teams are not valued as experts by the staff and management, and hence their findings are not given the attention they deserve.

External Consultants and Researchers

The disadvantages of the internal research teams are the advantages of the external teams, and the former's advantages are the latter's disadvantages. However, the specific advantages and disadvantages of the external teams may be highlighted.

Advantages First, the external team can draw on a wealth of experience from having worked with different types of organizations that have had the same or similar types of problems. This wide range of experience would enable them to think both divergently and convergently rather than coming to a solution immediately on the basis of the apparent facts of the situation. They would be able to think of several alternative ways of looking at the problem because of their extensive problem-solving experiences in various other situations. Having looked at the situation from several possible angles and viewpoints (divergently), they could then critically assess each of these, eliminate the less viable options and alternatives, and focus on selected feasible solutions (convergent thinking).

A second advantage is that external team members from established research or consulting firms are usually more current on the latest problem-solving models, statistical tools and techniques, and computer analysis. Because knowledge obsolescence is a real threat in the research area, the external research institutions ensure that their team members are kept current on the innovations through training programs. This may or may not be the case with the internal teams within the organization.

Disadvantages The major disadvantages in hiring an external research team are as follows:

1. The cost of hiring an external research team is usually high and is the main deterrent, unless the problems are very critical.

2. In addition to the considerable time required for the external team to understand the organization to be researched, they also are seldom welcomed or readily accepted by the employees in the organization. Therefore, eliciting employees' help and cooperation in the study is a

little more difficult and time-consuming for the external researchers, when compared to the internal teams.

3. The external team also charges more money for assisting in the implementation and evaluation phases.

Given these advantages and disadvantages of both the internal and external teams, the manager needing research services has to weigh the pros and cons of engaging either before making a decision.

If the problem is a complex one, or if there are likely to be vested interests, or if the very existence of the organization is imperiled because of one or more serious problems, it is probably advisable to engage external researchers despite the increased costs involved. However, if the problems that arise are fairly simple ones, and if time is of the essence in solving moderately complex problems, or if there is a systemwide need to establish procedures and policies of a fairly routine nature, the internal team would probably be the better suited option.

Knowing about research methods and the comparative advantages and disadvantages of the external and internal teams helps managers to make decisions on how to approach the problem solution.

SUMMARY

In this unit we have examined what research is, considered the two types of research, tried to understand what scientific investigation is, what the hypothetico-deductive method of research involves, why a manager should know about research, and the advantages and disadvantages of hiring internal and external teams of researchers or consultants.

We examine the research process in the next unit.

SUPPLEMENTAL READINGS

The following topic references will guide you to seek more information.

Topic	Reference	Chapter	Page
Definition of research	Clover & Balsley (1979)	1	1
	Emory (1980)	1	7
	Leedy (1974)	1	3–8
Applied and basic research	Clover & Balsley (1979)	1	2
	Murdick & Cooper (1982)	3	44–51

Topic	Reference	Chapter	Page
Scientific investigation	Clover & Balsley (1979)	2	13–29
	Emory (1980)	2	20–47
	Kerlinger (1973)	1	2–15
	Murdick & Cooper (1982)	2	15–31
	Roscoe (1975)	1	1–9
Hypothetico-deductive method	Clover & Balsley (1979)	3	13–29
	Emory (1980)	2	39–44
	Kaplan (1964)	1	9–11
Managers and research	Clover & Balsley (1979)	1	3–12
	Emory (1980)	1	11–13

REFERENCES

Clover, V. T., & Balsley, H. L. *Business research methods* (2nd ed.). Columbus, Ohio: Grid Publishing Co., 1979.

Emory, C. W. *Business research methods* (Rev. ed.). Homewood, Ill.: Richard D. Irwin, Inc., 1980.

Kaplan, A. *The conduct of inquiry: Methodology for behavioral science.* New York: Chandler Publishing Co., 1964.

Kerlinger, F. N. *Foundations of behavioral research* (2nd ed.). New York: Holt, Rinehart and Winston, 1973.

Leedy, P. D. *Practical research: Planning and design.* New York: Macmillan, 1974.

Murdick, R. G., & Cooper, D. R. *Business research: Concepts and guides.* Columbus, Ohio: Grid Publishing Co., 1982.

Roscoe, J. T. *Fundamental research statistics for the behavioral sciences* (2nd ed.). New York: Holt, Rinehart and Winston, 1975.

POINTS TO PONDER AND RESPOND TO

1. One hears the word research being mentioned by several groups such as research organizations, college and university professors, doctoral students, graduate assistants working for faculty, graduate and undergraduate students doing their term papers, research departments in industries, newspaper reporters, journalists, lawyers, doctors, and several other professionals and nonprofessionals.

In the light of what you have learned in this unit, how would you rank the aforementioned groups of people in terms of the extent to which they might be doing "scientific" investigations. Why?

2. If research in the management area cannot be 100 percent scientific, why bother to do it at all?

3. Because basic research is not applied immediately to a problem, it is less valuable and useful than applied research.

4. If managers learn how to do good research by taking a course such as this book gives, there would be no need to hire anybody to solve problems in organizations.

UNIT 2
THE RESEARCH PROCESS

Steps 1 to 3:
The Broad Problem Area
Preliminary Data Gathering
Problem Definition

ISSUES DISCUSSED

The Broad Problem Area

Preliminary Data Collection

Some Information Vital for Research
- Background Information on the Organization: Contextual Factors
- Structural Factors, Job Factors, Management Philosophy
- Perceptions, Attitudes, and Behavioral Responses

Literature Survey
- Reasons for Literature Survey
- Organizing for Literature Survey
  - Bibliographical Indexes
  - Bibliography Format
  - Selecting Relevant Materials

Writing up the Literature Survey

Problem Definition

UNIT OBJECTIVES

After completing Unit 2 you should be able to:

1. Identify the steps in the research process.
2. Identify problem areas that are likely to be studied in organizations.
3. Discuss how problem areas can be identified in work settings.
4. State research problems clearly and precisely.
5. Develop relevant and comprehensive bibliographies for any organizational research area.

6. Write a literature review on any given topic, documenting the references in the prescribed manner.

7. Apply all you have learned to a group project that might be assigned to you.

In this unit we will examine ways to identify the variables that would be relevant in any specific problem situation. Your instructor might also organize a simulation for the class that would help you to learn how to surface relevant variables in any problem situation through unstructured and structured interviews with employees at various levels in the organization. We will also see how a literature survey is done and how problems can be narrowed down and clearly defined.

THE RESEARCH PROCESS FOR APPLIED AND BASIC RESEARCH

The steps in the hypothetico-deductive method in research can be depicted in the form of a research process model (see Figure 2.1). The re-

Figure 2.1
The research process for basic and applied research.

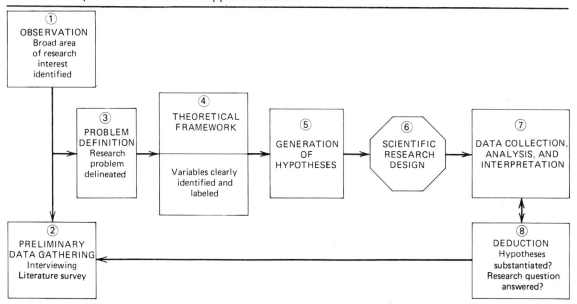

search process model facilitates the representation and organization of the research process through step-by-step logic, even though research is not always a linear process.

Each of the components of the research model will be discussed in this book. This particular unit will discuss steps 1 to 3 of the model, that is: (1) the broad problem area; (2) preliminary information gathering, especially through unstructured and structured interviews and literature survey; and (3) problem definition.

BROAD PROBLEM AREA

Identifying the broad problem area through the process of observing and focusing on the actual problem were discussed in Unit 1. Recall that the broad problem area refers to the entire situation where one senses a possible need for research and problem solving. The actual issues that need to be researched within this situation will not have been identified at this stage. Such issues might pertain to (1) problems currently existing in an organizational setting that need to be solved, (2) areas in the organization that a manager believes need to be improved, (3) a conceptual or theoretical issue that needs to be tightened up for the basic researcher to understand certain phenomena, and (4) some research questions that a basic researcher wants to answer empirically. Here are two examples of broad problem areas.

Example 2.1

A manager might sense that there could be a potential problem at the workplace, having observed that the employees seem somewhat disinterested and alienated from their jobs. The manager may not know exactly what the problem is—that is, whether it is with the jobs or the organization, or with the employees themselves. This then becomes the broad problem area from which the specific problem can be narrowed down. This issue would fall under category (2) above, where a situation could stand improvement to avert a potential problem. However, if the manager feels that people are presently alienated from their jobs and this is something that needs to be rectified right now, then the problem will fall under category (1).

Example 2.2

A basic researcher might be interested in investigating the concept of job involvement at the workplace, although the specific aspects of the topic may not yet be obvious. This is the broad problem base from which the researcher would work to derive a concise definition of the problem that she is interested in analyzing.

Other broad problem areas that a manager could observe in the workplace are as follows:

1. Training programs are perhaps not as effective as were anticipated.
2. Women are not willing to work overtime.
3. Minority groups are not participating as much as others in meetings.
4. The reward system in the organization is not effective.

The broad problem area would be narrowed down to specific issues for investigation after some preliminary data are gathered by the researcher. This may take the form of interviews and library research.

PRELIMINARY DATA COLLECTION

In Unit 1 it was mentioned that unstructured interviews, structured interviews, and library research would help the researcher to define the problem more specifically and evolve a theory delineating possible variables that might influence the problem. The nature of information that would be needed by the researcher for the purpose could be broadly classified under three headings:

1. Background information of the organization—that is, the contextual factors.
2. Managerial philosophy, company policies, and other structural aspects.
3. Perceptions, attitudes, and behavioral responses of organizational members.

Certain types of information such as the background information of the company can be obtained from available published records. Other types of written information such as company policies, procedures, and rules can be obtained from the organization's records and documents. Data gathered through such readily available sources are called *secondary data*. Some secondary sources of data are statistical and other bulletins, information published or unpublished and available from either within or outside the organization, data bases available from previous research, and library records. Certain other types of information, such as the perceptions and attitudes of employees, are best obtained by talking to individuals, by observing events, people, and objects, or by administering questionnaires to individuals. Gathering information on employee perceptions, attitudes, and feelings belongs in this category. Such data gathered for research from the actual situation where events occur are called *primary data*.

We will now see how the three broad types of information mentioned earlier can be gathered.

Background Information
on the Organization

It is important for the researcher or the research team to know some background information about the company or organization to be studied before even conducting the first interview with the officials of the institution. Such background information might include, among other things, the following contextual factors, which may be obtained from various published sources such as trade publications, the *Census of Business and Industry, Directory of Corporations*, several other business guides and services, and from records available with the organization that is researched:

1. The origin and history of the company—when it was started, business it is in, rate of growth, ownership and control, and so on.
2. Size in terms of employees, or assets, or both.
3. Charter—purpose and ideology.
4. Location—regional, national, or other.
5. Resources—human and others.
6. Interdependent relationships with other institutions and the external environment.
7. Financial position during the last five to ten years, and other financial data.

Information on Management
Philosophy and Structural Factors

Information on management philosophy, company policies, structure, workflow, and the like, can be obtained by asking direct questions of the management. When questions are directed at several managers individually, it is quite possible that some information received might be conflicting and contradictory. Frequent occurrences of such contradictions might in themselves indicate problems such as poor communication or misperceptions of the organization's philosophy, goals, values, and so forth. These issues can be pursued by the researcher in subsequent interviews and might indicate the extent to which differences in perceptions exist in the organization.

Quite frequently, aspects of structure influence the problem and need to be explored. Below are some of the structural factors.

1. Roles and positions in the organization and number of employees in each job level.
2. Extent of specialization.

3. Communication channels.
4. Control systems.
5. Coordination and span of control.
6. Reward systems.
7. Workflow systems and the like.

It is possible that the respondents' perceptions of the structural variables may not match the formal written structural policies and procedures of the organization. Where such is the case, these become relevant leads to follow during unstructured and structured interviews with various levels of employees in the organization.

Perceptions, Attitudes, and Behavioral Responses

Employee perceptions of the work and the work environment, and their attitudinal and behavioral responses can be tapped by talking to them, observing them, and seeking their responses through questionnaires. A general idea of people's perceptions of their work, the organizational climate, and other aspects of interest to the researcher can be obtained through both unstructured and structured interviews with the respondents. By establishing good rapport with the individuals and following the right questioning techniques—discussed in detail in Unit 5—the researcher will be able to obtain useful information from the respondents. An idea of the attitudinal and behavioral reactions of organizational members is often very helpful in arriving at a precise problem definition.

Attitudinal factors comprise people's reactions to the following:

1. Nature of the work.
2. Workflow interdependencies.
3. Superiors in the organization.
4. Participation in decision making.
5. Client systems.
6. Co-workers.
7. Rewards provided by the organization, such as pay, and fringe benefits.
8. Opportunities for advancement in the organization.
9. Family environment and relationships.
10. Involvement in community, civic, and other social groups.
11. Views on taking time off the job.

Behavioral factors include actual work habits such as being industrious or goofing off, extent of absenteeism, intention to remain in or to leave the organization, and the like.

The respondents could be encouraged at the interviewing stage to talk about their jobs, other work-related factors, non-work-related factors, and their attitudes, values, perceptions, and behaviors, some of which might influence the outcomes at the workplace. Detailed discussions on how the unstructured and structured interviews are to be conducted can be seen in Unit 5, where data-collection methods are discussed.

Talking to several people at various levels in the organization would give the interviewer a good idea of what is going on there. The next step for the researcher is to tabulate the various types of information that have been gathered and determine if there is a pattern to the responses. For instance, it might be observed that some problems are frequently mentioned by employees at several levels in the organization. Certain factors such as insufficient lighting, monotony on the job, or inadequate tools may be brought out forcefully in the interviews by several workers. When the tabulation reveals that such variables have surfaced quite frequently, it gives the researcher some good ideas about how to proceed with the next step of surveying the literature to see how others have perceived such factors in other work settings and defined the problem before arriving at solutions. Because literature survey is one way of summarizing secondary data and is an important step in the research process for defining the research problem, we will now discuss it in some detail as one of the preliminary data-gathering tools.

Literature Survey

Literature survey is the documentation of a comprehensive review of the published work from secondary sources of data in the areas of specific interest to the researcher. The library is a rich storage base for secondary data, and researchers usually spend several weeks, and sometimes months, going through books, journals, newspapers, magazines, conference proceedings, doctoral dissertations, master's theses, several government publications, and financial, marketing, and other reports, to find current published information on their research topic.

The researcher is ready to begin the literature survey even as the information from the unstructured and structured interviews is being gathered. Reviewing the literature on the topic area at this time helps the researcher to focus the interviews more meaningfully on certain aspects that were found to be important in the published studies, even if these had not surfaced during the interviews.

Reasons for Literature Survey

The purpose of the literature review is to ensure that no important variable is ignored that has in the past been found repeatedly to have had an impact on the problem. It is possible that some of the critical variables are never brought out in the interviews, either because the employees cannot articulate them or are unaware of their impact, or because the variables seem so obvious to the interviewees that they are not specifically stated. *If there are variables that are not identified during the interviews, but that influence the problem critically, then doing research without considering them would be an exercise in futility.* In such a case, the true reason for the problem would remain unidentified even at the end of the research. To avoid such mishaps, the researcher needs to read all the important research work relating to the particular problem area.

A survey of the literature not only helps the researcher to include all the relevant variables in the research project, it also facilitates the creative integration of the information gathered from the structured and unstructured interviews with what is found in previous studies. In other words, it gives a good basic framework to proceed further with the investigation.

A good literature survey thus ensures that

1. Important variables that are likely to influence the problem situation are not left out of the study.
2. A clearer idea emerges as to what variables would be most important to consider (parsimony), why they would be considered important, and how they should be investigated to solve the problem.
3. Testability and replicability of the findings of the current research are enhanced.
4. The problem statement can be made with greater precision and clarity.
5. One does not run the risk of "reinventing the wheel," that is, wasting efforts on trying to rediscover something that is already known.
6. The problem investigated is perceived by the scientific community as relevant and of significance.

Organizing for Literature Survey

The question that arises at this stage is how the researcher can know about and get access to the research that has been done earlier in his area of interest. The following sections deal with this issue.

Bibliographical Indexes Before setting out to survey the research work in the areas of interest, it is necessary to know how to obtain and locate materials. One cannot take each journal published in the management area and thumb through the pages of the last twenty years' issues. That would be unmanageable and inefficient. To facilitate the search for sources of published articles relevant to several areas in business and management, there are **bibliographical indexes** compiled periodically, which list articles published in periodicals, newspapers, books, and so on.

Some indexes particularly useful to students in the management area are (1) the *Business Periodicals Index* (BPI), which is a cumulative index of several management, business, and economic periodicals; (2) the *Public Affairs Information Services* (PAIS), which is an index of several sources; (3) the *Psychological Abstracts* and (4) *Sociological Abstracts,* both of which abstract articles in several areas that would include the psychological and sociological aspects relating to the management area; (5) the *Dissertation Abstracts International,* which gives details of doctoral dissertations done in specific areas in the social sciences; and (6) *Books in Print,* which is a valuable index listing all books written on most important topic areas.

All the above sources list the published work by subject, under which heading appears complete information on the title of the article, the author(s), the journal name, and the year, volume, and page numbers of the article. There will be some overlapping of references among several of the indexes; for example, both BPI and PAIS might cover many of the same references under a subject, but the distinction is that whereas the BPI would cover basically business-related topics, the PAIS would also include the public affairs area.

The next step for the researcher is to compile a bibliography of the references pertaining to her particular area of interest.

Bibliography and the Use of Index Cards   A bibliography is a systematic alphabetical listing of authors, the work done by them in the specific area, and where they can be found. In order to compile the bibliography conveniently from the information available from the various books of indexes referred to earlier, index cards can be used. Preparing 5 × 8 index cards from the bibliographical indexes is an efficient and systematic way of compiling a bibliography. The pertinent references from the indexes can be extracted on the index cards using the format shown in Figure 2.2, and the cards can be alphabetically arranged according to the last name of the first author. In essence, the cards will contain the names of the authors (last names first, and then their first and middle initials), the

Figure 2.2

Format for referencing the article on the 5 × 8 index card.

(Author)	(Catalogue Reference)	(Topic)
Dunham, R. B.	BF 1 J 82	Job Design

(Title of the article)
"The Measurement and Dimensionality of Job Characteristics"

(Source)
Journal of Applied Psychology, 1976, *61*(4), 404–409.

title of the article, the name of the journal where the article is published, the year, volume, and number of the publication, and the page numbers of the article. A 5 × 8 card is preferable because further details of the articles can later be noted on the back of the card when doing the literature survey, as detailed later in this unit. Once all the references in the index have been copied on the cards, the next step is to have the bibliography typed from the cards.

Bibliography Format The bibliography should conform to accepted formats. The American Psychological Association (1974) has prescribed a format that is followed by most of the journals in the management area. A specimen of the bibliography that conforms to the American Psychological Association format is given in Table 2.1. Note the differences with respect to the references for journal articles (items 1 and 3), books (items 2 and 7), dissertations (item 5), contributions to edited books (item 8), maga-

Table 2.1

Specimen Format for Bibliography

	Item*
Aldag, R. J., & Brief, A. P. Impact of individual differences on employee affective responses to task characteristics. *Journal of Business Research,* 1975, *3*(4), 311–322.	1
Alderfer, C. P. *Existence, relatedness and growth: Human needs in organizational settings.* New York: Free Press, 1972.	2
Dunham, R. B. The measurement and dimensionality of job characteristics. *Journal of Applied Psychology,* 1976, *61*(4), 404–409.	3
Hackman, J. R., & Oldham, G. R. *The job diagnostic survey: An instrument for the diagnosis of jobs and the evaluation of job redesign projects* (Tech. Rep. 4). New Haven, Conn.: Yale University, Department of Administrative Sciences, 1974.	4
Kidron, A. G. *Individual differences, job characteristics and commitment to the organization.* Unpublished doctoral dissertation, Ohio State University, 1976.	5
Kidron, A. G., & Osborn, R. N. *Satisfaction and the interaction between individual and job characteristics* (working paper). Carbondale, Ill.: Southern Illinois University, Department of Administrative Sciences, 1977.	6
Runkel, P. J., & McGrath, J. E. *Research on human behavior: A systematic guide to method.* New York: Holt, Rinehart and Winston, 1972.	7
Sekaran, U., Martin, T., Trafton, R., & Osborn, R. N. Nomothetical nets and higher order factor analysis in middle range theory development. In C. Pinder & L. R. Moore (Eds.), *Middle range theory and the study of organizations.* Boston: Martinus Nijhoff, 1980.	8
Editorial. *The Times,* June 29, 1979, pp. 1–2.	9

*Numbers for discussion purposes only.

zine and newspaper articles without the author's name (item 9), technical reports (item 4), and working papers (6). The format prescribes that with respect to articles, the journal name be underlined, whereas in the case of books and book chapters, the name of the book is underlined, as well as other style points. These are to be noted carefully.

Note the following important additional hints:

1. It is a good idea for students who prepare index cards for writing term papers or other reports to file these alphabetically in an index box, so that they can be referred to as frequently as necessary for writing term projects for different management courses.

2. A short list of the journals most frequently referred to by organizational behavior researchers, and some examples of academic, practitioner-oriented, and other types of reading materials can be seen in Tables 2.2 and 2.3, respectively.

3. Students might like to know that computerized literature searches are now available, and many universities have on-line search systems that would retrieve information on the areas of research interest. Depend-

Table 2.2

Some Journals Most Commonly Referred to by Organizational Behavior Researchers

Academy of Management Journal (AMJ)
Academy of Management Review (AMR)
Administrative Science Quarterly (ASQ)
American Sociological Review
Business Horizon
California Management Review (CMR)
Group & Organization Studies
Harvard Business Review (HBR)
Human Relations
Industrial and Labor Relations
Journal of Applied Behavioral Science (JABS)
Journal of Applied Psychology (JAP)
Journal of Business
Journal of Occupational Psychology
Journal of Vocational Behavior
Management Science
Organizational Behavior and Human Performance (OBHP)
Organizational Dynamics
Personnel
Personnel Administration
Personnel Management
Psychological Bulletin
Sex Roles
Sloan Management Review

Table 2.3

Examples of Academic, Practitioner-Oriented, Trade, and Light-Material References

Academic	Practitioner-Oriented	Trade	Light, Easy to Read
Academy of Management Journal	California Management Review	Business Week	Newspaper articles
Academy of Management Review	Group & Organization Studies	Fortune	mba
Journal of Applied Psychology	Harvard Business Review	Industrial Week	Campus Business
Organizational Behavior and Human Performance	Sloan Management Review	Wall Street Journal	Information pamphlets
	Business Horizon		

ing on the amount of available money that could be expended for such searches, one could ask for a listing of sources of information on the topics of interest from any given year, and also, if necessary, ask for full texts of the articles.

Finding the Materials in the Library   Once the bibliography has been compiled, the location of the materials in the library is determined from the card catalogue. The card catalogue lists each book and journal in the library by subject matter as well as by author(s). Each such card would contain an identifying Dewey decimal number such as HB 245.1s, and each library usually posts where the materials containing these prefixes would be stacked. While going through the card catalogues, the researcher should note the catalogue numbers for each of the references on the index cards, in order to facilitate locating the materials on the library shelves.

Selecting Relevant Material for the Literature Survey   Whereas the bibliography should list all the work done in the area of interest, not all of the references will be relevant to the particular problem under investigation. The researcher can eliminate a number of these by merely reading the title or by glancing at the abstracts of the articles. While going through the other articles, it would be efficient to note some pertinent details of the study in shorthand form on the backs of the 5×8 cards as shown in Figure 2.3. Thus the front of the card would contain the identifying details of the article (author, journal name, etc.), and the back would list details of the problem statement, the variables used, the sample, data-collection and data-analytic methods, and the results of the study. A set of such cards would help in writing the literature survey without too much confusion and wasted time. One would later go through the cards and determine which

Figure 2.3

Back of the 5 × 8 index card containing details of the study referenced in the front.

Study on: <u>Absenteeism</u>   Nath, E. (1945)
           (Topic)   Author/Year

Problem STT

What factors have the greatest influence on absenteeism?

Variables

Age, education, working conditions, marital status, type of job.

Sample

67 mine workers from the XYZ Mine Co., Illinois. Mean age = 35; all males.

Data Collection

All 67 employees were interviewed by three researchers within a period of 3 months inside the mine.

Data Analysis

Correlational and multiple-regression analysis used.

Results

Working conditions influenced absenteeism the most—especially toxic dust and explosions. None of the other variables were significantly related to absenteeism.

Conclusions

Chemicals that would absorb the toxic dust and mechanisms for explosion danger warnings should substantially reduce absenteeism.

Any Other Info/Comments

variables have been found to be important in most of the studies, and summarize the details of such studies. Often during this process, the researcher might find that certain other areas of research are closely related to the problem at hand. For instance, while reading the articles on the problem area of *turnover,* the researcher might find that organizational structure has been found to influence turnover in these studies. The researcher might then want to know more about the definition of organizational structure and its various components. Thus the researcher might be reading materials on organizational structure and making cards and notes on these also. Such comprehensive knowledge in all the related areas helps to develop a logical and meaningful problem statement later.

Writing Up the Literature Survey Section

The documentation of the relevant studies citing the author and the year of the study is called literature survey. The literature survey is a clear and logical presentation of the research work done thus far in the area of investigation. As stated earlier, the purpose of literature survey is to identify and highlight the important variables, and to document the significant findings from earlier research that will serve as the foundation on which the subsequent theoretical framework for the current investigation can be based. Such documentation is important to convince the reader·that (1) the researcher is knowledgeable about the problem area, and has done the preliminary homework that is necessary to be able to conduct research; and (2) the theoretical framework will be built on work already done and will add to the solid foundation of existing knowledge.

A point to note is that the literature survey should bring together all relevant information in a cogent and logical manner instead of presenting all the studies in chronological order with bits and pieces of uncoordinated information. A good literature survey also leads one logically into a good problem statement.

A Note on Referencing and Quotations

A note on referencing and quotations would be useful at this point. Honesty and ethical considerations demand that original ideas and work of others, on which the research is based, be given proper credit and appropriately referenced. Doing this also adds credibility to the skill of the researcher. Besides, failure to do so can have unpleasant consequences because plagiarism is punishable by the author's expulsion from the profession and professional affiliations. The following guidelines, which draw heavily on the American Psychological Association (1974) format, would be an acceptable referencing procedure to follow in writing the literature survey and other parts of the research paper.

References in Text Cite all references in the body of the paper by enclosing in parentheses the author's surname and the year of the publication. *Example:* A recent study (Sekaran, 1981) has shown . . . .

If no author can be identified, use the first two or three crucial or critical words of the title, which will help locate the reference in the reference list. *Example:* (*Webster's Dictionary,* 1965).

If the name of the author is in the text, the reference citation needs only the year of publication. *Example:* Sekaran (1981) has said . . . .

If the reference has two authors, the citation includes the surnames of both connected with an ampersand. *Example:* A recent study (Sekaran & Mowday, 1981) has shown . . . .

If a reference has more than two authors, the citation includes the surnames of all authors the first time it appears; later citations of the same reference include only the surname of the senior author and the abbreviation, et al. *Examples:* A recent study (Sekaran, Martin, Trafton, & Osborn, 1978) has shown . . . . The study previously cited (Sekaran et al., 1978) has shown . . . .

References to different works cited at the same point in the text are separated by semicolons and enclosed in one pair of parentheses, the names appearing in alphabetical order. *Example:* (Argyris, 1964; Bowen, 1980; Hunt, 1976).

References to various works by the same author are separated by commas sequenced by year of publication, and with a suffix where there is more than one work referenced for the same year. *Example:* Recent studies (McKelvey, 1964, 1967, 1977a, 1977c; Sekaran, 1977, 1978a, 1978b) have shown . . . .

References to pages or chapter in books are cited. *Example:* (Jones, 1958, pp. 15–21) or (Crozier, 1973, Ch. 5).

Quotation in Text Quotations should be given exactly as they appear in the source. The original wording, punctuations, spelling, and italics must be preserved even if they are erroneous. The citation of the source of a direct quotation should always include the page number(s) as well as the reference; this citation should directly follow the quotation before the final period. *Example:*

Perceptions of job characteristics, like the perceptions of organizational climate would seem to be an integration and consolidation of the totality of one's job-related experiences (Sekaran & Trafton, 1978, p. 259).

Note: All the references cited in the literature survey should be found in the bibliography or references section of the final research report. Whereas a bibliography is a comprehensive list of all important work done in the topic area, arranged according to the alphabetical order of the last name of the first authors, references contain only a list of such documents as have been used and cited in the literature survey.

An example of a good literature survey can be found at the beginning of any article in the *Academy of Management Journal* and most other academic journals. A specimen of a literature survey can also be found on pages 280–281 of this book in Unit 8.

Apart from all the other points cited earlier on the usefulness of a good literature survey, one important benefit derived from a well-written literature survey section is that the researcher would be able to delineate a logical, well-defined, and sharply focused problem for research investigation. This delineation or definition of the problem, which is the next step in the research process, is now discussed.

PROBLEM DEFINITION

After the interviews and the literature review, the researcher is in a position to narrow down the problem from its original broad base and define the issues more effectively. This problem definition or problem statement, as it is also often called, is a clear, precise, and succinct statement of the question or issue that is to be investigated with the goal of finding an answer or solution. As mentioned earlier, problem definitions could pertain to (1) existing business problems where a manager is looking for a solution, (2) situations that may not be posing any problems at present but where the manager feels that things may be improved, (3) areas where some conceptual clarity is needed for better theory building, or (4) situations in which a researcher is trying to answer a research question empirically. The former two fall within the realm of applied research, and the latter two are basic research.

Examples of Problem Definition

Example 2.1 pertaining to the broad problem area (page 27) would be defined more clearly and precisely after the interviews with employees have been completed and a literature survey has been done on the area of alienation of employees at the workplace. In other words, in an effort to improve the situation in which the manager sensed that people were disinterested and unenthusiastic about their jobs, the researcher would have talked to the employees in depth and perhaps found that their disinterest stems from the nature of the jobs, which happens to be routine and monotonous. The literature survey would have also reinforced this. At this stage, the researcher might define the problem as follows:

Example 2.3

How can the jobs in this organization be designed so that people interfacing with them are not likely to get bored and distanced or alienated from their jobs?

The second problem area (Example 2.2), where the basic researcher was interested in investigating the concept of job involvement, might be narrowed down and defined after a thorough literature review on job involvement and the important variables affecting it as follows.

Example 2.4

Which contributes more to the job involvement of white-collar clerical workers—the nature of the jobs or the organizational climate?

Thus the problem to be researched is defined after more knowledge is gained about the subject being studied through direct observation, interviewing people, discussions with people having experience in the field of study, and a thorough review of the existing literature.

Further examples of problem statements are shown in this next example.

Example 2.5

1. What are the correlates of job satisfaction?
2. Does job satisfaction increase job performance?
3. Can turnover be reduced by increasing wages in this organization?
4. How effective is our advertising for product X?
5. Do dual-career couples pose more mobility problems for organizations than employees of single-career families?
6. Are the leadership styles of female managers different from those of male managers?

SUMMARY

In this unit we have looked at the first three steps of research: the broad problem area to be researched, preliminary data gathering through unstructured and structured interviews and literature survey, and problem definition. We have additionally learned about the bibliography search and how to document the literature survey from secondary data sources.

In the next unit we look at how the researcher proceeds with the next few steps outlined in the research process model.

SUPPLEMENTAL READINGS

The following topic references will guide you to seek more information.

Topic	Reference	Chapter	Page
Problem area and problem definition	Clover & Balsley (1979)	3	31–36

Topic	Reference	Chapter	Page
Problem area and problem definition	Emory (1980)	3	63–73
	Murdick & Cooper (1982)	6	83–104
	Selltiz, Jahoda, Deutsch, & Cook (1959)	2	26–35
Primary and secondary sources of data	Clover & Balsley (1979)	3	53–65
	Emory (1980)	7	191–211
	Williams & Wolfe (1979)	3	
Literature survey and bibliography	Emory (1980)	7	197–211
		Appendix A	489–505
	Leedy (1974)	5	58–63

REFERENCES

American Psychological Association. *Publication manual* (2nd ed.). Washington, D.C.: American Psychological Association, 1974.

Clover, V. T., & Balsley, H. L. *Business research methods* (2nd ed.). Columbus, Ohio: Grid Publishing Co., 1979.

Emory, C. W. *Business research methods* (Rev. ed.). Homewood, Ill.: Richard D. Irwin, Inc., 1980.

Leedy, P. D. *Practical research: Planning and design*. New York: Macmillan, 1974.

Murdick, R. G., & Cooper, D. R. *Business research: Concepts and guides*. Columbus, Ohio: Grid Publishing Co., 1982.

Selltiz, C., Jahoda, M., Deutsch, M., & Cook, S. W. *Research methods in social relations* (Rev. ed.). New York: Holt, Rinehart and Winston, 1959.

Williams, C. T., & Wolfe, G. K. *Elements of research: A guide for writers*. Sherman Oaks, Calif.: Alfred Publishing Co. Inc., 1979.

POINTS TO PONDER AND RESPOND TO

1. Why is it important to know background information about the organization that is to be researched?

2. Should a researcher *always* find information on the structural and job characteristics from those interviewed?

3. How much library work is involved in compiling a bibliography on the mental health of employees and writing a literature review on the subject: a day? a week? a month? Find out for yourself.

4. Why should one get hung up on problem definition if one already knows the broad problem area to be studied?

5. After studying and extracting information from all the relevant work done previously, how does the researcher know which particular references, articles, and information should be given prominence in the literature survey?

PROJECTS THAT WOULD HELP YOU ACHIEVE LIBRARY SKILLS

Project 2.1

Compile a bibliography on the topic of *job design* with at least fifteen references, including books, academic- and practitioner-oriented journal articles, and articles from magazines and newspapers.

Project 2.2

From the bibliography you compiled in Project 2.1, take three journal articles that you consider important, and write a literature review of two to three paragraphs based on those three articles, properly citing the references. Try to use the several different examples of reference citations shown in the preceding discussions and illustrations in the text.

Project 2.3

Based on the literature review you did for the preceding project, write your problem definition.

UNIT 3
THE RESEARCH PROCESS

Steps 4 to 6:
Theoretical Framework
Hypothesis Development
Elements of Research Design

ISSUES DISCUSSED

The Need for a Theoretical Framework

Variables
- Dependent Variable
- Independent Variable
- Moderating Variable
- Intervening Variable

The Theoretical Framework and Its Five Basic Features

Hypothesis Development
- Definition
- If-Then Statements
- Directional and Nondirectional Hypotheses
- Null and Alternate Hypotheses

The Research Design
- Type of Investigation: Causal versus Noncausal
- Purpose of the Study: Exploratory, Descriptive, Hypothesis Testing (Analytical, Predictive)
- Extent of Reseacher Interference with the Study
- Study Setting: Contrived versus Noncontrived
- Unit of Analysis: Individuals, Dyads, Groups, Organizations, Cultures
- Time Horizon of Study: Cross-sectional versus Longitudinal

UNIT OBJECTIVES

After completing Unit 3 you should be able to:

1. Identify and label variables associated with a given situation.
2. Trace and establish the links among the variables and evolve a theoretical framework.

3. Develop a set of hypotheses to be tested and state them in the null and the alternate.

4. Identify and appropriately select the choice points in the research design, that is, type of investigation, purpose of study, extent of researcher interference, study setting, unit of analysis, and the time horizon of the study.

5. Apply the concepts to a research project.

In the previous unit, the focus was on learning how to narrow down and clearly define the research problem. We can now examine steps 4, 5, and 6 in the research process model in Figure 2.1. Step 4 relates to evolving a theoretical framework, step 5 is concerned with deriving testable hypotheses, and step 6 relates to basic research design issues. This unit will focus on these three steps.

Unit 3 is probably one of the most important units to understand. All your future work in this course will be based on a sound knowledge of developing appropriate theoretical frameworks and deriving logical hypotheses therefrom. This unit will aid in the development of these skills and the additional skill of being able to think systematically. It may be well worth your time and effort to study this unit not merely to know and understand the contents but to work diligently on the exercises. Working conscientiously on the exercises will help sharpen conceptual skills, organize thoughts logically, and enhance communication skills.

The exercises are organized and immediate feedback is provided so that you can constantly evaluate your ability to apply what you have learned. It is important to answer each exercise at the end of this unit carefully and diligently as if it were an examination question. Correct answers are provided at the end of the book for the sole purpose of enabling you to evaluate how organized, systematic, and logical you are in thinking and writing. Careful comparison of your answers with those provided, coupled with an understanding of right and wrong answers, would prove to be very valuable. If you have any doubts about the answers provided, you should be willing and able to discuss it in class. A thorough understanding of how a theoretical framework is developed will enable you to organize variables or concepts logically in order to conduct a research project. A good comprehension of the theoretical framework will not only help you perform better on class exams but will also improve your overall writing skills for other term papers.

Finally, this unit has direct application and relevance to a manager's problems. Throughout the book, examples are provided that in some way relate to problems managers may be forced to confront. In summary. mastering this unit will not only be useful for doing well in this course and other classes, but will also help in understanding a few of the organizational problems you may face as a manager.

THE NEED FOR A
THEORETICAL FRAMEWORK

After conducting the interviews, completing a literature survey, and defining the problem, we are ready to develop a theoretical framework. A theoretical framework is a conceptual model of how we theorize the relationships among the several factors that have been identified as important to the problem. This theory flows logically from the documentation of previous research in the problem area. Integrating one's logical beliefs with published research is pivotal in developing a scientific basis for the research problem. The basis is deemed scientific only if the relationships have been built upon a previously tested and established theory base. Only then can hypotheses be logically developed and subjected to statistical analysis. By being able to test and replicate the findings we will have more faith in the rigor of our research.

The theory and the hypotheses developed will address the problem issues, and the research will focus on finding appropriate solutions. Thus, in order to find solutions to the problems or find answers to research questions, we should first understand the factors or variables that are important in a given problem situation. This, of course, would be identified through the interviews and literature survey. The factors influencing the problem are called variables. Before proceeding to the development of a theoretical framework, it is essential to understand what a variable means and how many types of variables there are.

VARIABLES

A variable is anything that can take on differing or varying values. The values can differ at various times for the same object or person, or the values could differ at the same time for different objects or persons. Examples of variables could be exam scores, absenteeism, or motivation.

Example 3.1

Exam score: Your scores could differ on the different exams you take in this and other classes, or the exam score can take on differing values for each individual in this class for exam one, exam two, and so on.

Example 3.2

Absenteeism: Today three class members may be absent, tomorrow five students may not show up in class; the day after, there may be no one absent. The value can thus theoretically range from "zero" to "all" being absent on the absenteeism variable.

Example 3.3

Motivation: The levels of motivation to learn among members in the class might take on varying values ranging from "very low" to "very high." Your motivation to learn from different classes might also take on differing values.

Types of Variables

Four main types of variables are discussed in this unit:

1. The dependent variable (also known as the criterion variable).
2. The independent variable (also known as the predictor variable).
3. The moderating variable.
4. The intervening variable.

Extraneous variables that confound cause → effect relationships are discussed in the next unit, "Experimental Design."

Dependent Variable

The dependent variable is the variable of primary interest to the researcher. The researcher's goal is to explain or predict the variability in the dependent variable. In other words, it is the main variable that poses the problem for our study. Through the analysis of the dependent variable (i.e., what variables influence it), information about the problem is obtained. This helps us find possible answers and solutions to the problem. The researcher is interested in quantifying and measuring this variable, as well as the other variables that influence this variable.

Example 3.4

A manager is concerned about the productivity of his employees. If he engaged in research, the dependent variable would be *productivity*.

The productivity levels of employees vary—some employees are highly productive, some are average, and others are below average. Obviously, the manager would like to increase the productivity of all employees. In other words, the manager would want to find why the variability exists among the employees and if the low levels of productivity can be controlled in some way. The goal here is thus to explain the variance in productivity.

Example 3.5

A basic researcher is interested in understanding and explaining the concept of job involvement. The dependent variable in her study would be *job involvement.*

Parallel to the explanation in Example 3.4, the job involvement of different employees varies—some have high involvement, some average, and some low involvement. If a researcher wants to find why there is a variability in the level of involvement of employees in their jobs, and how the low levels of some employees' job involvement can be increased, the researcher is, in essence, trying to explain the variability in the job involvement of employees.

Example 3.6

A personnel manager is concerned that the employees are not loyal to the organization and, in fact, switch their loyalties to other institutions. The dependent variable in this case would be *organizational loyalty.*

Here again, there is variance found in the levels of organizational loyalty in employees. The personnel manager wants to know what accounts for the variance in the loyalty of organizational members, so that he can control the variance. Supposing he finds that high pay would keep members loyal to the organization and they will not leave the job for another position with another organization; pay increases given to employees might then help control the variability, and people may stick to this organization.

Now respond to Exercises 3.1 and 3.2 and write your answers in the space provided therein.

Independent Variable

An independent variable is one that influences the dependent variable and accounts for or explains the variance in the dependent variable. In establishing causal relationships, the independent variable is manipulated as described in the next unit.

Example 3.7

Research studies show that a challenging job motivates the employees to work hard. Here, the challenging job is the one that influences motivation and explains the variance in the level of motivation of the employees. That is, the higher the challenge in the job, the greater the motivation of the employees. By increasing or decreasing the challenge in the job, the moti-

Figure 3.1

Diagram showing the relationship between the independent variable (challenging job) and the dependent variable (motivation).

vation of the employee can be increased or decreased. So, **challenging job** is the **independent** variable that would explain the variance in **motivation,** which is the **dependent** variable. This relationship and the labeling of the variables can be diagrammed as in Figure 3.1.

Example 3.8

A professor believes that the time of day that classes are held is an important factor in students' attendance. Early-morning classes usually have poor student attendance, but not the later classes. In this case, **attendance** is the **dependent** variable, and **time** is the **independent** variable that influences or makes a difference in the number of students attending a class. This can be diagrammed as in Figure 3.2.

Now do Exercises 3.3 and 3.4 and write your answers in the space provided.

Moderating Variable

The moderating variable is one that has a strong contingent effect on the independent variable–dependent variable relationship. That is, only when this variable is present (or absent) will the theorized relationship between the independent variable and the dependent variable exist—not otherwise. This becomes clear through the following examples.

Figure 3.2

Diagram showing the relationship between the independent variable (time) and the dependent variable (attendance).

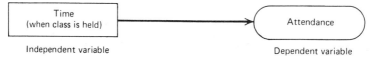

Figure 3.3a

Diagram showing the relationship between the independent variable (number of books) and the dependent variable (reading abilities).

Number of books

Independent variable

Reading abilities

Dependent variable

Example 3.9

It has been found that there is a relationship between the number of books that five- and six-year-old children have access to at home, and their reading abilities. That is, if five- and six-year-olds are provided with a lot of children's books, their reading skills and abilities will improve because the children have greater opportunities to read more books—an activity in which they are assisted by their parents—and hence read better. As a corollary, if children are reared in homes where there are no books, they will have no opportunities to cultivate the reading habit, and hence their reading skills and abilities will be deficient. It is thus argued that there is a relationship between the independent variable, *number of books,* and the dependent variable, *reading abilities,* which is diagrammed in Figure 3.3a.

Although this relationship can be said generally to hold true for all children, there is a group of children for whom this relationship will not exist. Supposing there are illiterate parents in some homes—as is the case in some developing countries; irrespective of the number of children's books that the parents may buy, these children's reading skills and abilities may not develop because they are not being helped by their parents during their preschool years. The relationship between the independent variable, number of books, and the dependent variable, reading skills, has thus become contingent or dependent on the fact that the children have literate parents. In other words, the relationship does not hold true for a subset of six-year-old children who have illiterate parents; for the rest of the children the relationship should generally hold good. In essence, we have divided all children into two groups: those who have literate parents and those who do not, and we are saying that for one group (the children with literate parents who help them) the relationship exists, but for the other group (the children with illiterate parents who do not help), the relationship does not. Thus *parents' literacy* moderates the relationship between the number of books and reading abilities. To put it differently, the relationship between the number of children's books at home and the reading abilities of the six-year-old children is contingent or dependent on the fact that the children have literate parents. This influence of parents' literacy on the relationship between the independent and the dependent variable can be diagrammed as in Figure 3.3b.

Figure 3.3b

Diagram of the relationship between the independent variable (number of books) and the dependent variable (reading abilities) as moderated by the moderating variable (parents' literacy).

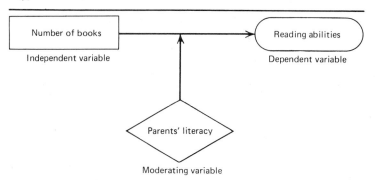

As in the above case, whenever the relationship between the independent variable and the dependent variable becomes contingent or dependent on another variable, we say that the third variable has a moderating effect on the independent variable–dependent variable relationship. The variable that moderates the relationship is known as the moderating variable.

Example 3.10

Let us take another example of a moderating variable related to the organizational setting. Research has shown that the variance in employees' motivation to work (the dependent variable) can be explained by the two independent variables of enriched jobs and organizational support. That is, the extent to which the two latter variables are present influences people's motivation to work. However, research also indicates that this relationship between the two independent variables and the dependent variable does not hold for *all* employees. Only those employees who are high in need for growth would increase their motivation to work through enriched jobs and organizational support. For those who do not have high growth need (say, those who have medium or low growth need strength), enriched jobs and greater organizational support will have no effect on their motivation to work.

In this case, employees have been divided into two distinct groups: those who have high growth needs and all others who do not have high growth needs. For the first group, the relationship between the independent variables and the dependent variable holds; for the second group it does not. Hence, *growth need strength* is the moderating variable in this case.

The relationships discussed above can be depicted as in Figure 3.4.

Figure 3.4

Diagram of the relationships among the four variables: Enriched job, support from the organization, growth need strength, and motivation to work.

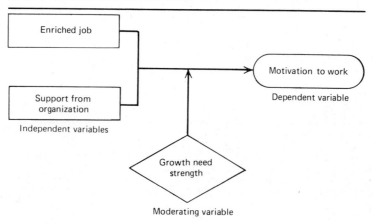

The Distinction Between an Independent Variable and a Moderating Variable

At times, one could get confused as to when a variable is to be treated as an independent variable and when it would become a moderating variable. For instance, there may be two situations as follows:

Situation 1

A research study indicates that the better the quality of the training programs in an organization, and the greater the growth needs of the employees, the greater their willingness to learn new ways of doing things.

Situation 2

Another research study indicates that the willingness of the employees to learn new ways of doing things is not influenced by the quality of the training programs offered by the organizations for all people. Only those who have high growth needs seem to be willing to learn to do new things through specialized training.

In the above two situations, we have the same three variables. In the first case, the training programs and growth need strength are the independent variables that influence employees' willingness to learn—the dependent variable. In the second case, however, the quality of the training

Figure 3.5a

Illustration of the influence of independent variables on the dependent variable when no moderating variable operates in the situation.

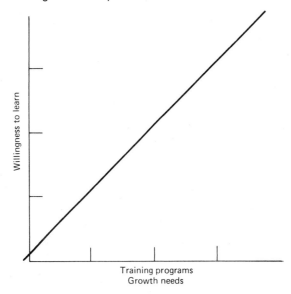

program is the independent variable, and while the dependent variable remains the same, growth need strength becomes a moderating variable. In other words, only those who have high growth needs (i.e., the growth need is strong) will become more willing to learn to do new things when the quality of the training program is increased. Thus the relationship between the independent and dependent variables has now become contingent on the existence of a moderator.

The above illustration makes it clear that even though the variables used may be the same, the decision whether to label them dependent, independent, or moderating would depend on how they affect one another. The differences between the effects of the independent and the moderating variables could be visually depicted as in Figure 3.5a and b.

Now do Exercises 3.5 and 3.6.

Intervening Variable

An intervening variable is one that surfaces between the time the independent variables operate to influence the dependent variable and their impact on the dependent variable. There is thus a temporal quality or time

Figure 3.5b

Illustration of the influence of an independent variable
on the dependent variable when a moderating variable is
operating in the situation.

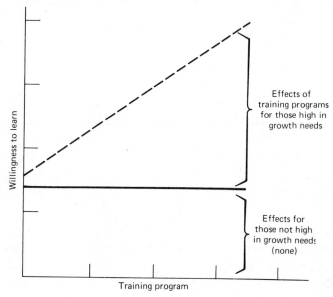

dimension to the intervening variable. The intervening variable surfaces as
a function of the independent variable(s) operating in any situation, and
helps to conceptualize and explain the influence of the independent vari-
able(s) on the dependent variable. The following example illustrates this
point.

Example 3.11

In Example 3.10 where the independent variables (enriched jobs and organizational support) influenced the dependent variable (motivation to
work), an intervening variable that might surface as a function of enriched
jobs and organizational support could be *employee satisfaction*. Because
enriched jobs—that is, jobs that are challenging, use skills, and provide
feedback—will generally be satisfying to most employees, one could see
how employee satisfaction would surface. This is also the case when the
organization supports and encourages employees to do their work in improved and efficient ways. People who derive satisfaction in this manner
are also likely to be more inclined to engage in work behavior. That is,
employees will become more motivated to work. Thus employee satisfaction, the intervening variable that surfaced as a function of the two independent variables, has helped us to conceptualize and understand how,
through the intermediate step of the satisfaction process, one becomes

Figure 3.6

Diagram of the relationships among the independent, intervening, and dependent variables.

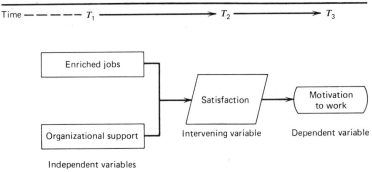

motivated to work. Temporally, satisfaction occurs after the enriched job is handled and the support from the organization is received, and before motivation actually occurs. That is, satisfaction intervenes or comes at some intermediate point between the time the independent variables operate in the situation and the dependent variable is influenced by the independent variables. The dynamics of these relationships can be illustrated as in Figure 3.6.

Example 3.12

It would now be interesting to see how the inclusion of the moderating variable of *growth need strength* in the above example would change the model or affect the relationships. The new set of relationships that would emerge in the presence of a moderator can be depicted as in Figure 3.7. The relationship between the two independent variables and the intervening variable—job satisfaction—will now be moderated by the growth need strength of the employees in the work environment where jobs are enriched and organizational support is given. That is, only those employees who have a high need to grow on the job will achieve increased satisfaction in handling an enriched job and receiving support from the organization, and subsequently, will increase their level of motivation to work. Those who do not have this high growth need will not experience increased satisfaction despite increases in the two independent variables, enriched jobs and organizational support. Thus, growth need strength not only moderates the influence of the independent variables on the dependent variable, it even moderates their influence on the intervening variable. That is, at time T_2 only a subset of the employees experience satisfaction as a function of the two independent variables. They are the ones who have high growth needs. The satisfaction of the others is not influenced.

Figure 3.7

Diagram of the relationships among independent, intervening, moderating, and dependent variables.

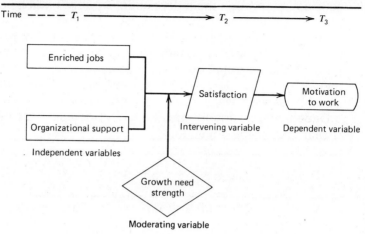

Example 3.13

Now, if we change the situation and say that enriched jobs and organizational support make all employees happy and satisfied, but it is only those who have a high need for growth that actually become motivated to work, then we have a different situation that can be depicted as in Figure 3.8. As can be seen, here the moderating variable influences the relationship between the intervening and dependent variables. In this case, the interven-

Figure 3.8

Representation of the dynamics of variables in the situation described in Example 3.12.

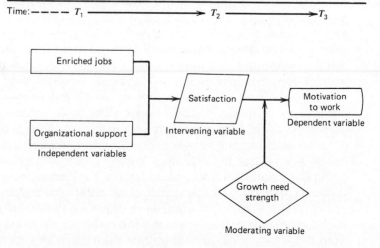

ing variable still helps us to conceptualize and understand how the two independent variables can result in people's motivation to work; the moderating variable, however, explains how only some, but not all who derive satisfaction through the independent variables, will be motivated to work.

Whether a variable is an independent variable, a dependent variable, an intervening variable, or a moderating variable should be determined by a careful reading of the dynamics operating in any particular situation. For instance, a variable such as motivation to work could be a dependent variable, as we have seen in the several situations above; it could also be an independent variable, an intervening variable, or a moderating variable, depending on the situation.

> Now do Exercises 3.7, 3.8, and 3.9.

THEORETICAL FRAMEWORK

Having examined the different kinds of variables that could operate in a situation and how the relationships among these can be established, it is now possible to see how we can develop conceptual models, or theoretical frameworks for our research.

The theoretical framework is the foundation on which the entire research project is based. It is a logically developed, described, and elaborated network of associations among variables that have been identified through such processes as interviews, observations, and literature survey. These variables are deemed important to the problem situation. It becomes evident at this stage that to find good solutions to the problem, one should first identify the problem correctly and then identify variables that contribute to the problem. The importance of conducting good surveys and doing a thorough literature review now becomes clear. After the identification of the proper variables, the network of associations among the variables needs to be elaborated so that relevant hypotheses can be developed and subsequently tested. Based on the results of the tests of hypotheses (which would indicate whether or not the hypotheses have been supported), the extent to which the problem can be solved through the findings of the research becomes evident. The theoretical framework is thus an important step in the research process.

The relationship between the literature survey and the theoretical framework is that the literature survey provides a solid basis for developing the theoretical framework. That is, the literature survey identifies the variables that might be important, as determined by previous research findings. The theoretical framework draws on these findings. It elaborates the relationships that exist among the variables, explains the theory underlying these relations, and describes the nature and direction of the relationships. Just as the literature survey sets the stage for the theoretical framework, a good theoretical framework, in turn, provides the logical base for developing testable hypotheses.

The Components of the Theoretical Framework

A good theoretical framework first identifies and labels the important variables in the situation that are relevant to the problem defined. It then logically describes the interconnections among these variables. The relationships among the independent variables, the dependent variables, and if applicable, the moderating and intervening variables are elaborated. If there are any moderating variables, it is important to explain how and what specific relationships they would moderate. An explanation of why they operate as moderators should also be presented. If there are any intervening variables, a discussion on how or why they are treated as intervening variables would be necessary. Any interrelationships among the independent variables themselves, or among the dependent variables themselves (in case there are two or more dependent variables of interest to the researcher), should also be clearly spelled out and adequately explained.

The elaborations in the theoretical framework thus address the issues of why or how we expect certain relationships to exist, and the nature and direction of the relationships among the variables of interest. A schematic diagram of the conceptual model described in the theoretical framework will also help the reader to visualize the theorized relationships. Thus there are five basic features that should be incorporated in any theoretical framework.

1. The variables considered relevant to the study should be clearly identified and labeled in the discussions.

2. The discussions should state how two or more variables are related to each other. This should be done for the important relationships that are theorized to exist among the variables.

3. If the nature and direction of the relationships can be theorized on the basis of the findings from previous research, then there should be an indication in the discussions as to whether the relationships would be positive or negative.

4. There should be a clear explanation of why we would expect these relationships to exist. The arguments could be drawn from the previous research findings.

5. A schematic diagram of the theoretical framework should be given so that the reader can visualize the theorized relationships.

Let us see how these five features can be incorporated in a theoretical framework in a given problem situation.

Example 3.14

A teacher is wondering how students can be motivated to learn. Her hunch is that if the students are interested in the subject, and the teacher is enthusiastic about teaching the subject, there will be an exciting classroom climate that will motivate students to learn.

**The Theoretical Framework
for the Research in Example 3.14**

The variable of primary interest to this study is the dependent variable of *student motivation*. An attempt is made to explain the variance in students' motivation by the two independent variables of *student interest* and *teacher's enthusiasm. Classroom climate* is the intervening variable that helps us to understand why the relationship between the independent variables and the dependent variable exists.

The greater the students' interest in the subject and what goes on in the class, the higher will be their level of motivation to come to the class and learn. If students are not interested, they will not be highly motivated to learn because the subject taught will seem dull and boring. Likewise, the greater the enthusiasm shown by the teacher in teaching the subject, the more likely the students are to be motivated to attend classes and learn the subject. There would also be a high positive correlation between the two independent variables, because the greater the interest shown by the students, the greater will be the teacher's enthusiasm to teach. This would happen because the teacher draws energy from the interest displayed by students, and teachers usually respond with enthusiasm to student interest in the subject. Having an enthusiastic teacher, likewise, kindles the student's interest and motivation. Students usually respond favorably to teachers who are enthusiastic about teaching. Thus, student interest and teacher's enthusiasm reinforce each other, and when both are present, the climate in the classroom would be one of lively discussion, participation, and excitement. This would be a direct function of both student interest and teacher enthusiasm, and would not happen except for the presence of these two independent variables. In an exciting classroom climate, students would be naturally motivated to learn because their interest level and curiosity would be stimulated. Thus, the classroom climate intervenes between the two independent variables and the ultimate criterion variable. We could think of the two independent variables happening at time T_1, the intervening variable surfacing at time T_2, and the criterion variable happening sometime thereafter, at time T_3. This is diagrammed in Figure 3.9.

Note how the five basic features of the theoretical framework have been incorporated in the above example.

Figure 3.9

Schematic diagram of the theoretical framework in Example 3.14.

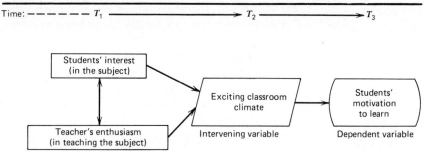

1. **Identification and labeling** of the variables relevant to the study have been completed in the first paragraph. The dependent variable, the two independent variables, and the intervening variable have been introduced and an explanation of their role provided.

2. **The relationships** among the variables were discussed in paragraph two by establishing that:
   a. The independent variable, student interest, is related to the dependent variable, motivation to learn.
   b. The independent variable, teacher enthusiasm, is related to the dependent variable.
   c. The two independent variables influence each other and the intervening variable, classroom climate.
   d. The intervening variable, classroom climate, influences the dependent variable, motivation to learn.

3. **The nature and direction** of the relationships was established by saying that there is a positive correlation (i.e., when one is high, the other is also high) between the following sets of variables:
   a. Student interest and motivation.
   b. Teacher's enthusiasm and student motivation.
   c. Student interest and teacher's enthusiasm.
   d. The two independent variables and classroom climate.
   e. The classroom climate and motivation.

4. **Why these relationships** can be expected was explained through several logical statements, including the following:
   a. Student interest and motivation to learn will be related because without student interest the subject would seem boring, and there would be no inclination to learn.
   b. An enthusiastic teacher would motivate students to learn because such enthusiasm would draw students to class and arouse their curiosity.
   c. Teacher enthusiasm and student interest will be related because

the more the students are interested in learning, the greater will be the teacher's energy level to make it a worthwhile experience for students, who then become even more interested in learning. Thus the one reinforces the other continuously.

d. The two independent variables and classroom climate will be related because with a roomful of interested students and a very enthusiastic teacher, the classroom is going to be very lively with a lot of student participation, discussion, and the like.

e. The intervening variable will be related to motivation because when there is a lively classroom, who would not be inclined to participate in what goes on in the classroom and make it even a better learning experience? Thus motivation to learn will be high.

5. The schematic diagram has been given in Figure 3.9 so that the reader can visually follow the relationships that are theorized.

Now do Exercises 3.10 and 3.11.

HYPOTHESES DEVELOPMENT

Once we have identified the important variables in a situation and established the relationships among them through logical reasoning in the theoretical framework, we are in a position to test whether the relationships that have been theorized do in fact hold true in the particular situation we are examining. By testing these relationships scientifically, through appropriate statistical analyses, we are able to obtain some reliable information on what kinds of relationships exist among the variables operating in the problem situation. The results of these tests offer us some clues as to what could be changed in the situation to solve the problem. Formulating such testable statements is called hypotheses development.

Definition of Hypothesis

A hypothesis is an educated guess about a problem's solution. It can be defined as a logically conjectured relationship between two or more variables expressed in the form of testable statements. These relationships are conjectured on the basis of the network of associations established in the theoretical framework formulated for the research study.

Example 3.15

Several testable statements or hypotheses can be drawn from the theoretical framework formulated in Example 3.14. One of them could be as follows:

If teacher's enthusiasm is high, then student motivation to learn will be high.

The above is a testable statement. If we can measure the extent of teachers' enthusiasm and students' motivation in several classes (we will later learn how to measure these), we can then statistically examine the relationship between these two variables to see if there is a significant positive correlation between the two. If we do find a significant positive correlation, then the hypothesis is substantiated; if a significant positive correlation is not found, then the hypothesis would not have been substantiated.

We would of course expect our hypothesis to be substantiated through the data analysis, because it is a logically conjectured relationship. However, if the hypothesis is not substantiated, we would search for possible reasons for this. We might even suspect that some other important variable that has a contingent influence on the relationship between the two variables was ignored. After reviewing the educational literature, we might in fact discover that previous research has identified a moderating variable— *basic skills.* That is, although initially students might exhibit interest toward a course, unless they have the basic prerequisite skills to meet the goals of the course, their motivation to learn might drop off because learning then becomes a very frustrating experience. Thus we might discover, perhaps a little too late, that the theoretical framework missed an important moderating variable. Incidentally, a situation such as this sensitizes us to the fact that a thorough literature survey is essential to insure against inadequate and inappropriately developed theoretical frameworks. In other words, a good literature survey helps to develop a good theoretical framework, and a good theoretical framework enables us to develop good, testable hypotheses, where the conjectured relationships would hold.

Statement of Hypotheses: Formats

If-Then Statements

As already stated, a hypothesis is a testable statement of the relationship among variables. A hypothesis can also test whether there are differences between two groups (or among several groups) with respect to any variable or variables. To examine whether the conjectured relationships or differences exist or not, these hypotheses can be set either as ordinary statements or in the form of **if-then** statements. The two formats can be seen in the following two examples.

Example 3.16

Students who are more interested in the subject will be more motivated to attend classes regularly.

Example 3.17

> **If** students are more interested in the subject, **then** they will be more motivated to attend the classes regularly.

> ### Directional and Nondirectional Statements

> Where the direction of the relationship between two variables is known, it is possible to state the hypothesis so as to indicate the direction of the relationship. These take the form of **more** or **less,** or **positive** or **negative,** as in the following examples.

Example 3.18

> Women are **more** motivated than men.
> or
> Men are **less** motivated than women.

Example 3.19

> The greater the effort put in, the greater the volume of production (positive relationship).
> or
> The greater the strain experienced by the workers, the less their productivity (negative relationship between the two variables).

> Thus, statements that give an indication of the direction of the relationship are called *directional* hypotheses.
> Sometimes, however, the direction of the relationship between two variables is not definite or is not known. This could happen either because the relationships have not ever been explored in previous research or there have been conflicting findings in the previous research. That is, sometimes the relationship might have been found to be positive and sometimes negative. Hence, the current researcher might only be sure that there is some relationship, but the direction may not be clear. In such a case, the hypotheses might be stated *nondirectionally.* Examples of such hypotheses follow.

Example 3.20

> There is a difference between the motivational levels of men and women.

Example 3.21

> There is a relationship between stress experienced on the job and production levels.

Note that in the first example above, we do not know whether it is the men or the women who have more motivation, and in the second example, whether there is a positive or a negative relationship between stress and production.

Null and Alternate Hypotheses

A *null* hypothesis is usually one that sets the parameters you expect not to find, whereas the *alternate* hypothesis is one that sets the parameters you do expect to find. In other words, the null hypothesis is a statement of *no* difference between two groups or *no* relationships between two variables. The alternate is a statement of differences between groups or relationship between variables.

The null hypothesis in respect to group differences stated in our Examples 3.18 or 3.20 would be

$H_0: \mu_M = \mu_W$

or

$H_0: \mu_M - \mu_W = 0$

where H_0 represents the term null hypothesis

μ_M is the mean motivational level of the men

μ_W is the mean motivational level of the women

The alternate for the above example would statistically be set as follows:

$H_A: \mu_M \neq \mu_W$ (for nondirectional hypothesis according to Example 3.20)

or

$H_A: \mu_M < \mu_W$ (for the directional hypothesis according to Example 3.18)

or

$H_A: \mu_W > \mu_M$ (for the directional hypothesis according to Example 3.18)

where H_A represents the term alternate hypothesis and μ_M and μ_W are the mean motivation levels of men and women, respectively.

The null hypothesis for the relationship between the two variables in Example 3.21 would be

H_0: There is no relationship between stress experienced on the job and the production levels.

This would be statistically expressed by

$H_0: \rho = 0$

where ρ represents the correlation between stress and production, in this case equal to 0 (i.e., no correlation).

The alternate hypotheses for the above null, which has been expressed both directionally in the latter half of Example 3.19, and nondirectionally in Example 3.21, can be statistically expressed as

$H_A: \rho < 0$ (The correlation is negative.)
$H_A: \rho \neq 0$ (There is a correlation—either positive or negative.)

Having thus formulated the null and the alternate hypotheses, the appropriate statistical tests would indicate whether the null is to be accepted or rejected. When the null is accepted (i.e., there are indeed no significant differences between two groups or there is no relationship between two variables), then we could find no support for our alternate hypothesis. However, when we reject the null (i.e., there is a difference between groups or there is a relationship between two variables), then we would have found support for the alternate. *It is thus the alternate hypothesis that is tested in order either to accept or reject the null.*

If we find support for our alternate hypothesis, then we can think of ways of solving the problem (e.g., we can lessen the stress levels experienced by workers in order to increase production, say, by introducing relaxation sessions during work hours).

Now do Exercises 3.12 and 3.13.

THE RESEARCH DESIGN

The research process model in Figure 2.1 shows that the step after the formulation of the hypotheses is the research design stage. Although it is shown as one step in Figure 2.1 for the sake of convenience, research design involves several issues. How scientific a research project is, is often a function of the critical choices made by the researcher at this stage. The design decisions involve several aspects, including the purpose of the study, the type of investigation, the extent to which the researcher would interfere with the normal flow of events, the setting for the study, what should be the unit of analysis, the time horizon for the study, what sampling design should be used, how the variables are to be measured, how the data are to be collected, and how they are to be analyzed. These decision points are shown in the research design model in Figure 3.10.

Figure 3.10

The research design.

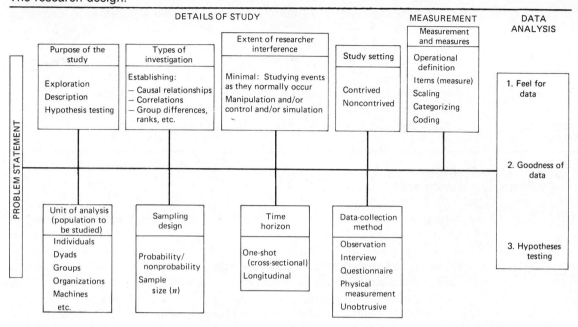

It is important for the researcher to consider carefully each one of the choices in the several boxes in the figure. The purpose of the study and the extent of exactitude needed in the findings would considerably influence the researcher's choice of the sampling design and the data-collection methods. Sometimes as a result of paucity of such resources as time, money, or help, the researcher might settle for less than what would be the "ideal" research design. For example, instead of using both interviewing and questionnaire administration for data collection, the researcher might decide to make use of only questionnaires. Likewise, the researcher might have to make compromises on the ideal sampling design. Thus the researcher might often be forced to suboptimize the design decisions and settle for a lower level of scientific quality in the study because of resource constraints. This trade-off between rigor and resources would be a deliberate and conscious decision made by the researcher based on the scope and objectives that are set for the study. Such trade-offs, as we can see, also partially explain why studies in the management area are not 100 percent scientific, as discussed in Unit 1. Hence, understanding the design choices becomes important in doing research.

In this unit we will look into the alternative choice points with regard to the purpose of the study, the type of investigation, the extent of researcher interference, the study setting, the unit of analysis, and the time horizon of the study. The measurement and data-collection methods and the sampling design will be discussed later in the book.

It should be borne in mind that different researchers have come up with different types of design classifications. Though distinctions and categorizations of study designs have been attempted by several authors, it is difficult to come up with clear and nonoverlapping, distinct categorizations. Emory (1980) has described and discussed these problems. The design classification discussed below and illustrated in Figure 3.10 also suffers from some of the same problems, but should help the student understand the complex research design issues involved.

Type of Investigation: Causal versus Noncausal

A researcher should determine whether a causal or a noncausal study is needed to answer the research question. The former type of study is done when it is necessary to establish a definitive "cause → effect" relationship. However, if the researcher merely wants to identify the important factors "associated with" the problem, then a correlational study is called for. In the former case, the researcher is keen on delineating one or more factors that are undoubtedly *causing* the problem. In other words, the intention of the researcher conducting a causal study is to be able to state that variable X causes variable Y. So, when variable X is removed or altered in some way, the problem Y is solved. Quite often in organizations, though, it is not just one or two variables that cause a problem. Given the fact that most of the time there are multiple factors that influence each other and the problem in a chainlike fashion, the researcher might be more interested in identifying the crucial factors that are associated with the problem, rather than establishing a cause → effect relationship.

When the researcher wants to delineate the cause of a problem, then the study is called a **causal** study. When the researcher is interested in delineating the important variables that are associated with the problem, it is called a **correlational** study. It may be of interest to know that attempts are sometimes made to establish cause → effect relationships through certain types of correlational or regression analyses, such as cross-lagged correlations and path analysis (Billings & Wroten, 1978; Namboodri, Carter, & Blalock, 1975). Whether a study is a causal or a correlational one thus depends on the type of research questions asked and how the problem is defined. The following example will illustrate the difference.

Example 3.22

A causal study question: Does smoking *cause* cancer?
A correlational study question: Are smoking, drinking, and chewing tobacco *associated* with cancer? If so, which of these contributes most to the variance in the dependent variable?

The answer to the first question will help determine whether people who do not smoke will not be affected by cancer. The latter situation recognizes that there are perhaps several other factors that influence cancer apart from the three identified, but do these three help to explain a significant amount of the variance in cancer? If they do, then which among the three variables examined is the one that has the greatest association with it, which is the next important, and which is the third? The answer to the correlational study would help us to determine the extent of risk people take of getting cancer by smoking, drinking, and chewing tobacco.

Whether one wants to do a causal or a correlational study is important, because the decisions regarding the extent of researcher interference with the flow of events and/or the time frame of the study (discussed next) would be influenced by this choice. If it is a causal study, then some variables may have to be manipulated and others controlled. If, in contrast, it is a correlational study, the study can be conducted in the natural setting where events occur without researchers' interfering with the variables. However, as mentioned earlier, it is possible to attempt the establishment of causal relationships without researcher interference with the natural flow of events by using special analytical techniques, or by collecting data at different points in time.

Other types of noncausal studies deal with finding significant differences among groups on some variables of interest, studying the preferences of individuals on various aspects of the environment, and so on. These studies are descriptive in nature and may not be interested either in establishing cause → effect relationships or in knowing the correlations among variables.

The Purpose of the Study: Exploratory, Descriptive, Hypothesis Testing (Analytical and Predictive)

Studies can be either exploratory in nature, or descriptive, and/or conducted to test hypotheses. The nature of the study depends on the stages of advancement of knowledge in the research area. The design decisions become more rigorous as we proceed from the exploratory stage, where we try to explore new areas of organizational research, to the descriptive stage where we try to describe certain characteristics of the phenomena we are interested in knowing about, to the hypotheses-testing stage where we examine whether or not the conjectured relationships have been substantiated and an answer to the research question obtained. We will now look at each of these in some detail.

Exploratory Study

An exploratory study is undertaken when we do not know anything about the situation at hand, or when we have no information on how similar problems or research issues have been solved in the past. In such a case, extensive preliminary work needs to be done to gain familiarity with the phenomena in the situation, and to understand what is happening, before we can even set up a rigorous design for more complete investigation.

Example 3.23

An anthropologist might want to know about the behavior patterns of employees working in organizations in Pennathur.

We hardly know where the place is, much less about the organizations or the people working in the organization, and certainly we have no idea of their behavior patterns! The library may have no information on organizations in Pennathur, or at best, may have very limited information. So, we may need to do extensive exploratory work to find out the details of the place, the organizations, and the people even before we start thinking of how to describe their behavior. Such a study is called an exploratory study.

In the management and organizational behavior areas, almost every topic of interest and concern to management has been studied, and information is available in the library on almost any subject area. Although there are very few exploratory studies done in the management area, from time to time researchers do explore new grounds with the changing dynamics that occur at the workplace. Not long ago, for instance, the topic of women in management was explored. Because of the subsequent studies, the topic has now gone beyond the exploratory stage. The same is possibly true, albeit to a lesser extent, of research on dual-career families and its implications for management.

It is important to note that doing a study for the first time in a particular organization does *not* make the research exploratory in nature; only when no study has ever been done and knowledge is scant in a particular field of investigation, does the study become exploratory.

Descriptive Study

A descriptive study is undertaken in order to ascertain and to be able to describe the characteristics of variables in a situation. For instance, describing a class in terms of the percentage of members who are in their senior and junior years, sex composition, age groupings, number of semesters left for graduation, and number of business courses taken, would be descriptive in nature. Quite frequently, descriptive studies are undertaken in organizations in order to learn about and describe the perceptions of the employees on such variables as the structure, the job, and other factors of interest to the manager. This kind of study is done to obtain a good idea of the characteristics of the variables of interest in any given situation.

Example 3.24

The dean of the college of business wants to know the mean age, IQ, GPA, and gender composition of the administrative science, marketing, finance, and accounting majors in the college. This would be a descriptive study, that is, one can provide the information to the dean, by collecting the data on the variables of interest which would describe the profile of the majors in each area.

Hypotheses Testing

Studies that engage in hypotheses testing could be either analytical or predictive in nature. When, as in applied research, we are mainly interested in investigating the relationships among variables in a particular system that are of interest to us, with the intention of solving the problems immediately at hand, we could be said to be engaged in an analytical study. However, basic research sets out to predict the relationships in other similar situations, and these studies could be called predictive studies. Thus, a subtle distinction is being made between analytical and predictive studies under the hypotheses-testing head. These two subtypes of studies are now discussed.

Analytical Study An analytical study would be undertaken when the problem definition goes beyond describing variables in a situation to knowing why or how certain things are associated with, or contributing to a problem. In other words, the research interest here is in finding the factors that contribute to the problem, and the extent to which they influence the problem. At this phase, one goes beyond merely trying to understand what is happening to analyzing why or how something is happening. Here one tries to explain the variance in the dependent variable by examining which variables impact on it, and why or how.

Example 3.25

If in Example 3.24, the dean had asked what is the relationship between students' GPA and their age, IQ, and sex, then the researcher would analyze the data to determine the extent to which the variance in the GPA of students is explained by these three variables. Such a study definitely goes beyond merely describing the IQs, the age, the sex composition, and the GPA of the students, to analyzing and explaining, through an analysis of the data, the variance in GPA as a function of these three independent variables.

Example 3.26

A manager wants to know how much of the variance in the motivation of the workers can be explained by the amount of bonus they are given. In this situation the manager is trying to analyze the influence of bonus on employee motivation and the study can be categorized as an analytical study.

Predictive Study   A predictive study would go beyond the analytical study inasmuch as it would analyze not only what, how, or why something is happening in a particular situation, but also what, how, or why some things could happen in several other situations with respect to the same problem. In other words, we would be aiming at broader generalizability in predictive studies, where solutions to a problem in a particular study will be applicable in similar cases in other organizational settings. To what extent we would be able to predict similar results for other organizations would depend on how rigorously we design the study in terms of sampling and other methodological issues.

Example 3.27

If the dean of the college of business had wanted to know not only how the three variables of IQ, sex, and age impacted on and explained the variance in students' GPA, but also to determine other significant variables that would influence the GPA of all students in any college of business, the study would be a predictive study. That is, the study is not only looking at a current situation, but also trying to figure out how to maximize the GPA for all students, now and for the future. Thus a predictive study tries to determine how the variance in the dependent variable can be maximally explained, which knowledge will be applicable to many other situations as well.

Review of the Purpose of the Study

It is not difficult to see that in the exploratory stages of a study, the researcher is basically interested in exploring the situational factors so as to get a grip on the characteristics of the phenomena of interest. The descriptive study is undertaken when the characteristics or the phenomena to be tapped in a situation are known to exist, and one wants to be able to describe them better. The analytical study tries to get a handle on how something happening in a situation can be explained, and a predictive study tries to draw more precise conclusions that can be applied to other similar situations. An analytical or predictive study would also be designed to establish cause → effect relationships, so that we would be able to explain and predict that if variable X is introduced into a situation, variable Y will be affected in a given way. The methodological rigor and sophistication increase as one moves from an exploratory study to a predictive study. This usually implies more costs to the researcher. Hence, the nature of the study is a critical decision that needs to be made by the researcher, depending on the objectives of the study and the resources available.

Extent of Researcher Interference with the Study

Most research studies are conducted in the natural environment of the organizational setting with a minimal amount of researcher interference in the normal flow of events in the organization. In other words, the researcher does not deliberately attempt to change or manipulate variables in the work setting. A study conducted in this manner in any particular organization is usually called a **field** study. Where data are collected from several organizations in this manner, the study is usually called a **comparative** study.

Sometimes, however, the researcher must deliberately interfere with the normal flow of events in the natural setting and manipulate certain variables to establish cause → effect relationships. For instance, the researcher might want to study the influence of lighting on worker performance, and hence manipulate the intensity of lighting in the work situation. Here, there is a certain amount of researcher interference with the natural and normal setting. In other cases the researcher might want to create an altogether new setting where the cause → effect relationships can be studied by manipulating certain variables and tightly controlling certain others. Thus there could be varying degrees of interference by the researcher in the manipulation and control of variables in the research study, either in the natural setting or in an artificial research setting. A convenient way to label the two types of studies, where the researcher deliberately interferes with the normal flow of events and where there is no such interference, is to call the former **experimental** designs, and the latter **field** designs.

An example of an experimental design would be a study in which the researcher, trying to examine the effects of pay on employee performance, deliberately asks the president of the company to raise the salary of employees in one department, decrease the pay of employees in another department, and leave the pay of the employees as it is in the third department. Here the researcher is tampering with or manipulating the pay system to establish a cause → effect relationship between pay and performance.

Examples of field designs would be a researcher's plan to study the behavior of students in the classroom, or the behavior of bank employees while they are working in the bank (field studies). Other examples would be studying police chiefs' response patterns to crime in several major cities in the country, or examining employee behavior in several types of industries—banking, manufacturing, service, and so on (comparative studies).

Study Setting: Contrived and Noncontrived

Research could be done in the natural environment where events normally occur. Most organizational research is done in this manner. Even when the experimenter interferes with the natural flow of events in order to establish cause → effect relationships, the manipulation of the variables is quite frequently done in the natural environment of the subjects. Usually, such experimental designs are called *field experiments* because they are conducted in the natural physical environment of the subjects. However, the researcher might sometimes want to contrive an artificial setting for the research. Taking the earlier example of the manipulation of the pay variable on performance, for instance, the researcher might consider that several extraneous variables such as age, training, previous work experience, and other factors might have a direct impact on performance that might contaminate the assessment of the extent of influence of pay alone on performance. In this case, the researcher would like to control for all the contaminating factors, but this may not be possible in the workplace, where there would be varying mixes of these contaminating factors, and the researcher may not be able to isolate their influence because it is impractical to shift personnel for the purpose. Here the researcher might want to contrive a new setting away from the place where events normally occur. For example, the researcher might use a different set of subjects—say university students—and through a stringent control of the contaminating factors (how this is done will be explained in the next unit), manipulate the pay for some simulated task in an artificial setting in order to examine the effects of pay on performance. In this case, the researcher has contrived a setting for the research study that is different from the setting where the phenomena investigated normally and naturally happen. Such artificially contrived settings are usually called **lab** settings, and the experiments conducted in such settings are usually called **lab experiments.**

The researcher has thus to make a decision on whether the study will be conducted in the organizations where the events naturally occur or in an artificial contrived setting.

Unit of Analysis: Individuals, Dyads, Groups, Organizations, Cultures

The unit of analysis refers to the level of aggregation of the data during subsequent analysis. If, for instance, the problem statement focuses on how to raise the motivational levels of employees in general, then we are interested in individual employees in the organization and would like to know what we can do to raise their motivation. Here, obviously, the unit of analysis is the individual. We will be looking at the data gathered from each individual and treating each employee's response as an individual data source. If the researcher is interested in studying two-person interactions, then several two-person groups, also known as dyads, will become the unit of analysis. Analysis of husband-wife interactions in families, and supervisor–immediate boss relationship in the workplace, are good examples of dyads as the unit of analysis. However, if the problem statement is related to group effectiveness, then obviously the unit of analysis would be at the group level. In other words, even though we may gather relevant data from all individuals comprising, say, six groups, we would aggregate the individual data into group data so as to see the differences among the six groups. If we are comparing different departments in the organization, then the data analysis will be done at the departmental level—that is, the individuals in the department will be treated as one unit, and comparisons will be made treating the department as the unit of analysis.

Example 3.28

1. If I am interested in knowing about the performance of employees, then my unit of analysis would be each individual employee (i.e., *individuals*).

2. If I am interested in comparing the performance of six classes I teach, and in determining which class performs best, then my unit of analysis is the *class*. Because my interest is in comparing class performance, I will aggregate the data of all students in each class and compare only the class averages. Hence, my unit of analysis is the class.

3. If I am interested in two different cultures—say, the United States and India—then my cross-cultural comparisons would be at the national level, even though I may collect data from several individuals in several different organizations, in each of the two cultures. Here I will aggregate the data of each country. My unit of analysis is the *culture* or *country,* not individuals or organizations.

It is obvious that the unit of analysis has to be clearly identified as dictated by the problem statement, so that when the data have been collected, the researcher knows how they are to be analyzed; that is, at what level they should be aggregated, if at all. Sampling plan decisions would also be governed by the unit of analysis.

Time Horizon: Cross-Sectional versus Longitudinal Studies

Cross-Sectional Studies

A study can be done in which data are gathered just once, perhaps over a period of days or weeks or months, in order to answer a research question. Such studies are called one-shot or cross-sectional studies.

Example 3.29

Data were collected from bank employees between April and June of last year to investigate a research question. Data with respect to this research have not been collected before from these banks, nor will they be collected again.

Longitudinal Studies

In some cases, however, the researcher might want to study people or phenomena at several points in time in order to answer a research question. For instance, the researcher might want to study employees' behavior before and after there is a change in the top management so as to know the effects of the change on their behavior. Here, because data are gathered at two different points in time, it is not a cross-sectional or a one-shot study, but it is a study carried longitudinally across a period of time. Such studies are called longitudinal studies. That is, the same organizations are studied at different times to answer the research question.

Review of Elements of Research Design

This concludes the discussions on the basic design issues involving the type of investigation, purpose of the study, extent of researcher interference, study setting, the unit of analysis, and the time horizon. The reseacher would determine the appropriate decisions to be made in the study design based on the problem definition and the research objectives.

Do Exercise 3.14.

SUMMARY

In this unit we examined the four types of variables: dependent, independent, moderating, and intervening. We also discussed how theoretical frameworks are developed and testable hypotheses generated therefrom. Finally, we looked at some of the basic research design issues and the choice points available to the researcher.

In the next unit we discuss how experimental designs are set up and what is meant by exogenous and endogenous variables.

SUPPLEMENTAL READINGS

The following topic references will guide you to seek more information.

Topic	Reference	Chapter	Page
The research process	Clover & Balsley (1979)	2	13–29
	Emory (1980)	3	51–80
	Murdick & Cooper (1982)	2	23–24
	Selltiz, Wrightsman, & Cook (1976)	1, 2	1–48
	Stone (1978)	2	15–34
Types of variables	Emory (1980)	4	96–112
	Kerlinger (1973)	3	28–46
	Stone (1978)	2	22–32
Theory and theoretical framework	Emory (1980)	2	34–40
	Kaplan (1964)	8	294–326
	Selltiz, Jahoda, Deutsch, & Cook (1959)	14	480–499
Hypotheses development	Kerlinger (1973)	2	16–27
	Murdick & Cooper (1982)	3	48–49
	Roscoe (1975)	1	7–9
	Selltiz et al. (1959)	2	35–40
	Zetterberg (1955)		533–540
Research design	Emory (1980)	4	82–116
	Katz (1966)	2	56–97
	Murdick & Cooper (1982)	8	127–136
	Selltiz et al. (1959)	10	153–178
	Selltiz et al. (1959)	3	49–78

REFERENCES

Billings, R. S., & Wroten, S. P. Use of path analysis in industrial/ organizational psychology: Criticisms and suggestions. *Journal of Applied Psychology*, 1978, *63*(6), 677–688.

Clover, V. T., & Balsley, H. L. *Business research methods* (2nd ed.). Columbus, Ohio: Grid Publishing Co., 1979.

Emory, C. W. *Business research methods* (Rev. ed.). Homewood, Ill.: Richard D. Irwin, Inc., 1980.

Kaplan, L. *The conduct of inquiry: Methodology for behavioral science.* New York: Chandler Publishing Co., 1964.

Katz, D. Field studies. In L. Festinger & D. Katz (Eds.), *Research methods in the behavioral sciences.* New York: Holt, Rinehart and Winston, 1966.

Kerlinger, F. N. *Foundations of behavioral research* (2nd ed.). New York: Holt, Rinehart and Winston, 1973.

Murdick, R. G., & Cooper, D. R. *Business research: Concepts and guides.* Columbus, Ohio: Grid Publishing Co., 1982.

Namboodri, N. K., Carter, L. F., & Blalock, H. M. *Applied multivariate analysis and experimental designs.* New York: McGraw-Hill, 1975.

Roscoe, J. T. *Fundamental research statistics for the behavioral sciences* (2nd ed.). New York: Holt, Rinehart and Winston, 1975.

Selltiz, C., Jahoda, M., Deutsch, M., & Cook, S. W. *Research methods in social relations* (Rev. ed.). New York: Holt, Rinehart and Winston, 1959.

Selltiz, C., Wrightsman, L. S., & Cook, S. W. *Research methods in social relations* (3rd ed.). New York: Holt, Rinehart and Winston, 1976.

Stone, E. *Research methods in organizational behavior.* Santa Monica, Calif.: Goodyear Publishing Co., 1978.

Zetterberg, H. On axiomatic theories in sociology. In P. F. Lazarsfeld & M. Rosenberg (Eds.), *The language of social research.* New York: The Free Press, 1955.

POINTS TO PONDER AND RESPOND TO

1. Because literature survey is a time-consuming exercise, a good, indepth interview should suffice to develop a theoretical framework.

2. There is an advantage to stating the hypothesis both in the null and in the alternate; it adds clarity to our thinking about what we are testing.

3. It is advantageous to develop a directional hypothesis whenever we are sure of the predicted direction.

4. If one needs to establish a cause → effect relationship, a field study is out of the question.

5. An exploratory study is as useful as a predictive study.

6. The unit of analysis is not an important issue in research design.

7. A good literature survey is a prerequisite for a good theoretical framework, and a good theoretical framework is an essential prerequisite for the development of good hypotheses.

EXERCISES

Exercise 3.1

An applied researcher wants to increase the commitment of organizational members in a particular bank.
What would be the dependent variable in this case?

Exercise 3.2

A production manager is wondering why the workers in her department are reluctant to communicate with her.
What would be the dependent variable in this case?

Exercise 3.3

List the variables in this and the next exercise, individually, and label them as dependent or independent, giving brief reasons and explaining why they are so labeled. Diagram the relationships.

> A manager believes that good supervision and training will increase the production level of the workers.

Variable   **Label**   **Reason**

Explanation

Diagram

Exercise 3.4

> A consultant is of the opinion that increasing the pay and fringe benefits, contrary to common belief, decreases job satisfaction instead of increasing it.

Variable   **Label**   **Reason**

Explanation

Diagram

Exercise 3.5

List and label the variables in the following situation and explain and diagram the relationships among the variables.

> A manager finds that off-the-job classroom training has a great impact on the productivity of the employees in his department. However, he also observes that employees over fifty years of age do not seem to derive much benefit and do not improve from such training.

Variable   **Label**

Explanation

Diagram

Exercise 3.6

List and label the variables in the following situation and explain and diagram the relationships among the variables.

A visitor to a factory observes that the workers in the packing department have to interact with each other to get their jobs done. The more they interact, the more they seem to tend to stay after hours and go to the local pub together for a drink. However, the women packers, even though they interact with the others as much as the men, do not stay late and visit the pub after work hours.

Variable   **Label**

Explanation

Diagram

Exercise 3.7

Make up three different situations in which motivation to work would be an independent variable, an intervening variable, and a moderating variable. Write your answers in the space provided below or on a separate piece of paper.

Situation 1: Motivation to Work as an **Independent** Variable.

Situation 2: Motivation to Work as an **Intervening** Variable.

Situation 3: Motivation to Work as a **Moderating** Variable.

Exercise 3.8

List and label the variables in the following situation, explain the relationships among the variables, and diagram these.

> The multiple roles that members of dual-career families take impose considerable stress on them that, in turn, impairs the satisfactions they derive from their lives. The life satisfaction of those members who have a high self-concept, however, is not influenced by stress.

Variable   **Label**

Explanation

Diagram

Exercise 3.9

List and label the variables in the following situation. Explain the relationships among the variables and diagram them. What might be the problem
statement or problem definition for the situation?

> The manager of Haines Company observes that the morale of employ-
> ees in her company is low. She thinks that if the working conditions,
> the pay scales, and the vacation benefits of the employees are bet-
> tered, the morale will improve. She doubts, though, that increasing
> the pay scales is going to raise the morale of all employees. Her guess
> is that those who have good side incomes will just not be "turned on"
> by higher pay. However, those without side incomes will be happy
> with increased pay and their morale will improve.

Variables   **Label**

Explanation

Diagram

Problem Statement

Exercise 3.10

Develop a theoretical framework for the following situation after stating what the problem definition of the researcher would be in this case.

A family counselor, engaged in counseling married couples who are both professionals, is caught in a dilemma. He realizes that the focus of the counseling sessions should be on both family satisfaction and job satisfaction; however, he is not sure how job and family satisfactions can be integrated in the dual-career family. Husbands, who are the traditional breadwinners, seem to derive more job satisfaction as they get more involved in their jobs and also spend more discretionary time on job-related activities. This, however, does not seem to be true in the case of the wives who perform the dual role of careerperson and homemaker. However, both husbands and wives seem to enjoy high levels of family satisfaction when they spend more time together at home and help each other in planning family-oriented activities.

Problem Statement

Theoretical Framework

Exercise 3.11

Define the problem and develop the theoretical framework for the following situation.

The probability of cancer victims successfully recovering under treatment was studied by a medical researcher in a hospital. She found three variables to be important for recovery.

• Quick and correct diagnosis by the doctor.
• The nurses' careful following of the doctor's instructions.
• Peace and quiet in the vicinity.

In a quiet atmosphere, the patient rested well and recovered sooner. Patients who were admitted in advanced stages of cancer did not respond to treatment even though the doctor's diagnosis was done immediately on arrival, the nurses did their best, and there was plenty of peace and quiet in the area.

Problem Statement

Theoretical Framework

Exercise 3.12

For the theoretical framework developed for the Haines Co. in Exercise 3.9, develop five different null hypotheses and the alternate hypothesis for each null.

1. H_0:

H_A:

2. H_0:

H_A:

3. H_0:

H_A:

4. H_0:

H_A:

5. H_0:

H_A:

Exercise 3.13

A *production* manager is concerned about the low output levels of his employees. The articles that he read on job performance frequently mentioned four variables as important to job performance: skill required by job, rewards, motivation, and satisfaction. In several of the articles it was also indicated that only if the rewards were valent (attractive) to the recipients, did motivation, satisfaction, and job performance increase—not otherwise.

Given this situation, do the following in your own assignment book.

1. Define the problem.
2. Evolve a theoretical framework.
3. Develop at least six hypotheses.

Exercise 3.14

A machine tool operator thinks that fumes emitted in the workshop are instrumental in the low efficiency of the operators. She would like to prove this to her supervisor through a research study.

1. Would this be a causal or a correlational study? Why?

2. Is this an exploratory, descriptive, analytical, or predictive study? Why?

3. What would be the study setting: field, comparative, lab experiment, or field experiment? Why?

4. What would be the unit of analysis? Why?

5. Would this be a cross-sectional or a longitudinal study? Why?

UNIT 4
EXPERIMENTAL DESIGNS

ISSUES DISCUSSED

Causal versus Correlational Analysis

Lab Experiments

Controlled and Uncontrolled Variables

Manipulation of the Causal Factor

Controlling Exogenous Variables
- Matching
- Randomization

Internal Validity

Field Experiments

External Validity

Trade-off Between Internal and External Validity

Factors Affecting Internal Validity
- History Effects
- Maturation Effects
- Testing Effects
- Instrumentation Effects
- Selection Effects
- Statistical Regression Effects
- Mortality Effects

Factors Affecting External Validity

Types of Experimental Designs and Internal Validity

Simulation

UNIT OBJECTIVES

After completing Unit 4 you should be able to:

1. Distinguish between causal and correlational analysis.
2. Explain the difference between lab and field experiment.
3. Explain the following terms: controlled variables, uncontrolled variables, manipulation, experimental and control groups, treatment effect, matching, and randomization.
4. Discuss internal and external validity in experimental designs.

5. Discuss the seven possible threats to internal validity in experimental designs.

6. Describe the different types of experimental designs.

7. Discuss the Solomon four-group design and its implications for internal validity.

8. Apply what has been learned to class assignments, and exams.

In this unit we will discuss experimental designs—both lab experiments and field experiments. Experimental designs are set up to study cause → effect relationships among variables. These are in contrast to the correlational studies that we have discussed thus far. Correlational studies can be done as field studies (i.e., the phenomena can be studied as they occur in their natural environment), but causal studies usually have varying degrees of artificial constraints imposed on them, interrupting the natural sequence or flow of events. We will discuss the various aspects of experimental designs in this unit.

CAUSAL VERSUS CORRELATIONAL ANALYSIS

Sometimes managers may not be content with knowing what the correlates of a dependent variable of interest are. They may want to know which independent variable "causes" the dependent variable. For example, a manager might want to know what causes a decrease or drop in production or which variable causes absenteeism of employees, and so on. The manager in these cases is not content with knowing all the variables that are associated with the dependent variable, but wants to know which particular variable causes the dependent variable. Knowing this, the manager could eliminate the variable in question so that its adverse consequences on the dependent variable would be eliminated. The causal variable is identified by studying the situation through experimental designs. Thus experimental designs help determine cause → effect relationships.

A field study is distinguished from an experimental design in that the former is concerned with identifying the important correlates that explain the variance in the dependent variable, and the study is conducted in the environment where events naturally occur without any artificial constraints being imposed in the setting. The latter, in contrast, helps to isolate the variable that causes the dependent variable, and the researcher does interfere with the natural flow of events to some degree. Setting up an experimental design thus calls for careful and well-thought-out strategies. Isolating a causal factor is difficult because we have to establish beyond the shadow of a doubt that variable X causes variable Y. That is, we are no longer content as in the correlational field studies, with making statements such as the following: variables X, D, and C covary with variable Y—that is, whenever these variables are present, variable Y is also present; whenever these variables are present only to a very small degree, variable Y is also present only to a small extent; and when these variables are present to a high degree, variable Y is also present to a high degree. Instead, in a causal study we want to be able to say that if variable X is not present, then variable Y will not occur, no matter how many other factors may be present in the situation.

Also, in establishing a causal relationship, we have to be sure that variable X causes variable Y, and that there is no possibility that variable Y could or would cause variable X. The following example illustrates this. Suppose a doctor tells his patient, who is a heavy smoker, that she should stop smoking because her lungs are becoming affected by it. The patient might ask the doctor whether smoking is the cause for the deterioration in the lungs, and the doctor might say yes. The patient might understandably get upset by this statement and argue with the doctor that it is not really smoking that is causing her lung condition, but it is the other way around. That is, she is smoking so much because her lungs are craving for a smoke and find relief through her smoking. In other words, the patient is saying, in her own words, that it is not smoking that causes the lung condition, but it is the lung condition itself that is causing her to smoke. Seeing how upset the patient is (she is now visibly trembling with anxiety) and not wanting to upset her any further during this particular visit, the doctor might say that he could not agree with the patient's logic, but at this stage he would only be willing to say that there is a connection between smoking and lung condition. What the doctor did was to change his argument from "smoking *causes* weak lungs," to "smoking and weak lungs are *associated* very strongly—that is, each influences the other and there could be reciprocal causation."

The dialogue between the doctor and the patient can be depicted as in Figure 4.1 through the direction of the arrows. If the doctor has to prove to the patient that smoking causes cancer, and it is not the weak lungs that cause people to smoke, the doctor will have to show that people with weak lungs do not always smoke, and that those who smoke have weak lungs.

To establish causal relationships in an organizational setting, several variables that might covary with the dependent variable (i.e., influence each other mutually and vary together either positively or negatively) have to be controlled in order to allow us to say that variable X and variable X alone causes the dependent variable Y. Establishing this also implies that when variable X is eliminated, variable Y will also be eliminated. Useful as it is to know the cause → effect relationships, establishing them is not easy, because several other variables that covary with the dependent variable have to be controlled. It is not always possible in research on organi-

Figure 4.1

Distinction between causal and correlational influences.

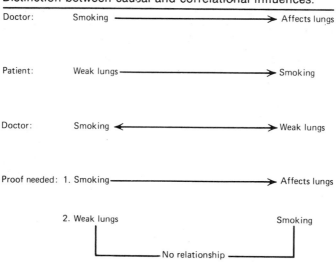

zations where the events are allowed to occur and follow their natural sequence, to control several variables while manipulating the causal factor—that is, the one independent variable that is causing the dependent variable. It is, however, possible to first isolate the effects of a variable in a tightly controlled artificial setting (the lab setting), and after testing and establishing the cause → effect relationship under these tightly controlled conditions, see how generalizable these cause → effect relationships are to the natural settings (field setting).

Let us illustrate this with an example. Suppose a manager or a researcher believes that staffing the accounting department completely with females will increase its productivity; it is well nigh impossible to transfer all the men currently in the department to other departments, and then recruit or transfer other women to this department, because this would disrupt the work of the entire organization—that is, many new people would have to be trained in the various departments, work would slow down, employees would be upset, and so on. However, the hypothesis that gender influences the productivity of the accounting department can be tested in an artificially created setting in which men can be asked to perform an accounting job, women can be asked to do the same job, and a mix of men and women can be asked to perform the same accounting task to determine whether the hypothesis is substantiated. If it is, then the manager or researcher could arrange to have planned and systematic transfers effected in the organization such that, in due course, the entire accounting department can be staffed with female members. We can see then if the productivity goes up or not.

Thus, experimental designs fall into two categories: the lab experiment and the field experiment.

THE LABORATORY (LAB) EXPERIMENT AND THE FIELD EXPERIMENT

The Lab Experiment

As stated earlier, when cause → effect relationships are clearly established between an independent and a dependent variable of interest, then all other variables that might contaminate or confound the relationship have to be tightly controlled. In other words, the possible effects of other variables on the dependent variable have to be in some way accounted for, so that the actual causal effects of the investigated independent variable on the dependent variable can be determined. It is also necessary to manipulate the independent variable so that the extent of its causal effects can be established. The controls and manipulations are best done in an artificial setting called the laboratory, where the causal effects can be tested. Such experimental designs, where artificial controls and manipulations are introduced to establish cause → effect relationships, are called laboratory experimental designs or simply lab experiments.

Because we are using the terms control and manipulation, let us examine what these concepts mean.

Controlled and Uncontrolled Variables

In the context of experimental designs, a distinction is often made between exogenous or extraneous variables, and endogenous or explanatory variables. The endogenous or explanatory variables are none other than the independent, dependent, intervening, and moderating variables that we have already discussed in Unit 3; exogenous variables are those variables or factors that are not directly considered in the causal study but that could possibly have a contaminating or confounding effect on the cause → effect relationships. For instance, a new advertising campaign might have been started to increase the sales of, say, a mod product. That is, the new advertising is expected to cause an increase in sales. However, this cause → effect relationship might be influenced by an extraneous factor, for example, the life stage of the consumer. For instance, teenagers with a mod life-style might really be induced by the advertisement to buy more of the product. People in their middle years, with a more sober life-style, might not be influenced to the same degree; and senior citizens may, with few exceptions, be influenced even less by the advertisement. Thus, here is a variable—life stage—extraneous to the study, which might confound the results of studying the impact of advertisement (the independent variable) on sales (the dependent variable). Such a possible confounding variable is called a controlled exogenous variable. Note that this is not the same as the moderating variable. We are not saying here that there is a

Figure 4.2

Controlled and uncontrolled exogenous variables in experimental designs.

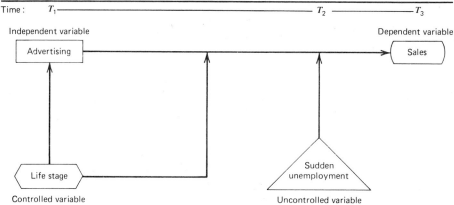

causal relationship only for one group and for others there is none. We are merely stating that there is another variable that might confound the relationships between the independent and dependent variables. The effects may be very pronounced with one or more groups, and less pronounced with one or more other groups, such that when we put all the groups together and examine the relationship, we would fail to distinguish the true extent of the cause → effect relationship. However, this confounding variable can be controlled, inasmuch as we can study the cause → effect relationship among teenagers where the impact will be most pronounced.

There is also another type of exogenous variable that could confound the cause → effect relationship but that cannot be controlled. This type of variable is called the uncontrolled exogenous variable. Let us consider the same example of the effects of advertisement on consumer buying. Suppose that in the middle of the advertising campaign, there is severe unexpected unemployment in the country. Now, because the purchasing power of the consumers is down, we would not be able to determine whether a failure of sales of the mod product to pick up indicates a failure of the advertisement or simply a reaction to the general state of the economy. It could be either, or both; but it would be difficult to estimate the true cause → effect relationship that we had originally set out to establish. The state of the economy is not a variable we can control as advertisers. Such variables are called uncontrolled exogenous variables. Figure 4.2 shows the different variables in experimental designs.

Even though we may not be able to do much to control for the effects of the uncontrolled variables, the possible confounding effects of the controlled exogenous variable have to be carefully thought through before experimental research designs are set up. Later, in Example 4.1, we will see how we control for some of the controlled confounding variables.

Manipulation of the Independent Variable

In order to examine the causal effects of an independent variable on a dependent variable, certain manipulations need to be tried in the lab setting. For instance, if we want to test the effects of lighting on worker production among sewing machine operators, then we might want to manipulate the intensity of the light beams. To do this, we might first want to measure the production levels of all the operators over a 15-day period with the usual amount of light they work with—say 60-watt bulbs. We might then want to split the group of 50 operators into five groups of ten members each, and while allowing one subgroup to work under the same conditions as before (60-watt electric bulbs) we might want to manipulate the intensity of the light for the other four subgroups, by making one group work with 80-watt bulbs, another with 90 watts, the third with 100 watts, and the fourth with 120 watts. After the different groups have worked with these varying degrees of light exposures for 15 days, each group's total production for these 15 days may be checked to see if the difference between the preexperimental production and the postexperimental production among the groups is directly proportional to the intensity of the light beams to which they have been exposed. If our hypothesis that more light increases the production levels is correct, then the subgroup that did not have any change in the lighting—called the control group—should have no increases in production; all the other groups should show increases in production levels; and the ones having more light should show greater increases than those who had lesser amounts of increased lighting.

In this case the independent variable, lighting, has been manipulated by having a control group who had no change in the lighting, and various other groups who were exposed to different degrees of changes in the lighting. This manipulation of the independent variable is also known as the *treatment*, and the results of the treatment are called *treatment effects*.

Let us illustrate how variable X can be both controlled and manipulated in the lab setting through Example 4.1.

Example 4.1

Let us say that a production manager is rather disappointed with the productivity of his workers, who are paid wages at an hourly rate. He might be wondering whether paying them piece rates would increase their productivity. However, before implementing the piece-rate system he would want to know for sure that switching over to the new system will result in an increase in productivity.

In a case like this, the researcher might first want to test the causal relationships in a lab setting, and if the results are encouraging, the experiment might then be conducted in a field setting. For the lab experimental design, the researcher should first think of possible factors that might affect the productivity of the workers, and then try to control these. Other than piece rates, previous job experience might influence productivity because familiarity with the job makes it easy for people to increase their productivity levels; gender differences may affect productivity, especially if the jobs are very strenuous and require muscular strength; age may also influence the productivity of employees, and for some types of jobs, educational levels may be important, too. Let us say that for the type of production job in question, age, gender, and prior experience of the employees are the factors that would influence the performance and productivity of the employees. Hence, the researcher needs to control these three exogenous variables. Let us see how this can be done.

Suppose the researcher is going to set up four groups of 15 people each for the lab experimental design—one group to be used as the control, and the other three to be subjected to three different manipulations. Now, the three variables can be controlled in two different ways—either by matching the groups or through randomization. These concepts should be explained before we proceed further.

Controlling Exogenous Variables

Matching Groups

One way of controlling for exogenous controlled variables is to match the various groups by taking the confounding characteristics and deliberately spreading them across groups. For instance, if there are 20 women among the 60 members, then each group will be assigned 5 women, so that the effects of gender are distributed across the four groups. Likewise, age and experience factors can be matched across the four groups, such that each group has a similar mix of individuals in terms of gender, age, and experience. Because the suspected contaminating factors are matched across the groups, we can be comfortable in saying that variable X alone causes variable Y, if such is the finding after the experiment.

Randomization

Another way of controlling for the exogenous variables is to assign the 60 members randomly to the four groups. That is, every member would have a known and equal chance of being assigned to any of these four groups. For instance, we might throw the names of all the 60 members into a hat, and draw their names. The first 15 names drawn may be assigned to the first group, the second 15 names to the second group, and so on. By thus randomly assigning members to the groups—remember, random assignment means there is no predetermination as to which group each person would be assigned to—we would be distributing the controlled variables

Table 4.1

Determining the Cause → Effect Relationships After Randomization

Groups	Treatment	Treatment effect (% increase in productivity rate)
Experimental group 1	$1.00 per piece	10
Experimental group 2	$1.50 per piece	15
Experimental group 3	$2.00 per piece	20
Control group (no treatment)	Old hourly rate	0

among the groups equally. That is, the variables of age, sex, and previous experience—the controlled variables—will have an equal probability of being distributed among the groups. The process of randomization would ideally ensure that each group is comparable to the other. To put it differently, we could expect that the effects of age, sex, and previous experience will be controlled. That is, each of the groups will have some members who have more experience mingled with those who have less or no experience. All groups will have members of different age and sex composition. Thus randomization would ensure that if these variables do indeed have a contributory or confounding effect, by distributing these confounding effects across groups, we have controlled their confounding effects. This is achieved because when we manipulate the independent variable of piece rates by having no piece-rate system at all for one group (control) and having different piece rates for the other three groups (experimental), we can determine the causal effects of the piece rates on productivity; any errors or biases caused by age, sex, and previous experience are now normally distributed with equal probability among all four groups. Any causal effects found would be over and above the effects of the confounding variables.

To make it clear, let us illustrate this with some actual figures as in Table 4.1. Note that because the effects of experience, sex, and age have been controlled in all the groups by randomly assigning the members to the four groups, and the old hourly rate control group had no increase in the productivity rates, it can be safely concluded from the table that the percentage increases in productivity are a result of the piece-rate treatment effects. In other words, piece rates are the cause of the increase in productivity. We cannot now say that the cause → effect relations have been confounded by other exogenous variables, because they have been controlled through the process of randomly assigning members to the groups.

Advantages of Randomization

The difference between matching and randomization is that in the former case individuals are deliberately and consciously matched for the various controlled characteristics, whereas in the latter case we expect that the process of randomization will distribute the inequalities among the groups, based on the laws of normal distribution, and we need not be particularly concerned about any confounding factors. Matching could be less effective than randomization because we may not be cognizant of all the confounding variables that might affect the cause → effect relationship or the internal validity of the experiment, discussed more fully later. We may thus fail to match groups on some critical factors. Sometimes, even if we know the confounding variables, we may not be able to find a match for all such variables. For instance, if gender is a confounding variable, and if there are only two women in a four-group experimental design, we will not be able to match all the groups with respect to gender. Randomization solves this kind of problem as well.

In sum, experimental designs involve controlling the contaminating variables through the process of either matching or randomization, and the manipulation of the treatment.

Internal Validity

Because of the tightly controlled and carefully manipulated treatments in the lab setting, it is possible to establish cause → effect relationships more precisely and confidently. To put it differently, there is much truth or validity to our findings in regard to the cause → effect relationship in the lab experiments. The internal validity of the lab experiments is thus high; that is, we can be sure that variable X *causes* variable Y. Within the artificial lab setting, where a high degree of control and manipulation have taken place, the cause → effect relationships found are valid or true. Thus internal validity refers to the validity or truth of any conclusions drawn about causal relationships, and internal validity is usually high in lab experiments where statistical results substantiate cause → effect relationships.

So far we have talked about establishing cause → effect relationships within the lab setting, which is an artificially created, controlled situation. You might yourself have been a subject taking part in one of the lab experiments conducted by the psychology or other departments on campus at some time. You might not have been told exactly what cause → effect relationships the experimenter was looking for, but if you have been a participant in any of the lab experiments, they surely would have had a cover story for you. That is, some vague reason for the experiment would have been given to you so as not to sensitize you to the real issues. At the end of the experiment, the researcher would have provided the total reasoning for the actual purpose of the experiment. That is how lab experiments are usually done. Subjects are selected and assigned to different groups through a matching or randomization process; they are put into a lab (i.e., a controlled setting); they are given a cover story and a task to perform; and some kind of questionnaire or other tests will be administered both before and after the task is completed. The results of these studies would indicate the cause → effect relationships under investigation.

Incidentally, it should be noted that the cover stories used cannot be too deceptive because the human subjects committees on campuses, who protect the interests of the subjects, will not approve the research if they consider it in any way impinging on the rights or the dignity of the subjects. In such cases it becomes the researcher's job to obtain informed consent signed by the subjects before the committee will permit the researcher to conduct the study. This makes it difficult for researchers to come up with cover stories that would completely mask the purpose of the experiments to the subjects.

Now let us see to what extent the findings in the lab setting would be transferable or generalizable to the actual organizational or field settings. For instance, if in the lab experimental design in Example 4.1 the groups were given the simple production task of screwing nuts and bolts onto a piece of iron, and the results were that the groups who were paid piece rates were more productive than those who were paid hourly rates, to what extent can we say that this would be true in the live organizational setting? The tasks in organizations might be far more complex, and there might be several confounding variables that cannot be controlled. For instance, the persons who are there are a "given"—we cannot lay off some people because of their inadequate age or experience or because of their sex. Under such circumstances, we cannot be sure that what was true in the lab experiment is necessarily likely to hold good in the field setting. To test the causal relationships in the organizational setting, field experiments are done. These will now be briefly discussed.

The Field Experiment

A field experiment, as the name implies, is an experiment done in the natural environment in which events normally occur, but with the difference that there will be a treatment given to one or more groups. Thus in the field experiment, even though it may not be possible to control all of the exogenous variables because members cannot be either randomly assigned to groups or matched, treatments can still be manipulated. Control groups could also be set up in field experiments. The experimental and control groups in the field experiment could be made up of the people working at several plants within a certain radius, or from the different shifts in the same plant, or in some other way. If there are three different shifts in a production plant, for instance, and the effects of the piece-rate system are to be studied, one of the shifts can be used as the control group, and the two other shifts could be given two different treatments or the same treatment—that is, different piece rates or the same piece rate. Any cause → effect relationship found under these conditions would have wider generalizability to other similar production settings, even though we may not be sure to what extent the piece rates alone were the cause of the increase in productivity because some of the other confounding variables could not be controlled.

External Validity

What we just discussed can be referred to as an issue of external validity versus internal validity. External validity refers to the extent of generalizability of the results of a causal study to other field settings, and internal validity refers to the extent of the accuracy of the causal effects—that variable X causes variable Y. Field experiments or quasi-experiments have more external validity (i.e., the results may be more generalizable to other similar organizational settings); but they have low internal validity (i.e., we cannot be certain of the extent to which variable X alone caused variable Y). Note that in the lab experiment, the reverse is true. The internal validity is high but the external validity is rather low. In other words, in lab experiments we can be sure that variable X causes variable Y because we have been able to keep the other confounding exogenous variables under control, but we have so tightly controlled several variables to establish the cause → effect relationship that we do not know to what extent the results of our study could be generalized, if at all, to field settings. In other words, the lab setting does not reflect the "real world" setting; we do not know to what extent the lab findings validly represent the reality in the outside world. Thus the generalizability of lab experimental findings to organizations becomes restricted.

Trade-off Between Internal and External Validity

There is thus a trade-off between internal and external validity. If we want high internal validity, we should be willing to settle for low external validity, and vice versa. To ensure both types of validity, researchers usually try first to test the causal relationships in a tightly controlled artificial or lab setting, and once the relationship has been established they try to test the causal relationship in a field experiment. Lab experimental designs in the management area have thus far been used to sort out, among other things, gender differences in leadership styles, managerial aptitudes, and so on. However, gender differences and other factors found in the lab settings are frequently not found in field studies (Osborn & Vicars, 1976). These problems of external validity usually limit the use of lab experiments in the management area, even though they are frequently used as a first step to establish cause → effect relationships before extending causal theories to field settings. Because field experiments often have unintended consequences—such as personnel becoming suspicious, rivalries and jealousies being created among departments—researchers conduct field experiments only infrequently.

FACTORS AFFECTING INTERNAL VALIDITY

Even the best designed lab studies could include some factors that might affect the internal validity of the lab experiment. That is, some confounding factors might still be present. Seven main factors that pose a threat to internal validity should be mentioned. The effects of these seven factors on the causal relationships are history, maturation, testing, instrumentation, selection bias, statistical regression, and mortality effects. Each of these is explained briefly with examples.

History Effects

Certain events (or factors) that would have an impact on the independent variable–dependent variable relationship might unexpectedly occur while the experiment is in progress, and this history of events would confound the cause → effect relationship between the two variables, thus affecting the internal validity. For example, let us say that a teacher tries different teaching methods to determine which particular pedagogy has the greatest impact on student performance. The teacher might have been able to control for confounding variables such as previous exposure of the students to the same topic, or student age. Although the experimental design is properly set up to enhance the internal validity of the experiment, certain events may occur that could have an impact on the independent variable–dependent variable causal relationship. Recall our earlier discussions in the context of the uncontrolled exogenous variable. In this case, it could be the university president introducing a new scholarship for the three students who score the highest points in this and some other classes. This move on the part of the president might have been totally unexpected and there might have been no way of controlling the president's announcement in the middle of the experiment. When the students' performance in the class increases, there is no way of establishing how much of the increase is attributable to the changed teaching methods adopted by the instructor, and how much to the induced motivation to study and perform through the announcement of the president's award. Thus the uncontrolled flow of events has ruined the internal validity of the experiment because we would be unable to determine the amount of improvement in student performance that is caused by the changed pedagogy, as compared to the amount caused by the historical flow of events. The effects of history can be illustrated as in Figure 4.3.

Figure 4.3

Illustration of history effects in experimental designs.

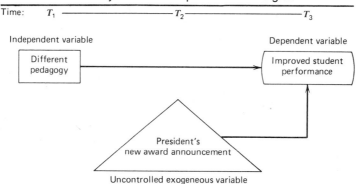

To give another example, let us say a bakery is studying the effects of adding to its bread a new ingredient that is expected to enrich it and offer greater strength and vitality to children under 14 years of age within 30 days, if certain prescribed quantities of the bread are consumed daily. At the start of the experiment the bakery takes a measure of the strength and vitality of the children through a special measuring device, and matches 80 children in four groups—two of which are subjected to the experimental treatment, and two used as control groups. On the twentieth day of the experiment, a flu virus hits the city in epidemic proportions affecting most of the city, including many of the children studied. This unforeseen and uncontrollable specific event, flu, has contaminated the cause → effect relationship study for the bakery.

Maturation Effects

Cause → effect relations can also be contaminated by the effects of the passage of time—another uncontrollable variable. Such contamination is called maturation effects. The maturation effects are a function of the processes—both biological and psychological—operating within the respondents as a result of the passage of time. Examples of maturation processes could include growing older, getting tired, feeling hungry, and getting bored. In other words, there could be a maturation effect on the independent variable–dependent variable relationship purely because of the passage of time. For instance, let us say that students in the classroom complain that the course has so little structure that there is a lot of ambiguity, which is inhibiting their performance. Let us also say that the instructor develops handouts during the rest of the semester in order to reduce the ambiguity that might have adverse effects on their performance. At the end of the semester, when the students perform well, it would be difficult for the instructor to determine how much of their perfor-

Figure 4.4

Illustration of maturation effects on cause → effect relations.

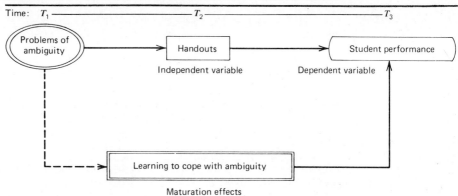

mance improvement during the semester is attributable to her providing handouts and trying to give more structure, and how much resulted from the students having learned to deal with ambiguity as the semester proceeded—the maturation effects. The mere passage of time might have allowed the students to learn to cope with ambiguity and perform well, even without the handouts! The maturation effects in this case can be illustrated as in Figure 4.4.

Thus, maturation effects might also contaminate the internal validity of experimental designs.

Testing Effects

In order to test the effects of a treatment, subjects will often be given what is called a pretest. For instance, if a teacher wants to know the effects of his lecture on the learning of the students in a class, he might first administer a quiz containing questions on the material to be covered in the lecture, and score the test. This pretest score will give the teacher an indication of how much the students already know about the subject. If the students then score higher on a posttest given after the lecture—that is, they are found to have gained in knowledge—then the teacher can determine the extent to which his lecture has been effective. Thus the pretest is used to gauge the effects of the treatment by comparing it with the posttest scores. However, the very fact that the students were exposed to a pretest would sensitize them to some of the key issues in the material, which they would then respond to much better at the time of the posttest than if they had not been sensitized to the issues through the pretest. This sensitizing through previous testing, called the testing effects, also affects the internal validity of experimental designs. Although teaching effectiveness can be legitimately measured through pre- and posttests, the pretest could confound the cause → effect relationship by sensitizing the respondents to the posttest.

Instrumentation Effects

Instrumentation effects are another source of threat to internal validity. These effects might arise because of a change in the measuring instrument between pretest and posttest, and not because of the treatment's differential impact at the end (Cook & Campbell, 1979). For instance, an observer who is involved in observing the types of behaviors that occur in a respondent might become more experienced and sensitive in observing behaviors between a pretest and a posttest. Thus the posttest might be measured with greater sophistication than was the pretest, and there would be an exaggerated difference reflected as a result. Another example would be the loss in tension of a spring balance or other finely calibrated instrument with frequent use, which would result in an erroneous final measurement. The internal validity in such cases would suffer from instrumentation effects.

In a classroom experimental design situation, if different instructors dealing with different groups of students have different grading standards, then this will introduce instrumentation biases that would contaminate the results. Thus instrumentation effects pose a threat to the internal validity in experimental designs.

Selection Bias Effects

The threat to internal validity could also come from improper or unmatched selection of subjects for the experimental and control groups. For example, if a behavior-modification consultant wants to study the effects of electric shock on student behavioral responses, not many students would want to participate in the study. Those who volunteer for money or grades might be totally different from the ones who are put in the control group to whom shock is not administered. Thus any causal effects detected from the differences between the control and experimental groups' behaviors may not reflect the true cause → effect relationships. Hence, newcomers, volunteers, and others who cannot be matched with the control groups would pose a threat to internal validity in certain types of experiments.

Statistical Regression

The effects of statistical regression occur when the experimental or control group or both happen to include members with extreme scores on some important variables. Let us say that the effects of a new teaching technique are to be tested on a class of students. Let us also say that students with very low IQs or very high IQs have been selected for the experimental and control groups. The effects of the teaching pedagogy cannot be accurately reflected in the performance of these two groups because we know from the laws of probability that the students with very low IQs have a greater probability of showing improvement and scoring closer to the mean on the posttest (i.e., after the treatment) than before. This is called regressing toward the mean. Likewise, students with very high IQs would also have a greater probability of tending to regress toward the mean—that is, of scoring lower on the posttest than before. Thus the very high or very low IQ students are not good samples on which to base our findings about the treatment effects. Hence we must ensure that subjects selected for the experimental and control groups do not belong to the extremes of a continuum on some critical variables. Failing to do so will only contaminate the cause → effect relationship and decrease the internal validity. Randomization, however, would avert or at least considerably reduce the problem of statistical regression.

Mortality

Another confounding effect on the cause → effect relationship comes from the mortality or attrition of the members in the experimental or control group or both, as the experiment progresses. When the group composition changes over time across the groups, comparison between the groups becomes difficult, because those who dropped out of the experiment may confound the results. Again, we would not be able to say how much of the effect observed arises from the treatment, and how much is attributable to the nature of the members who dropped out; those who stayed with the experiment could be quite different from those who dropped out.

FACTORS AFFECTING EXTERNAL VALIDITY

Whereas internal validity raises questions about whether it is the treatment alone or some other exogenous factor that causes the effects, external validity raises issues about the generalizability of the findings to other settings. For instance, the extent to which the experimental situation differs from the setting to which the findings are expected to be generalized is directly related to the degree of threat it poses to external validity. To illustrate, subjects in a lab experiment might be given a pretest and a posttest. Those findings, however, cannot be generalized to the organizational world, where a pretest is seldom administered to employees to be followed up by a posttest. Thus the effects of the treatment will not be the same in the field, which reduces the generalizability. Another threat is the selection of the subjects. In a lab setting, the types of subjects selected for the experiment could be very different from the types of employees recruited by the organizations. For example, students in a university might be given an artificial job and a treatment to study the effects on their performance. The findings from this experiment cannot be generalized to the real world of work, however, where the employees and the nature of the jobs would both be quite different. Thus subject selection and its interaction with the treatment would also pose a threat to external validity. These are just some of the factors that restrict generalizability. Maximum external validity can be obtained by ensuring that the experimental conditions are as close and compatible as possible to the real-world situation. It is in this sense that field experiments have greater validity than lab experiments. That is, the effects of the treatment can be generalized to other settings similar to the one where the field experiment was conducted.

Review of Factors Affecting
Internal and External Validity

In summary, at least seven contaminating influences exist that might affect the internal validity of experimental designs. These are the effects of history, maturation, testing, instrumentation, selection, statistical regression, and mortality. However, it is possible to reduce the biases by increasing the sophistication of the experimental design. Whereas some of the more sophisticated designs, discussed below, would help increase the internal validity of the experimental results, they could also become expensive and time consuming.

Threats to external validity can be combated by creating experimental conditions that are as close as possible to the situations to which the results of the experiment are to be generalized.

TYPES OF EXPERIMENTAL
DESIGNS AND INTERNAL VALIDITY

Let us consider some of the commonly used experimental designs and determine the extent to which they guard against the seven factors that could contaminate the internal validity of experimental results. It goes without saying that the shorter the time span of the experiments, the less the chances of encountering history, maturation, and mortality effects. Experiments lasting for an hour or two do not usually face many of these problems. It is when experiments take place over an extended period, say several months, that the confounding factors increase.

Some studies expose an experimental group to a treatment and mea-

Figure 4.5

Pretest and posttest experimental group design.

Group	Pretest Score	Treatment	Posttest Score
Experimental group	O_1	X	O_2

Treatment effect $= (O_2 - O_1)$

sure the effects of the treatment. Such an experimental design is the weakest of all designs, and it does not measure any true cause $\rightarrow$ effect relationship because there is no comparison, or any recording of the status of the dependent variable as it was prior to the experimental treatment and how it changed after the treatment. In the absence of such control, the study is of no scientific value in determining cause $\rightarrow$ effect relationships. Hence, such a design is not discussed as an experimental design here.

Pretest and Posttest Experimental Group Design

An experimental group (without a control group) may be given a pretest, exposed to a treatment, and then given a posttest to measure the effects of the treatment. This can be diagrammed as in Figure 4.5. Here, the effects of the treatment can be obtained by measuring the difference between the posttest and the pretest. Note, however, that the testing effects might contaminate the internal validity. If the experiment is extended over a period of time, history effects and maturation effects may also confound the results.

Posttests Only with Experimental and Control Groups

Some experimental designs are set up with an experimental and a control group, the former being exposed to a treatment and the latter not being exposed to it. The effects of the treatment are studied by assessing the difference in the outcomes—that is, the posttest scores of the experimental and control groups. This is illustrated in Figure 4.6. Here is a case where the testing effects have been avoided because there is no pretest, only a posttest. Care has to be taken, however, to make sure that the two groups are matched for all the possible contaminating exogenous variables. Otherwise, the true effects of the treatment cannot be determined by

Figure 4.6

Posttest only with experimental and control groups.

Group	Treatment	Outcome
Experimental group	X	O_1
Control group		O_2

Treatment effect $= (O_1 - O_2)$

merely looking at the difference in the posttest scores of the two groups. Randomization would take care of this problem.

Pretest and Posttest Experimental and Control Group Designs

This design can be visually depicted as in Figure 4.7. Two groups—one experimental and the other control—are both exposed to the pretest and the posttest. The only difference between the two groups is that the former is exposed to a treatment whereas the latter is not. Measuring the difference between the differences in the post- and pretests of the two groups would give the net effects of the treatment. Both groups have been exposed to both the pre- and posttests, and both groups have been randomized; thus we could expect that the history, maturation, testing, and instrumentation effects have been controlled. This is true because whatever happened with the experimental group (e.g., maturation, history, testing, and instrumentation) also happened with the control group, and by measuring the net effects (the difference in the differences between the pre- and posttest scores) we have controlled these contaminating factors.

Figure 4.7

Pre- and posttest experimental and control groups.

Group	Pretest	Treatment	Posttest
Experimental group	O_1	X	O_2
Control group	O_3		O_4

Treatment effect $= [(O_2 - O_1) - (O_4 - O_3)]$

Through the process of randomization, we have also controlled the effects of selection biases and statistical regression. This design still does not insure against mortality.

Solomon Four-Group Design

To gain more confidence in internal validity in experimental designs, it is advisable to set up two experimental groups and two control groups for the experiment. One experimental group and one control group can be given both the pretest and the posttest, as shown in Figure 4.8. The other two groups will be given only the posttest. Here the effects of the treatment can be calculated in several different ways as indicated in the figure. To the extent that we come up with almost the same results in each of the different calculations despite mortality in one or more groups, we can attribute the effects to the treatment. This increases the internal validity of the experimental design and its results. This design, known as the Solomon four-group design, is probably the most comprehensive and the one with the least problems with internal validity. However, it is rather cumbersome, more time consuming, and more expensive, and hence not as widely used as might be desirable, especially in field experiments.

Other experimental designs such as the multigroup designs, randomized block design, Latin square design, and factorial design are not discussed here. The interested student is referred to Emory (1980) and Campbell and Stanley (1963).

Figure 4.8

Solomon four-group design.

Group	Pretest	Treatment	Posttest
Experimental	O_1	X	O_2
Control	O_3		O_4
Experimental		X	O_5
Control			O_6

Treatment effect (E) could be judged by:

$$E = (O_2 - O_1)$$
$$E = (O_2 - O_4)$$
$$E = (O_5 - O_6)$$
$$E = (O_5 - O_3)$$
$$E = [(O_2 - O_1) - (O_4 - O_3)]$$

If all Es are similar, the cause $\rightarrow$ effect relationship is highly valid.

Simulation

An alternative to lab and field experimentation currently being used in business research is simulation. Simulation uses a model-building technique to determine the effects of changes, and computer-based simulations are becoming popular in business research. The day may not be far off when management decisions involving motivation, leadership, and other behavioral and administrative areas will be scientifically simulated as a matter of course using programmed, computer-based simulation models.

SUMMARY

This unit covered experimental designs, with particular reference to the lab and field experiments. Issues of internal and external validity and the seven factors that could affect internal validity were discussed. Also, some types of experimental designs that can be used to test cause $\rightarrow$ effect relationships and the usefulness of these in the context of validity versus practicality were examined.

The next unit discusses how the variables—whether in a field survey or in an experimental design—could be measured, and how data may be collected.

SUPPLEMENTAL READINGS

The following topic references will guide you to seek more information.

Topic	Reference	Chapter	Page
Experimental designs	Campbell & Stanley (1963)	The entire book offers an excellent treatment covering all subtopics.	
	Carlsmith, Ellsworth, & Aronson (1976)	1 8	8–52 234–280
	Clover & Balsley (1979)	4	76–90
	Emory (1980) Kirk (1968)	4	106–114
Exogenous and endogenous, and controlled and uncontrolled variables	Emory (1980)	4	96–99

Topic	Reference	Chapter	Page
Matching and randomization	Carlsmith et al. (1976)	5	134–169
	Emory (1980)	4	107
		11	343–346
	Kerlinger (1973)	20	348–359
Lab experiments and field experiments	Carlsmith et al. (1976)	7	220
	Festinger (1966)	4	136–172
	French (1966)	3	98–135
	Kerlinger (1973)	23	395–409
	Stone (1978)	7	116–128
	Runkel & McGrath (1972)	4	103–107
Internal and external validity	Emory (1980)	11	332–336
	Stone (1978)	6	108–110
Quasi-experimental design	Emory (1980)	11	346–353
	Stone (1978)	6	100–104
Simulation	Emory (1980)	11	353–361
	Runkel & McGrath (1972)	4	96–99
	Stone (1978)	7	120–124

REFERENCES

Campbell, D. T., & Stanley, J. C. *Experimental and quasi-experimental designs for research.* Chicago: Rand-McNally, 1963.

Carlsmith, J. M., Ellsworth, P. C., & Aronson, E. *Methods of research in social psychology.* Reading, Mass.: Addison-Wesley, 1976.

Clover, V. T., & Balsley, H. L. *Business research methods* (2nd ed.). Columbus, Ohio: Grid Publishing Co., 1979.

Cook, T. D., & Campbell, D. T. *Quasi-experimentation: Design and analysis issues for field settings.* Boston: Houghton-Mifflin, 1979.

Emory, C. W. *Business research methods* (Rev. ed.). Homewood, Ill.: Richard D. Irwin, Inc., 1980.

Festinger, L. Laboratory experiments. In L. Festinger & D. Katz (Eds.), *Research methods in the behavioral sciences.* New York: Holt, Rinehart and Winston, 1966.

French, J. R. P. Experiments in field settings. In L. Festinger & D. Katz (Eds.), *Research methods in the behavioral sciences.* New York: Holt, Rinehart and Winston, 1966.

Kerlinger, F. N. *Foundations of behavioral research* (2nd ed.). New York: Holt, Rinehart and Winston, 1973.

Kirk, R. E. *Experimental design: Procedures for the behavioral sciences.* Belmont, Calif.: Brooks/Cole, 1968.

Osborn, R. N., & Vicars, W. M. Sex stereotypes: An artifact in leader behavior and subordinate satisfaction analysis? *Academy of Management Journal,* 1976, *19,* 439–449.

Runkel, P. J., & McGrath, J. E. *Research on human behavior.* New York: Holt, Rinehart and Winston, 1972.

Stone, E. *Research methods in organizational behavior.* Santa Monica, Calif.: Goodyear Publishing Co., 1978.

POINTS TO PONDER AND RESPOND TO

1. If a control group is a part of an experimental design, one need not worry about controlling for other exogenous variables.

2. A researcher wants to set up a lab experiment to test the effects of different kinds of leadership styles on followers' attitudes. The three particular kinds of leadership styles she is interested in testing are autocratic, democratic, and participative. You are asked to enlist some students to play the part of followers. What cover story would you give the participants?

3. Because the external validity of lab experiments is not usually high, they are useless for investigating cause → effect relationships in organizations.

4. Covariance—that is, two variables varying together either positively or negatively—and control are integral aspects of experimental designs.

5. The Solomon four-group design is the answer to all our research questions pertaining to cause → effect relations because it guards against all the threats to internal validity.

UNIT 5
MEASUREMENT OF VARIABLES AND DATA-COLLECTION METHODS

ISSUES DISCUSSED

Measurement of Variables

Operational Definition
- Dimensions and Elements of Concepts
- What an Operational Definition Is Not

Scales

Data-Collection Methods
- Interviewing
  - Unstructured and Structured Interviews
  - Tips for Interviewing
  - Face-to-Face and Telephone Interviews
- Questionnaires and Questionnaire Designing
  - Personally Administered Questionnaires and Mail Questionnaires
  - Principles of Wording
  - Principles of Measurement (validity and reliability)
  - General Appearance of the Questionnaire
- Observation: Structured and Unstructured
- Motivational Research
- Panel Studies: Static and Dynamic Panels
- Unobtrusive Methods
- Multimethods of Data Collection
- Multisources of Data

UNIT OBJECTIVES

After completing Unit 5 you should be able to:

1. Operationally define (or operationalize) concepts.
2. Distinguish among the characteristics of the four different scales.
3. Be conversant with the various data-collection methods.
4. Know the advantages and disadvantages of each method.

5. Make the logical decisions as to the appropriate data-collection method(s) for specific studies.

6. Demonstrate your skills using interviewing as a data-collection technique.

7. Design questionnaires to tap different variables.

8. Apply appropriate scales and scaling, and the principles of questionnaire design, with particular sensitivity to issues of reliability and validity.

9. Evaluate questionnaires, distinguishing between ''good'' and ''bad'' questions therein.

10. Identify and minimize the biases in various data-collection methods.

11. Discuss the advantages of multisources and multimethods of data collection.

12. Apply what you have learned to class assignments and projects.

Measurement of variables in the theoretical framework and collection of data are two important methodological issues in research, as shown in Figure 3.10. Unless the variables are measured and the data collected, we will not be able to test the hypotheses generated from the theoretical framework. This unit will show how the variables can be measured and will also discuss the different data-collection methods that can be used in research.

MEASUREMENT OF VARIABLES

Objects that can be physically measured by some calibrated instruments pose no measurement problems. For example, the length and breadth of an office table can be easily measured with a measuring tape or a ruler. The same is true for measuring the office floor area. Data representing several demographic characteristics of the office personnel are also easily obtained by asking employees simple, straightforward questions; for example:

How long have you been working in this organization?

How long have you been working on this particular assignment?

What is your job title?

What is your marital status?

One can also check the company records to obtain or verify the information. Even certain physiological phenomena pertaining to humans such as blood pressure, heart rates, and body temperature, as well as certain physical attributes such as height and weight, lend themselves to measurement through the use of appropriate measuring instruments. When we get into the realm of peoples' subjective feelings, attitudes, and perceptions, however, the measurement of these factors or variables becomes difficult. This is one of the aspects of organizational behavior and management research that adds to the complexity of studies.

There are at least two types of variables, as just delineated: One of these lends itself to some objective and precise measurement; the other is more nebulous and does not lend itself to precise measurement because of its subjective nature. However, despite the lack of objective physical measuring devices to measure the latter type, there are ways of tapping the subjective feelings and perceptions of individuals. One technique is to reduce the abstract notions, or concepts such as motivation, involvement, or satisfaction, to observable behaviors and characteristics exhibited by those who possess these abstract qualities. In other words, the abstract notions are simplified into observable characteristic behaviors. For instance, the concept of thirst is abstract; we cannot see thirst. However, we would expect a thirsty person to drink a lot of fluids. In other words, the expected behavior of people who are thirsty is to drink fluids. If several people say they are thirsty, then we can measure the thirst levels of each of these individuals by measuring the quantity of fluids that they drink when they are thirsty. We would thus be able to measure their levels of thirst, even though the concept of thirst itself is abstract and nebulous. Reducing abstract concepts so that they can be measured is called operationalizing the concepts.

Operational Definition

Operationalizing, or operationally defining a concept so that it becomes measurable, is achieved by looking at the behavioral dimensions, facets, or properties denoted by the concept, and categorizing these into observable and measurable elements. An example will help to illustrate how a concept is operationally defined.

Example 5.1

Let us try to operationally define achievement motivation, a concept of interest to educators, managers, and students alike. What behavioral dimensions or facets or characteristics would we expect to find in people high in achievement motivation? Such people would probably have the following five typical broad characteristics which we might call *dimensions.*

1. They would be driven by work; that is, they would be constantly working in order to derive the feeling of having "achieved and accomplished."

2. Many of them would generally find it hard to relax and think of things other than their work.

3. Because they always want to be achieving and accomplishing, they would prefer to work on their own rather than with others.

4. In order to derive the sense of accomplishment and achievement, they would rather engage in challenging jobs than easy, routine ones. However, they would not want to take on excessively challenging jobs because the probability of accomplishment and achievement in such jobs may not be very high.

5. They would like to know how they are doing in their jobs as they go along. That is, they would like to seek frequent feedback in direct and subtle ways from their superiors, colleagues, and sometimes even their subordinates, to know how they are performing on their jobs.

Thus we would expect those high in achievement motivation to be driven by work, unable to relax, preferring to work alone, engaging in challenging—but not too challenging—jobs, and seeking feedback. Although breaking the concept into these five dimensions has somewhat reduced its level of abstraction, we still have not operationalized the concept into measurable elements of behavior. This could be done by examining each of the five dimensions and breaking it further into its elements, thus delineating the actual behaviors that would be exhibited. These behaviors should be quantitatively measurable. Let us see how this can be done.

Elements of Dimension 1

We can describe the behaviors of a person who is driven by work. Such a person will (1) be constantly working, (2) be reluctant to take any time off from work, and (3) persevere even if there are some setbacks. All these three behaviors would lend themselves to measurement.

For instance, we can count the number of hours employees engage themselves in work-related activities during work hours, beyond working hours at the workplace, and at home where they are likely to carry their unfinished assignments. Thus, merely observing and keeping track of the number of hours that they work would provide an indication of the extent to which work "drives" them.

Next, keeping track of how frequently people continue to persevere on their job despite failures would give a good idea of how persevering people are in achieving their goals. A student who drops out of school because he could not pass the first exam does not represent a highly persevering, achievement-oriented individual. However, a student who, despite getting D grades on three quizzes, works night after night in order to understand and master a course he considers difficult, say statistics, would exhibit persevering and achievement-oriented behaviors. Achievement-motivated individuals would not usually want to give up on their tasks when faced by some failures. They would have the drive to persevere. Hence, the extent of perseverance could be measured by counting the number of setbacks people experience on the task, yet continue to work. For example, a bank employee might find that she is unable to balance the books. After trying to detect the error for an hour or so, if she has still not detected it, she might give up and leave the workplace. Another employee in the same position might not want to leave until the mistake has been detected and the books are balanced, even if it takes the whole evening to accomplish the task. In this case we would get an idea of who is the more persevering by merely observing the two individuals.

Finally, in order to measure the reluctance to take time off, we need only know how frequently people take time off, and for what reasons. If an employee has taken seven days off during the last six months to watch football games, attend an out-of-town circus, and visit friends, we would have no trouble in concluding that the individual would probably not be reluctant to take time off the job at all. However, if an individual has never missed work even a single day during the past 15 months, and he is at work even when he is not feeling very well, it is evident that he is perhaps not one who would be willing to take time off from the job.

Thus, if we can measure how many hours per week individuals spend on work-related activities, how persistent they are in completing their daily tasks, and how frequently and for what reasons they take time off from their jobs, we would have a measure of the extent to which employees are driven by work. This variable, when thus measured, would place individuals on a continuum ranging from those who are driven very little by work to those who are driven all the time by work. This, then, would give a partial indication of the extent of their achievement motivation.

Figure 5.1 schematically diagrams the dimensions (the several facets or main characteristics) and the elements (representative behaviors) for the concept of achievement motivation. Frequent reference to this figure will help you follow the ensuing discussions.

Elements of Dimension 2

The extent of inability to relax can be measured by asking persons such questions as (1) how often they think of work while they are at home, (2) whether they have any hobbies, and (3) how they spend their time off the job. Those who are able to relax would indicate that they spend time on hobbies and leisure-time activities, and would say that they do not gener-

Figure 5.1

Dimensions (D) and elements (E) of the concept (C) of achievement motivation.

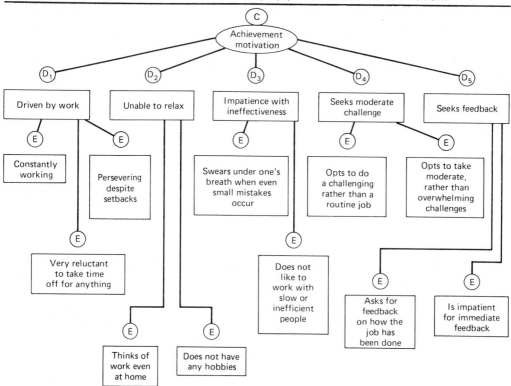

ally think about work or the workplace while at home. Such people are probably engaged in family or other social or cultural activities while away from work.

Thus we can here place employees on a continuum ranging from those who relax a lot to those who relax very little. This dimension also then becomes measurable.

Elements of Dimension 3

Individuals wanting to achieve on their own can be measured by their reluctance to work with others. Whereas some achievement-motivated persons in the organization may be very high on these behavioral predispositions, there may be others who are not highly achievement motivated. These latter people may not be upset with ineffectiveness either in themselves or others, and may be quite willing to work with almost anybody. Thus impatience with ineffectiveness can also be measured by observing behaviors.

Elements of Dimension 4

The extent to which people seek challenging jobs can be measured by asking employees what kinds of jobs they would prefer. A number of different job descriptions can be presented, with some jobs being described to reflect routineness and others to indicate differing degrees of challenges built into them. Employee preferences for different types of jobs could then be placed on a continuum ranging from those who prefer fairly routine jobs to those who prefer highly challenging jobs. Those opting for medium degrees of challenge are perhaps the ones that are more achievement motivated than those who opt for lower or higher degrees of challenge. They would represent a set of individuals who are realistic and would choose jobs that are reasonably challenging and yet possible to accomplish. The reckless and overconfident persons would perhaps choose the highly challenging jobs where the probability of success is rather low, oblivious to whether the end results will be achieved or not. Those low in achievement motivation would perhaps choose the more routine jobs. Thus, those who seek moderate challenge can also be identified.

Elements of Dimension 5

Those who want feedback would be seeking it from their superiors, co-workers, and sometimes even from their subordinates. They would want to know others' opinions on how well they are performing. Feedback, both positive and negative, would indicate to them how much they are achieving and accomplishing. If they receive messages indicating a need for improvement, they will act on them. Hence, they would be constantly seeking feedback from several sources. By keeping track of the number of times individuals seek feedback from others during a certain period of time—say, over several months—employees can again be placed on a continuum ranging from those who seek extensive feedback from all sources to those who never seek any feedback from anyone at any time.

Having thus operationalized the concept of achievement motivation by reducing its level of abstraction to observable behaviors, it is possible to develop a measure to tap the concept of achievement motivation. However, actually observing and counting the number of times individuals behave in particular ways, even if practical, would be too laborious and time consuming. So, instead of actually observing the behaviors of individuals, we could ask them to report their own behavior patterns by asking them appropriate questions. In other words, we could develop an instrument that would let the respondents communicate to us the extent of their achievement motivation. Such an instrument tapping the concept is described next.

Example 5.2

Answers to the following questions from respondents would be indicative of their level of achievement motivation.

1.   To what extent would you say you push yourself to get the job done on time?

2.   How difficult is it for you to keep on continuing to do your work in the face of initial failures or discouraging results?

3.   How frequently do you think of your work when you are at home?

4.   How disappointed would you feel if you did not reach the goals you had planned for?

5.   How much do you concentrate on achieving your goals?

6.   How annoyed do you get when you make mistakes?

7.   To what extent would you prefer to work with a friendly but incompetent colleague rather than a difficult but competent one?

8.   To what extent would you prefer to work by yourself rather than with others?

9.   To what extent would you prefer a job that is difficult but challenging to one that is easy and routine?

10.   To what extent would you prefer to undertake extremely difficult assignments rather than moderately challenging assignments?

11.   During the past three months, how often have you sought feedback from your superiors on how well you are performing your job?

12.   How often have you tried to obtain feedback on your performance from your co-workers during the past three months?

13.   How often during the past three months have you checked with your subordinates that what you are doing is not getting in their way of efficient performance?

14.   To what extent would it frustrate you if people did not give you feedback on how you are progressing?

The above example has illustrated that it is possible to measure variables relating to the subjective domain of people's attitudes, feelings, and perceptions by first operationally defining the concept. Operational definition implies our reducing the concept from its level of abstraction by breaking it into its dimensions and elements as discussed. Thus, by tapping the behaviors associated with a concept, we can measure the concept.

What an Operational Definition Is Not

Just as important as it is to understand what an operational definition *is*, equally important is it to remember what it is *not*. An operational definition does *not* describe the correlates of the concept. For example, performance or success cannot be a dimension of achievement motivation, even though a motivated person is likely to be highly successful in performing the job. Thus, achievement motivation and performance and/or success may be highly correlated, but we cannot measure an individual's level of motivation through success and performance. Performance and success could have occurred as a consequence of achievement motivation, but in and of themselves, the two are not measures of achievement motivation. To elaborate, a person may be high in achievement motivation, but for some reason, perhaps beyond her control, might have failed to perform the job successfully. Thus, if we judge the achievement motivation of this person by looking at performance, we would have measured the wrong concept. Instead of measuring achievement motivation—our variable of interest—we would have measured performance, another variable that we did not intend to measure and in which we were not interested.

Thus, it is clear that operationally defining a concept does *not* consist of delineating the reasons, antecedents, consequences, or correlates of the concept. Rather, it describes the observable characteristics of the concept in order to be able to measure it. This is important to remember because if we either operationalize the concepts incorrectly or confuse them with other concepts, then we will not have valid measures. This means that we will not have "good" data, and our research will not be scientific.

Having seen what an operational definition is and what it is not, let us now operationally define another concept that is relevant to the classroom: the concept of "learning."

Example 5.3

Learning is an important concept in the educational setting. Teachers tend to measure student learning by giving exams. Students quite often feel that exams really do not measure their learning—at least not the multiple-choice questions that are given in exams. The students are probably right.

How then might we measure the abstract concept called learning? As before, we need to define the concept operationally and break it down to observable and measurable behaviors. In other words, we should delineate the dimensions and elements of the concept of learning. The dimensions of learning may well be as follows:

1. Understanding.   **2.** Retention.   **3.** Application.

Figure 5.2

Dimensions (D) and elements (E) of the concept (C) of learning.

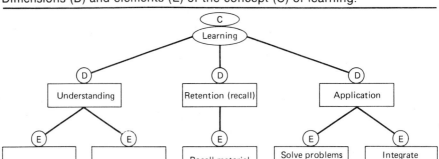

In other words, we can be reasonably sure that a student in the class is "learning" when the individual is (1) understanding what is going on in the classroom, (2) can remember what is understood, and (3) can apply whatever has been understood and remembered.

Terms such as understanding, remembering, and applying are still abstract even though they have helped us to get a better grasp of what learning is all about. It is necessary to break these three dimensions into elements so that we can measure the dimensions, and thus the concept of learning. A schematic diagram of the operational definition of the concept of learning is shown in Figure 5.2. The diagram will facilitate our understanding of the discussion that follows.

A teacher can assess whether students have understood by asking them to explain a concept that was just taught and to answer questions. If they answer correctly, the teacher can presume that the students have understood. By giving a test a week or month later, the teacher can measure the extent to which they have remembered what was explained. By asking them to apply the concepts learned in a new problem situation, the teacher can also measure how much they can apply what is understood. If they solve the problem successfully using the material taught to them in class, the teacher will be reasonably assured that learning has taken place. To the extent that they do not successfully apply the concepts taught, learning might not have occurred to the degree expected. Exams, when properly designed, could be a good instrument for assessing the learning that takes place during the semester. In other words, exams could reliably measure or tap learning when the questions therein are well constructed.

Again, it is very important to remember that learning is not the same as the amount of effort the teacher expends in explaining, or the amount of effort put in by the student to understand, though both of these will tend to enhance understanding. Although both may be correlated to learning, they do not measure actual learning.

A Measure of Student Learning

An exam that measures the extent of student learning on the topic of motivation would, according to our operational definition, include the following questions (the particular dimensions measured are given in parentheses):

1. Define the concept of motivation (*recall*).

2. State the various theories of motivation and explain them, giving examples (*understanding* and *recall*).

3. Describe three different situations in which a manager in a work organization would use equity theory, the expectancy theory, and job design to motivate employees (*understanding, retention,* and *application*).

4. (a) In the beginning of the semester, the class was split into two debate teams: one was to argue for the manager's role as a motivator, and the other that it is not a manager's job to motivate the employees. State three important arguments put forth by each group (*understanding* and *recall*).
   (b) What is *your* viewpoint regarding the manager's role as motivator (*understanding* and *analysis*).

5. In the Mylapore Camp case, how would Bob have been motivated to take an interest in the camp's activities? Adequately defend your answer, citing the appropriate theories and why they are superior to some of the other possible solutions (*understanding, retention,* and *application*).

6. How does motivation relate to leadership? How are both of these concepts related to a manager's job (*understanding, retention,* and *application*).

Review of Operational Definition

We have thus far examined how to operationally define concepts and to ask questions that are likely to measure the concept. Operational definitions are important for abstract concepts, which usually fall into the subjective areas of feelings and attitudes. More objective variables such as age or educational level are easily measured through simple straightforward questions and do not have to be operationally defined. Fortunately, measures for many organization-relevant concepts have already been developed by researchers. While you review the literature in a given area, you might want to note particularly the reference that discusses the instrument to tap the concept.

Now do Exercises 5.1 and 5.2.

SCALES AND MEASUREMENT

Learning how to define concepts operationally has helped us to see what questions might be asked to tap concepts. However, we still need to know how we can measure them. In other words, how would we know the extent to which these subjective feelings, attitudes, or perceptions might exist in different individuals? Is it possible to devise an instrument that would measure these variables?

Fortunately, certain scales have been devised that will allow us to measure our variables of interest in either a qualitative or a quantitative way. First we must become familiar with the scales themselves, and then we can examine how they can be used to measure the concepts.

Scales

A scale is a tool or mechanism by which individuals are distinguished on the variables of interest to our study, in some form or the other. The scale or tool could be a gross one in the sense that it would only broadly categorize individuals on certain variables; or it could be a fine-tuned tool that would differentiate individuals with varying degrees of sophistication on the variables.

There are four basic types of scales: nominal, ordinal, interval, and ratio. The degree of sophistication to which the scales are fine-tuned increases as we move from the nominal to the ratio scale. As the calibration or fine tuning of the scale increases in sophistication, the power of the scale increases; that is, more detailed information can be obtained on our variables. With more powerful scales, increasingly sophisticated data analyses can be performed, which means, in turn, that we can find more meaningful answers to our research questions as we tap the variables with more powerful scales. However, certain variables lend themselves more readily to more powerful scaling than others.

Let us now examine each of these four scales.

Nominal Scale

A nominal scale is one that allows the researcher to assign subjects to certain categories or groups. For example, with respect to the variable of gender, respondents can be grouped in two categories: males and females. These two groups can be assigned code numbers 1 and 2. Here we assigned respondents to one of two nonoverlapping or *mutually exclusive* categories. Note that the categories are also *collectively exhaustive.* In other words, there is no third category into which respondents would normally fall. Thus, nominal scales categorize individuals or objects into mutually exclusive and collectively exhaustive groups. The information provided by nominal scaling consists of the percentage (or frequency) of males and females in our sample of respondents. For example, if we had interviewed 200 people, and assigned a code number 1 to all male respondents and number 2 to all female respondents, then computer analysis of the data at the end of the survey might reveal that 98 of the respondents were men and 102 were women. This frequency distribution tells us that 49 percent of the survey's respondents are male and 51 percent female. Other than this marginal information (which, incidentally, is better than not knowing how many of each category responded to the survey), such scaling provides no other information. That is, we have no information as to whether women were superior to men or more enthusiastic about responding, or anything else. Thus the nominal scale gives some basic, categorical, gross information.

Example 5.4

Let us take a look at another variable that could have a nominal scale: the nationality of the individuals. We could nominally scale this variable in the following mutually exclusive and collectively exhaustive categories.

African	European
Asian	North American
Australian	South American

Other

Note that every respondent has to fit into one of the seven categories above, and that the scale will allow computation of the percentage of respondents who fit into each of these seven categories.

Now answer Exercise 5.3.

Ordinal Scale

An ordinal scale would not only categorize the variables in such a way as to denote qualitative differences among the various categories, it would also rank-order the categories in some meaningful way. With any variable for which the categories are to be ordered according to some preference, the ordinal scale would be used. The preferences would be ranked and numbered 1, 2, and so on. For example, respondents might be asked to indicate their preferences by ranking the importance they attach to five distinct characteristics in a job that the researcher might be interested in studying. Such a question might take the following form.

Example 5.5

> Rank the following five characteristics in a job in terms of how important they are for you. You should rank the most important item as 1, the second most important as 2, and so on, until you have given each of the five items a rank of 1, 2, 3, 4, or 5.

Job Characteristic   **Ranking of Importance**

The opportunity provided by the job to:

1. Interact with others.   _____
2. Use a number of different skills.   _____
3. Complete a whole task from beginning to end. _____
4. Serve others.   _____
5. Work independently.   _____

This ordinal scale would help the researcher to determine the percentage of respondents who consider interaction with others as most important, those who consider using a number of different skills as most important, and so on. Such knowledge might help in designing jobs that would be seen as most enriched by the majority of the employees.

We can now see that the ordinal scale provides more information than the nominal scale. The ordinal scale not only taps the differences in the categories, but also gives some information as to how respondents distinguish among these items by rank ordering them. Note, however, that the ordinal scale does not give any indication of the magnitude of the differences among the ranks. For instance, in the job characteristics example, the first-ranked job characteristic might be only marginally preferred over the second-ranked characteristic, whereas the characteristic that is ranked third might be preferred considerably more than the one ranked fourth. Thus, in ordinal scaling, even though we would know there are differences in the ranking of objects, persons, or events investigated, we would not know the magnitude of these differences. This deficiency is overcome by interval scaling, which is discussed next.

An advantage of the ordinal data over nominal data is that percentiles can be calculated. For instance, where there are large masses of data—such as students taking the Graduate Record Exam (GRE) or the Graduate Management Aptitude Test (GMAT)—it is often useful to describe the score in terms of percentile. If a student's score is in the 28th percentile, for instance, then we know that 72 percent of the students who took the exam scored better, and 27 percent scored worse than this student.

Now respond to Exercise 5.4.

Interval Scale

An interval scale tries to introduce an arithmetical element to the measurement of the variable. Whereas the nominal or the ordinal scale qualitatively distinguishes the groups by categorizing them into mutually exclusive and collectively exhaustive sets (nominal scale), and establishing priorities or preferences among these categories (ordinal scale), the interval scale adds a quantitative dimension to these categorical or qualitative data. In other words, here we go beyond compiling the percentiles with respect to each group, to computing the means and the standard deviation of the responses on the variables. In other words, the interval scale not only groups individuals according to certain categories, and taps the order of these groups; it also measures the magnitude of the differences in the preferences among the individuals. If, for instance, employees think that (1) it is more important for them to have a variety of skills in their jobs compared to doing a task from beginning to end, and (2) it is more important for them to be serving people than to be working independently on the job, then the interval scale would indicate whether the first preference is to the same extent, to a lesser extent, or to a greater extent than the second. This can be done by now changing the scale from the ranking type in Example 5.5 to make it appear as if there were several points on a scale that would signify the extent or magnitude of the importance of each of the five job characteristics. Such a scale could be indicated as follows for the job design example.

Example 5.6

Indicate the extent to which the following five job characteristics are important to you, by circling the number on the scale against each item that reflects your sentiment.

Job Characteristic	Extremely Important 1	Important 2	Neutral 3	Unimportant 4	Very Unimportant 5
The opportunity provided by the job to:					
1. Interact with others.	1	2	3	4	5
2. Use a number of different skills.	1	2	3	4	5
3. Complete a task from beginning to end.	1	2	3	4	5
4. Serve others.	1	2	3	4	5
5. Work independently.	1	2	3	4	5

The scale in Example 5.6 is so constructed that the respondents perceive the 5 points on a continuum from "extremely important" to "very unimportant," with "neutral" (neither important nor unimportant) signifying the midpoint on the scale. In their minds, the 5 points are spaced such that the distance between, say, 1 and 2 on the scale, would be of the same magnitude as the distance between 4 and 5, or 3 and 4, or 2 and 3. This interval scale, which connotes differences, order, and the equality between the points on the scale, is also known as an "equal-appearing" interval scale or "Likert-type" interval scale (Likert, excerpted in Fishbein, 1967). The scale could start at the *arbitrary* number 1 and could have as many points on the scale as the researcher considers necessary. Thus we could have a 5-point, or a 7-point, or a 9-point, or an 11-point interval scale. Research, however, indicates that the 5-point scale is probably as effective as any, and that an increase from 5 to 7 or 9 points on a rating scale does not statistically improve the reliability of the ratings (Elmore & Beggs, 1975). That is, responses on a 9-point scale do not contribute any more to the accuracy or the quality of the information than the responses on a 5- or a 7-point scale.

Let us illustrate how the equal-appearing, Likert-type interval scale establishes the equality of the magnitude of differences in the scale points. Let us suppose that employees circle the numbers 3, 1, 2, 4, and 5 for the five items in Example 5.6. We can say that the employees are trying to indicate to us that the extent of their preference for skill utilization by the job over doing the task from beginning to end, is the same as the extent of their preference for serving customers over their preference for working independently. That is, the magnitude of difference represented by the space between points 1 and 2 on the scale is seen by the respondents as the same as the magnitude of difference represented by the space between points 4 and 5. Any linear transformation preserves these differences. In other words, if you add any number to all the points on the scale, the magnitude of the differences would still be equal.

Thus the interval scale taps the differences, the order, and the equality of the magnitude of the differences in the variable. Any linear transformations made on the responses would still maintain the magnitude of the differences. As such, it is a more powerful scale than the nominal and ordinal scales, and has for its measure of central tendency the arithmetic mean. Its measures of dispersion are the range, the standard deviation, and the variance. Note, however, that the scale has been given an arbitrary origin point—1. It could have been given any other arbitrary number as well. The clinical thermometer is a good example of an interval-scaled instrument.

Now respond to Exercises 5.5 and 5.6.

Ratio Scale

The ratio scale overcomes the deficiency of the arbitrary origin point given to the interval scale, in that it has an absolute (in contrast to an arbitrary) zero point. Thus the ratio scale not only measures the magnitude of the differences between points on the scale but also taps the proportions in the differences. It is the most powerful of the four scales because it has a unique zero origin (not an arbitrary origin) and subsumes all the properties of the other three scales. The weighing balance is a good example of a ratio scale. It has an absolute (and not arbitrary) zero origin calibrated on it, which allows us to calculate the ratio of differences between the weights of two individuals. For instance, a person weighing 250 pounds is *twice* as heavy as one who weighs 125 pounds. Note that multiplying or dividing both of these numbers (250 and 125) by any given number will preserve the ratio of 2:1. Because of these properties, the measure of central tendency of the ratio scale is the geometric mean and the measure of dispersion is the coefficient of variation. Some examples of ratio scales are age, income, and the number of organizations an individual has worked for.

The properties of the increased fine tuning of the scales are summarized in Figure 5.3. We can also see from the figure how the power of the statistic increases as we move away from the nominal scale (where we group subjects under some categories), to ranking the categories (ordinal scale), to tapping the magnitude of the differences (interval scale), to measuring the proportion of the differences (ratio scale).

Figure 5.3

Properties of the four scales.

Scale		Highlights				Measures of Central Tendency	Measures of Dispersion	Some Tests of Significance
		Differ-ence	Order	Dis-tance	Unique Origin			
Nominal		Yes	No	No	No	Mode	—	χ^2
Ordinal	1st 2nd 3rd	Yes	Yes	No	No	Median	Quartiles	Rank-order correlations
Interval	1 2 3 4 5	Yes	Yes	Yes	No	Arithmetic mean	Standard devi-ation variance	t, F
Ratio	0 5 10 15 20	Yes	Yes	Yes	Yes	Geometric mean	Coefficient of variation	t, F

> Now respond to Exercise 5.7.

Measurement

Whereas the nominal and ordinal scales help us to group and to qualitatively identify the differences between the groups, the interval and the ratio scales help us to get some idea of the quantitative differences in the variables of interest.

Certain variables simply do not lend themselves to quantification, except in a very basic manner. For instance, when we split a sample of teachers into male and female teachers, we will at best only know the numbers and the percentage of men and women among the sample of teachers. If we ask the students to rank their preferences for male and female teachers, we could at best determine the percentage of students who prefer the male teacher and the percentage who prefer the female teacher. However, if instead of asking them to indicate their preferences for the two groups, we had asked the students to indicate the extent of their preferences for each of the two genders, then we would have a better feel not only for which gender is preferred but also for the magnitude of the difference in the preferences. We thus have more and better information through the interval scale.

Because the interval scale gives more information than the nominal and the ordinal scales, we should try whenever possible to measure variables on an interval scale. For instance, instead of asking respondents whether they are motivated or not ("yes or no" answer, nominal scale), we can ask them the extent to which they are motivated on a 5-point or a 7-point interval scale, with 1 denoting very little motivation and 5 or 7 denoting very high motivation.

It would be nice if we could measure all our variables on a ratio scale because we know it is even more powerful than the interval scale. Recall that the ratio scale can identify not only the magnitude but also the proportion of the differences. Unfortunately, however, attitudinal and perceptual variables do not have an absolute zero point. We could say that a person has very little motivation, or even negative motivation (i.e., turned off), but we would be unable to justify that someone can or will have an exact zero motivation, though we may loosely use the term in our conversations. Thus subjective feelings, attitudes, and perceptions cannot be measured on a ratio scale.

Review of Scales and Measurement

There are four scales that can be applied to the measurement of variables: the nominal, ordinal, interval, and ratio scales. The nominal scale highlights the differences by classifying objects or persons into groups, and of the four scales, provides the least amount of information on the variable. The ordinal scale provides some additional information by rank ordering the categories provided by the nominal scale. The interval scale, in addition to the ranking, provides us with information on the magnitude of the differences in the variable. Any linear transformation would preserve these differences. The ratio scale indicates not only the magnitude of the differences but also the proportion of the differences. Multiplications or divisions would preserve these ratios. As we move from the nominal to the ratio scale, we obtain more precision in quantifying the data, and greater flexibility in using more powerful statistical tests. Hence, wherever possible, and appropriate, a more powerful rather than a less powerful scale should be used to measure the variables of interest.

DATA-COLLECTION METHODS

Data can be collected from various settings and in many different ways. Data could be gathered through field surveys tapping variables in the natural environment where phenomena occur; they can be collected in lab experimental settings where variables are controlled and manipulated; they can be obtained from a panel of respondents specifically set up by the researcher whose opinions may be sought from time to time; and they can also be gleaned from other sources such as the company records or archives.

Interviewing, administering questionnaires, and observing people and phenomena are the three main data-collection methods in survey research. Projective tests are also sometimes used to tap variables. In such tests, respondents are usually asked to write a story, complete a sentence, or give their reactions to ambiguous cues such as inkblots or unlabeled pictures. It is assumed that the respondents project into the responses their own thoughts, feelings, attitudes, and expectations, all of which can be scored from the content of the responses.

Although interviewing has the advantage of flexibility in terms of adapting, adopting and changing the questions as the researcher proceeds with the interviews, questionnaires have the advantage of obtaining data more efficiently in terms of researcher time, energy, and costs. Unobtrusive methods of data collection such as extracting data from company records have the advantage of ensuring the accuracy of the information obtained. For instance, gathering information on the absenteeism of employees from company records will probably give more accurate information than asking the respondents how many days they have been absent during the past year. Projective tests are usually administered by those researchers who have had training in administering them and interpreting the results. Though some management research has been done using projective techniques, it is still not a very common data-collection method.

The choice of data-collection methods depends on the facilities available from the organization, the extent of accuracy required, the expertise of the researcher, the time span of the study, and other costs and resources associated with and available for data gathering.

We will now examine the various data-collection methods.

INTERVIEWING

One method of collecting data is to interview respondents to obtain information on the issues of interest to the researcher. Interviews can be unstructured or structured, and could be conducted either face to face or by telephone. The unstructured and structured interviews will be discussed first. Next, some important factors to be borne in mind while interviewing will be detailed, and finally, the advantages and disadvantages of face-to-face interviewing and telephone interviews will be enumerated.

Unstructured and Structured Interviews

Unstructured Interviews

Unstructured interviews are thus called because the interviewer does not enter the interview setting with a planned sequence of questions that he will be asking the respondent. The objective of the unstructured interview is to surface some preliminary issues so that the researcher can formulate a good idea of what variables need further in-depth investigation. In Unit 2 in the "Broad Problem Area" discussion, we saw several situations where the manager might have a vague idea of certain changes taking place in the situation without knowing what exactly is happening. Such situations call for unstructured interviews with the people concerned. In order to understand the total situation, the researcher will interview employees at several levels. At the initial stages of such conversations, only broad, open-ended questions would be asked, and the replies to these questions would give the researcher an indication of the perceptions of the individuals. The type and nature of the questions asked of the individuals might vary according to the job level and type of work done by respondents. For instance, whereas managers at top and middle levels might be asked more direct questions about their perceptions of the problem and the situation, employees at lower levels may have to be approached differently.

At the lower levels it is advisable to ask broad, open-ended questions during the unstructured interviews. If supervisors are interviewed, for example, they may be asked to talk about the work setting for which they are responsible. The researcher might ask a question like this:

> "Tell me something about your unit in terms of work, employees, and whatever else you think is relevant to your unit."

Such a question might elicit a voluminous response from some people, whereas others may briefly reply that everything is fine. Following the leads from the more vocal persons is comparatively easy, especially when the interviewer listens carefully for the important messages that might be transmitted in a very casual manner while responding to a general, global question. As managers and researchers, we should train ourselves to develop these listening skills and identify the critical topics that are being touched on. However, when some respondents give one-word, crisp, short replies that do not give out much information, the interviewer will have to ask questions that cannot definitely be answered in one or two words. Such questions might be phrased like this one:

> "I would like to know something about your job. Please describe to me in detail the things you do on your job on a typical day, from eight in the morning to four o'clock in the afternoon."

Several questions might then be asked as a follow-up to the answer. Some examples of such follow-up questions are as follows:

> "Compared to other units in this organization, what are the strengths and weaknesses of your unit?"

"If you would like to have one problem solved in your unit, or eliminate one bottleneck, or attend to something that affects your effectiveness, what would that be?"

If the respondent answers that everything is fine and she has no problems, the interviewer could say: "That is great! Tell me what contributes to this effectiveness of your unit, because most other organizations usually experience several difficulties." Such a questioning technique usually brings the respondent's defenses down and he then usually shows a greater willingness to share information. Typical of the revised responses to the original question is something like, "Well, it is not that we never have a problem. Sometimes, we are late in getting the jobs done, crash jobs have some defective items, ..." Encouraging the respondent to talk about both the good things and the not-so-good things in her unit can elicit a lot of information. Whereas some respondents do not need much encouragement to speak, others do; and they have to be questioned broadly. Some respondents may be reluctant to be interviewed, and may subtly or overtly refuse to cooperate. The wishes of such people must be respected and the interviewer should pleasantly terminate such interviews.

Employees at the shop-floor level, and other nonmanagerial and nonsupervisory employees, might be asked very broad questions relating to their jobs, work environment, satisfactions and dissatisfactions at the workplace, and the like—for example:

How do you like working here?

If you were to tell me what aspects of your job you like and which aspects of it you do not like, what would they be?

Tell me something about the reward systems in this place.

If you were offered a similar job elsewhere, how willing would you be to take it?

If I were to seek employment here and request you to describe your unit to me as a newcomer, what would you say?

After obtaining an impression of how the employees perceive the work and the work environment, it may become necessary to tap their reactions to certain other factors in the organization such as recreational facilities and the like. These reactions may help the researcher to get a feel for their attitudes and also their behaviors.

After a sufficient number of such unstructured interviews have been conducted with employees at several levels, the researcher would have a good idea of the variables that need more focus to elicit in-depth information. At this stage, the researcher is ready to conduct structured interviews.

Structured Interviews

Structured interviews are those conducted by the interviewer when he knows exactly what information is needed and has a predetermined list of questions that will be posed to the respondents. The interviewer will have written out these questions and will refer to this list while conducting the interviews. The questions are likely to focus on factors that were surfaced during the unstructured interviews and considered relevant to the problem. Examples of such questions on the structured interview schedule are given here:

		Very Little				Very Much
1.	To what extent are you satisfied with the feedback you get on how you perform your job?	1	2	3	4	5
2.	How much stress do you experience on the job?	1	2	3	4	5

As the respondent expresses her views, the researcher would note the response on the schedule. The same questions will thus be asked of everybody in the same manner. Sometimes, however, based on the exigencies of the situation, the researcher might follow a prospective lead from a respondent's answer by asking other relevant questions not on the schedule. Through this process new factors might be identified.

When a sufficient number of interviews have been conducted and the researcher feels he has sufficient information to understand and describe the important factors operating in the situation, the researcher would stop the interviews. The information collected from the various interviews would then be analyzed by tabulating the data. This would help the researcher to describe the phenomena, or quantify them, or identify the specific problem and evolve a theory of the factors that influence the problem.

Review of Unstructured and Structured Interviews

Thus the main purpose of the unstructured interview is to explore the several factors in the situation that might be central to the broad problem area. During this process it might become evident that the problem as identified by the client is only the symptom of a more serious and deep-rooted problem. Conducting unstructured interviews with many people in the organization could result in the identification of several critical factors in the situation. These factors would then be pursued further during the structured interviews, thus eliciting more in-depth information on the selected factors and perhaps aiding in the identification of the critical problem as well. In applied research, a tentative theory of the factors influencing the problem is often conceptualized on the basis of the information obtained from the unstructured and structured interviews.

Some Tips to Follow While Interviewing

The information obtained during the interviews should be as free as possible of bias. Bias can be minimized if not completely eliminated by establishing credibility and good rapport with the respondents, and also by following the right questioning mode. These techniques are discussed in detail in the following paragraphs.

Establishing Credibility and Rapport, and Motivating Individuals to Respond

Projecting professionalism, enthusiasm, and confidence is important for the researcher. A manager hiring outside researchers would be interested in assessing their abilities and personality predispositions. Researchers must establish rapport with and gain the confidence and approval of the hiring client before they can even start their work in the organization. Knowledge, skills, ability, confidence, articulateness, and enthusiasm are therefore qualities a researcher must demonstrate in order to establish credibility with the hiring organization and its members.

To obtain honest information from the respondents, the researcher should be able to establish rapport and trust with the interviewees. In other words, the researcher should be able to make the respondent comfortable enough to give information and truthful answers without fear of adverse consequences. To this end, the researcher should state the purpose of the interview and assure complete confidentiality about the source of the responses. Establishing rapport with the respondents may not be easy, especially at lower levels. The employees are likely to be suspicious of the intentions of the researchers; they may believe that the researchers are on the management's "side," and hence are likely to advocate reduction of the labor force, increase in the workload, and so on. Thus it is important to ensure that everyone concerned is aware of the researchers' purpose—simply to understand what is happening in the organization. The respondents must be assured that they are not on any particular side; they are not there to harm the staff, and they will provide the results of research to the organization only in aggregates, without disclosing the identity of the individuals.

The researcher can establish rapport by being pleasant, sincere, sensitive, and nonevaluative. Evincing a genuine interest in the responses and allaying any anxieties, fears, suspicions, and tensions sensed in the situation will help respondents to feel more comfortable with the researchers. If the respondent is told about the purpose of the study and how she was chosen to be one of those interviewed, there will be better communication flow between the parties. Researchers can motivate respondents to give honest and truthful answers by explaining to them that their contribution will help, and that they themselves may stand to gain from such a survey; for example, the quality of life at work for most employees might improve.

The Questioning Technique

Funneling   In the beginning of an unstructured interview, it is advisable to ask open-ended questions to get a broad impression, for example: "What are some of your feelings about working for this organization?" From the responses to this broad question, further questions that are progressively more focused may be asked as the researcher processes the interviewees' responses and determines some possible key issues relevant to the situation. This transition from broad to narrow themes is called the funneling technique.

Unbiased Questions   It is important to ask questions in a way that would ensure the least bias in the response. For example, "Tell me how you experience your job" is a better question than saying "Boy, the work you do must be really boring; let me hear how you experience it." The latter question is "loaded" in terms of the interviewer's own perceptions of the job. A loaded question might influence the types of answers the respondent gives. Bias could be also introduced by emphasizing certain words, by tone and voice inflections, and through inappropriate suggestions.

Clarifying Issues   To make sure that the researcher understands issues as the respondent means to represent them, it is advisable for the researcher to restate or rephrase important information given by the respondent. For instance, if the interviewee says, "There is an unfair promotion policy in this organization; seniority is not counted at all. It is the juniors who always get promoted," the researcher might interject, "So you are saying that juniors always get promoted over the heads of even capable seniors." Rephrasing in this way clarifies the issue of whether or not the respondent considers ability important. If certain things that are being said are not clear, the researcher should seek clarification. For example, if the respondent happened to say, "The facilities here are really poor; we often have to continue working even when we are dying of thirst," the researcher might ask if there is no water fountain or drinking water available in the building. The respondent's reply to this might well indicate that there is a water fountain across the hall, but the respondent would have liked one on his side of the work area.

Helping the Respondent to Think Through Issues If the respondent is not able to verbalize her perceptions, or replies, "I don't know," the researcher should ask the question in a simpler way, or rephrase it. For instance, if a respondent is unable to specify what aspects of the job he dislikes, the researcher might ask the question in a simpler way. For example, the respondent might be asked which task he would prefer to do: serve a customer or do some filing work. If the answer is "serve the customer," the researcher might use another aspect of the respondent's job and ask the paired-choice question again. In this way, the respondent can sort out which aspects of the job he likes better than others.

Taking Notes When conducting interviews, it is important that the researcher make written notes as the interviews are taking place, or as soon as the interview is terminated. The interviewer should not rely on her memory, because information recalled from memory is imprecise and often likely to be incorrect. Furthermore, if more than one interview is scheduled for the day, the amount of information received increases, as do possible sources of error in recalling from memory. In addition, information based solely on recall introduces bias into the research.

It is possible to record the interviews on tape if the respondent has no objection. However, taped interviews might sometimes bias the respondents' answers because they may be uncomfortable knowing that their voices are being recorded, and thus the interview is not completely anonymous. Hence, even if the respondents do not object, there could be some bias in their responses. Before taping or videotaping interviews, one should be reasonably certain that such a method of obtaining data is not likely to bias the research through biased information. Such taping or videotaping should always be done only with the respondent's permission.

**Review of Tips to Follow
in Interviewing**

Establishing credibility as able researchers with the client system and the organizational members is important for the success of the research project. Researchers need to establish rapport with the respondents and motivate them to give responses relatively free from bias by allaying whatever suspicions, fears, anxieties, and concerns they may have about the research and its consequences. This can be done by being sincere, pleasant, and nonevaluative. While interviewing, the researcher has to ask broad questions initially and then narrow the questions to specific areas, ask questions in an unbiased way, and clarify and help respondents to think through difficult issues. The responses have to be transcribed immediately and the information should not be trusted to memory and later recall.

Having looked at unstructured and structured interviews and learned something about how to conduct the interviews, we can now look at the face-to-face and telephone interviews.

Face-to-Face and Telephone Interviews

Interviews can be conducted either face to face or over the telephone. Although most unstructured interviews in organizational research are conducted face to face, structured interviews could be either face to face or through the medium of the telephone depending on the level of complexity of the issues involved, the time that the interview would take, the convenience of both parties, and the geographical area covered by the survey. Telephone interviews are best suited when many respondents are to be reached over a wide geographic area and the time that each interview takes is short—say, less than 10 minutes. Many market surveys, for instance, are conducted through structured telephone interviews.

Face-to-face interviews and telephone interviews have their other advantages and disadvantages. These will now be briefly discussed.

Face-to-Face Interviews

Advantages   The main advantage of face-to-face or direct interviews is that the researcher can adapt the questions as necessary, clarify doubts, and ensure that the responses are properly understood by repeating or rephrasing the questions. The researcher can also pick up nonverbal cues from the respondent. Any discomfort, stress, or problems that the respondent experiences can be detected through frowns on the face, nervous tapping, and other body language unconsciously exhibited by the respondent. This would obviously be impossible to detect in a telephone interview.

Disadvantages   The main disadvantages of face-to-face interviews are the geographical limitations they may impose on the surveys, and the vast resources needed if such surveys need to be done nationally or internationally. The costs of training interviewers to minimize interviewer biases (e.g., differences in questioning methods, interpretation of responses) are also high. Another drawback is that respondents might feel uneasy about the anonymity of their responses when they are interacting face to face with the interviewer.

Telephone Interviews

Advantages   The main advantage of telephone interviewing, from the researcher's point of view, is that a number of different people can be reached—if need be, across the country or even internationally—in a relatively short period of time. From the respondent's standpoint it would eliminate the discomfort that some respondents might feel in facing the interviewer. It is also possible that most respondents would feel less uncomfortable disclosing personal information over the phone than face to face.

Disadvantages A main disadvantage of telephone interviewing is that the respondent could unilaterally terminate the interview without warning or explanation by hanging up the phone. To minimize this problem it would be advisable to call the interviewee ahead of time to request participation in the survey, giving an approximate idea of how long the interview would last, and setting up a mutually convenient time. Interviewees tend usually to appreciate this courtesy and are more likely to cooperate. It is a good policy not to prolong the interview beyond the time originally agreed on. As mentioned earlier, another disadvantage of the telephone interview is that the researcher will not be able to see the respondent to read the nonverbal communication.

Interviewing is a useful data-collection method, especially during the exploratory stages of research. Where large interview surveys are conducted with a number of different interviewers, it is important to train the interviewers with care in order to minimize interviewer biases manifested in such ways as voice inflections, accentuations of particular words, and differences in interpretation. Good training increases interrater reliability.

Sources of Bias in Interview Data

Errors in data obtained through interviews could result from either respondent or interviewer bias. The respondent who is interviewed while very busy or in a bad mood may give answers that are strongly biased. Respondent bias could also occur when there is fear or distrust among the members in the organization. Social desirability of responses is another source of bias. This bias consists of respondents trying to answer the questions in a socially acceptable manner in order to win the approval of the interviewer (Crowne & Marlowe, 1964), and very likely occurs more frequently in face-to-face interviews. Emotionally loaded responses to certain topical questions (such as the abortion issue) could also produce biases. The interviewer himself could also be a source of bias. How the questions are asked, what words are emphasized, voice inflections, the personality of the interviewer, how the researcher introduces the subject, and how the answers are interpreted and recorded, could all be sources of interviewer bias. The interviewer needs to be aware of, and sensitive to these while collecting data.

Review of Interviewing

Interviews are one method of obtaining data; they can be either unstructured or structured, and can be conducted face to face or over the telephone. Unstructured interviews are usually conducted to obtain more definite ideas about what is and is not important and relevant to particular problem situations. Structured interviews give more in-depth information about specific variables of interest. To minimize bias in responses, the interviewer must establish rapport with the respondents and ask unbiased questions. The face-to-face interview and the interview conducted over the telephone each has its advantages and disadvantages; both are useful under different circumstances. We will now see how data can be gathered through questionnaires.

QUESTIONNAIRES

A questionnaire is a preformulated written set of questions to which respondents record their answers, usually within rather closely defined alternatives.

A questionnaire is an efficient data-collection mechanism when the researcher knows exactly what is required and how to measure the variables of interest. Questionnaires can be administered personally or mailed to the respondents.

Personally Administered Questionnaires

When the survey is confined to a local area, and the organization is willing and able to assemble groups of employees to respond to the questionnaires at the workplace, personally administering the questionnaires is the best way to collect data. The main advantage to this is that the researcher or a member of the research team can collect all the completed responses within a short period of time. Any doubts that the respondents might have regarding any question could be clarified on the spot. The researcher also has the opportunity to introduce the research topic and motivate the respondents to give their honest answers. Administering questionnaires to large numbers of individuals simultaneously is less expensive and less time consuming than interviewing; it also requires fewer skills to administer the questionnaire than to conduct interviews. Wherever possible, it is advantageous to administer questionnaires personally to groups of people because of these advantages. However, organizations often are not able or willing to allow company time for data collection, and other ways of getting the questionnaires completed and returned may have to be found. In such cases, employees may be given blank questionnaires that will be collected from them later personally, or they can be provided with self-addressed, stamped envelopes and asked to have them completed and mailed to the researcher by a certain date.

Mail Questionnaires

The main advantage of a mail questionnaire is that a wide geographical area can be covered in the survey. The questionnaires are mailed to the respondents, who can complete them at their own convenience, in their homes, and at their own pace. However, the return rates of mail question-naires are typically not as high as might be desired; sometimes they are very low. Another disadvantage to the mail questionnaire is that any doubts the respondents might have cannot be clarified. Also, with very low return rates it is difficult to establish the representativeness of the sample, because those who responded to the survey may be totally different from the population they were intended to represent. However, some effective techniques exist for improving the rates of response to mail question-naires. Sending follow-up letters, enclosing some small monetary incen-tives with the questionnaire, providing the respondent with self-addressed, stamped return envelopes, and keeping the questionnaire as short as pos-sible will all help to increase return rates of mail questionnaires (Kanuk & Berenson, 1975).

The choice of using the questionnaire as a data-gathering method might be restricted if the researcher has to reach subjects with very little education. Adding pictures to the questionnaires, if feasible, might help in such cases. For most organizational research, however, after the variables for the research have been identified and the measures for them have been found or developed, the questionnaire is a convenient data-collection mechanism. Field studies, comparative surveys, and the experimental de-signs often use questionnaires to measure the variables of interest. Be-cause questionnaires are commonly used in surveys, it is necessary to know how to design an effective questionnaire. A set of guidelines for questionnaire construction follows.

GUIDELINES FOR QUESTIONNAIRE DESIGN

Good questionnaire design principles should focus on three areas. The first relates to the wording of the questions. The second refers to issues of how the variables will be categorized, scaled, and coded after the ques-

Figure 5.4

Principles of questionnaire design.

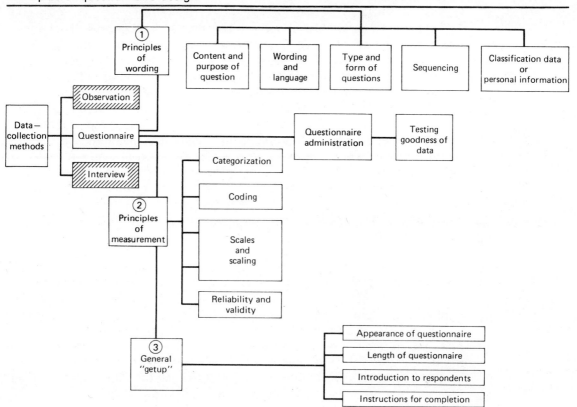

tionnaire responses are received. The third pertains to the general appearance of the questionnaire. All three are important issues in questionnaire design because they can minimize biases in research. These issues are discussed below. The important aspects are schematically depicted in Figure 5.4.

Principles of Wording

The principles of wording refer to such factors as (1) the appropriateness of the content of the questions, (2) how questions are worded and the level of sophistication of the language used, (3) the type and form of questions asked, (4) the sequencing of the questions in the questionnaire, and (5) the personal data sought from the respondents. Each of these is explained below. For further details, see the references given at the end of the unit.

Content and Purpose
of the Question

The nature of the variable tapped—subjective feelings or objective facts—will determine what kinds of questions will be asked. If the variables tapped are of a subjective nature (e.g., satisfaction, involvement), where respondents' beliefs, perceptions, and attitudes are being measured, the questions asked should tap the dimensions and elements of the concept (Lazarsfeld, 1935; Payne, 1951). Where objective variables such as age and educational levels of respondents are tapped, a single direct question—preferably a question that has an ordinally scaled set of categories—would be appropriate. Thus the purpose of each question should be carefully considered so that the variables are adequately measured and yet no unnecessary questions are asked.

The Language and Wording
of the Questionnaire

The language of the questionnaire should approximate the level of understanding of the respondents. The choice of words would depend on the educational level of the respondents sampled, the usage of terms and idioms in the culture, and the frames of reference of the respondents. For instance, even when English is the spoken or the official language in two cultures, certain words may be alien to one culture. Terms such as "working here is a *drag*," and "she is a *compulsive* worker," may not be interpreted the same way in two different cultures. Some blue-collar workers may not understand terminologies such as "organizational structure." Thus it is essential to word the questions in such a way that they are understood by the respondent. If some questions either are not understood or are interpreted differently by the respondent, the researcher will be getting the wrong answers to the questions, and responses will thus be biased. Hence, the questions asked, the language used, and the wording should be appropriate to tap respondents' attitudes, perceptions, and feelings.

Type and Form of Questions

Type of question refers to whether the question will be open-ended or closed. Form of the question refers to positively and negatively worded questions.

Open-Ended versus Closed Questions   Open-ended questions allow respondents to answer them in any way they choose. An example of an open-ended question is asking the respondent to state five things that are interesting and challenging in the job. Another example is asking how the respondents like their supervisors.

A closed question, in contrast, would ask the respondents to make choices among a set of alternatives given by the researcher. For instance, instead of asking the respondent to state any five aspects of the job that are interesting and challenging, the researcher might list ten or fifteen things that might seem interesting or challenging in any job and ask the respondent to rank the first five among these. All items in a questionnaire using a nominal, ordinal or Likert-type scale are considered closed.

Closed questions help the respondent to make quick decisions by making a choice among the several alternatives that are provided. They also help the researcher to code the information easily for subsequent analysis. Of course, care has to be taken to ensure that the alternatives are mutually exclusive and collectively exhaustive. If there are overlapping categories, or if all possible alternatives are not given (i.e., the categories are not exhaustive), the respondents might get confused and the advantage of their being able to make a quick decision may thus be lost.

Some respondents may find even well-delineated categories in a closed question rather confining, and might like the opportunity to make additional comments. This is the reason that many questionnaires end with open-ended questions that invite respondents to comment on topics that may not have been covered or might have been inadequately covered in the questionnaire. The responses to such open-ended questions have to be edited and categorized for subsequent data analysis.

Positively and Negatively Worded Questions   Instead of phrasing all questions positively, it is advisable to include some negatively worded questions so as to minimize "halo" effects and other response biases. The term *halo* refers to the respondent's tendency to continue responding at one end of the scale for all the questions. This can be easily illustrated.

Let us say that there are a set of six questions that tap the variable involvement on a five-point Likert-type scale, with 1 being "very low" and 5 being "very high" on the scale. A positively worded question to tap this variable would be "I am highly engrossed in the job." Let us assume that a respondent answers "5" to that question; but suppose he is not terribly interested or excited about responding to the questionnaire and is mechanically circling "5" for most of the responses. Now, to wake this person out of the stupor, it would help to include a question such as "I feel rather alienated from the job." This is in contrast to the earlier item that stated that the respondent is engrossed in the job. This individual now has to go to the other end of the scale (i.e., has to mark "1") if indeed the earlier response of "5" was correct. This person is now shaken from his lethargy and forced to be alert. The mechanical "one end of the scale" response is thus broken. Thus, including intermittent negatively worded questions would tend to reduce halo effects—that is, the respondent will have less tendency to stick to one end of the scale only. It also allows the researcher to identify respondents who are participating mechanically in the survey. A good questionnaire should therefore include both positively and negatively worded questions. The use of double negatives and excessive use of the words *not* and *only* should be avoided in the negatively worded questions because they tend to confuse respondents. For instance, it is better to say "Coming to work is no great fun" than to say "Coming to work is not any great fun at all." Likewise, it is better to say "The strong people need no tonics" than to say "Only the strong should be given no tonics."

Double-Barreled Questions A question that lends itself to different possible answers to its subparts is called a double-barreled question. Such questions should be avoided and two or more separate questions should be asked instead. For example, the question "Do you think there is a good market for the product and that it will sell well?" could bring a "yes" response to the first part (i.e., there is a good market for the product) and a "no" response to the latter part (i.e., it will not sell well—for various other reasons). In this case, it would be better to ask two questions: (1) "Do you think there is a good market for the product?" and (2) "Do you think the product will sell well?" The answers might be "yes" to both, "no" to both, "yes" to the first and "no" to the second, or "yes" to the second and "no" to the first. If we combined the two questions and asked a double-barreled question, we would obtain ambiguous responses. Hence, double-barreled questions should be avoided.

Ambiguous Questions Even questions that are not double-barreled might be ambiguously worded so that the respondent may not be sure exactly what they mean. An example of such a question is "To what extent would you say you are happy?" Respondents might not be sure whether the question refers to their state of feelings at the workplace, or at home, or in general. Because it is an organizational survey, she might presume that the question relates to the workplace. Yet the researcher might have intended to inquire about the general, overall degree of satisfaction that the individual experiences in everyday life—a very global feeling not specific to the workplace alone. Thus, responses to ambiguous questions have built-in bias inasmuch as different respondents might interpret such items in the questionnaire differently. The result would be a mixed bag of ambiguous responses that do not accurately reflect the respondents' true feelings.

Recall-Dependent Questions Some questions might require respondents to recall experiences from the past that are hazy in their memory. Answers to such questions might have bias. For instance, if an employee who has had 30 years' service in the organization is asked to state when he first started working in a particular department and for how long, he may not be able to give the correct answers and may be way off in his answers. A better source for obtaining that information would be the personnel records.

Leading Questions Questions should not be phrased in such a way that they lead the respondent to give the responses that the researcher would like to elicit. An example of such a question might be "Don't you think that we should demand a lot of our students now so that they become successful managers in the future?" By asking a question such as this, we are signaling and pressuring the respondents to say "yes," because many would want business students to become successful managers; and if being demanding now is going to achieve it, who is going to respond "no" to the question? Another way of asking the same question to get a less biased response would be "To what extent do you agree that we ought to be demanding a lot of our students now, in order to enable them to become successful managers?" If the respondent thinks that being demanding of the students now has nothing to do with their success as managers, the response would be "strongly disagree"; if a respondent somewhat agrees with the statement, the response would be in the middle of the scale, and so on. Here we are not asking the question in such a way that might bias the respondent to give an answer that she might think is what we want to hear.

Loaded Questions Another type of bias in questions occurs when they are phrased in an emotionally charged manner. An example of such a loaded question is "To what extent do you think abortion is the same as killing a live human being?" The issue of abortion is a highly controversial and emotional subject, and people tend to become polarized in their beliefs with regard to this issue. Hence, asking a question such as the above would elicit highly biased emotional responses. If the purpose of the question is to find out whether people are in favor of or against abortion and for what reasons, the following two questions would probably elicit less biased responses:

	Strongly Against		Neither for nor Against		Strongly in Favor of
1. What are your views on abortion? Indicate the extent to which you are in favor of it or oppose the issue.	1	2	3	4	5

2. Please briefly state, in two or three sentences, the reasons you responded the way you did.

Social Desirability Questions should not be worded so that they elicit socially desirable responses. For instance, a question such as "Do you think that old people should be abandoned?" would elicit a response of "no," mainly because society would frown on a person who would say that the elderly people should be abandoned or neglected. Hence, irrespective of the true feelings of the respondent, a socially desirable answer would be provided. If the purpose of the question is to tap the extent to which offspring feel obligated to provide for their parents, or society to elderly people, a less socially desirable way of wording the question might be, "Economic conditions today are such that some find it difficult to provide for their spouses and children. To what extent do you think we should be responsible for the elderly?" This can be scaled as a five-point Likert-type question.

Sometimes certain items that tap social desirability are deliberately introduced at various points in the questionnaire and an index of each individual's social desirability tendency is calculated therefrom. This index is then applied to all other responses given by the individual in order to adjust for his social desirability biases (Crowne & Marlowe, 1964; Edwards, 1957).

Length of Questions   Finally, simple, short questions are preferable to long ones. As a rule of thumb, a question or a statement in the questionnaire should not exceed 20 words, or exceed one full line in print (Horst, 1968; Oppenheim, 1966).

In sum, the language and wording of the questionnaire focus on such issues as the type and form of questions (i.e., open-ended and closed questions, and positively and negatively worded questions), as well as avoiding double-barreled questions, ambiguous questions, leading questions, loaded questions, questions prone to tapping socially desirable answers, and those soliciting distant recall. Questions should also not be unduly long.

Sequencing of Questions

The sequence of questions in the questionnaire should be such that the respondent is led from questions of a general nature to those that are more specific; and from questions that are relatively easy to answer to those that are progressively more difficult. This funnel approach, as it is called (Festinger & Katz, 1966), facilitates the easy progress of the respondent through the items in the questionnaire. The progression from general to specific questions might mean that the respondent is first asked questions of a global nature that pertain to the organization, and then is asked more incisive questions regarding the specific job, department, and the like. Easy questions might relate to issues that do not involve a lot of thinking; the more difficult ones might call for more thought, judgment, and decision making.

In determining the sequence of questions, it is advisable not to place consecutively a positively worded and a negatively worded question tapping the same element or dimension of a concept. For instance, two questions such as the following, placed one right after the other, is not only awkward but might also seem insulting to the respondent.

1. I have an opportunity to interact with my colleagues during work hours.

2. I have few opportunities to interact with my colleagues during work hours.

First, there is no need to ask exactly the same question in a positive and a negative way. Second, if for some reason this is deemed necessary (e.g., to check the consistency of the responses), the two questions should be placed in different parts of the questionnaire, as far apart as possible.

The way questions are sequenced could also introduce certain biases, frequently referred to as the ordering effects. Though randomly placing the questions in the questionnaire would reduce any systematic biases in the response, it is very rarely done.

Classification Data
or Personal Information

Classification data, also known as personal information or demographic questions, consist of such information as age, educational level, marital status, and income. Unless absolutely necessary, it is best not to ask for the name of the respondent. If, however, the questionnaire has to be identified with the respondents for any reason, then the questionnaire could be numbered and connected by the researcher to the respondent's name. This procedure should be clearly explained to the respondent, however. The reason for using the numerical system in questionnaires is to ensure the anonymity of the respondent even if the questionnaires fall into someone else's hands.

Whether questions seeking personal information should appear in the beginning or at the end of the questionnaire is a matter of choice for the researcher. Some people advocate asking for personal data at the end rather than at the beginning of the questionnaire (Oppenheim, 1966). Their reasoning may be that by the time the respondent reaches the end of the questionnaire she would have been convinced of the genuineness of the inquiry made by the researcher. Other researchers may prefer to elicit most of the personal information at the very beginning, on the grounds that respondents might have psychologically identified with the questionnaire and feel committed to responding, once they have said something about themselves at the very beginning. Thus whether one asks this information in the beginning or at the end of the questionnaire is a matter of individual choice. However, questions regarding details of income, if such information is absolutely necessary, may be best placed at the very end of the questionnaire, because some employees might be reluctant to disclose their income levels and become turned off, thus refusing to cooperate with the survey.

It is also a wise policy to ask for information regarding age, income, and other sensitive personal questions by providing a range of response options. For example, the variables can be tapped as shown here:

Example 5.7

Age (years)	Annual Income
☐ Under 20	☐ Less than $10,000
☐ 20–30	☐ $10,000–20,000
☐ 31–40	☐ $20,001–30,000
☐ 41–50	☐ $30,001–40,000
☐ Over 50	☐ More than $40,000

In organizational surveys, it is advisable to obtain certain demographic data such as age, sex, educational level, and number of years in the organization, even if the theoretical framework does not include these variables. Such data will help to describe the sample characteristics, as we will see later. However, when there are only one or two respondents in a department, then asking information that might reveal their identity might be threatening to employees. For instance, if there is only one female in a department, then she might not respond to the question on gender, because it might reveal the source of the data. In such cases, it would probably be inadvisable to force respondents to offer information that would make them uncomfortable.

Review of Principles of Wording for Questionnaires

Certain principles of wording need to be followed while designing a questionnaire. The questions asked must be appropriate for tapping the variable. The language and wording of the questionnaire should be at a level that is meaningful to the employees. The form and type of questions should be geared to minimizing respondent biases. The sequencing of the questions should facilitate the smooth progression of the respondent through the questionnaire. The personal data should be gathered with sensitivity to the respondents' feelings, and with respect for privacy.

Principles of Measurement

Just as there are rules or guidelines that have to be followed to ensure that the wording of the questionnaire is appropriate to minimize bias, so also are there some principles of measurement that are to be followed to ensure that the data collected are appropriate to test our hypotheses. These principles of measurement are really tests of the goodness of the data collected by the researcher. The two main criteria for testing the goodness of data are validity and reliability. Validity tests how well a technique, instrument, or process measures *the particular thing it is supposed to*

Figure 5.5

Testing goodness of measures—reliability and validity.

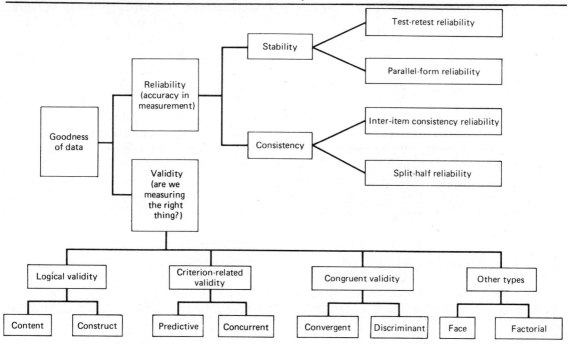

measure. Reliability tests how well or consistently a measuring instrument (or technique or process) measures *whatever it is measuring.* In other words, validity is concerned with whether we are measuring the right thing, and reliability is concerned with accuracy and consistency in measurement. Validity and reliability attest to the scientific rigor applied to the research study. These two criteria will now be discussed. The various forms of reliability and validity are depicted in Figure 5.5.

Validity

Earlier, in Unit 4, we examined the terms internal validity and external validity in the context of experimental design. That is, we were concerned about the issue of the authenticity of the cause → effect relationships and their generalizability to the external environment. Now we are going to examine the validity of the measuring instrument itself. That is, when we ask a set of questions (i.e., develop a measuring instrument) in hopes that we are tapping the concept, how can we be reasonably sure that we are measuring the concept we set out to measure and not something else? This can be determined by applying certain validity tests.

Several types of validity tests are used to test the goodness of measures. Various writers use different terms to denote these validity tests. For the sake of clarity, we can group these validity tests under three broad headings: logical validity, empirical validity, and other types of validity. Logical validity could be tested through content validity and construct validity. Empirical validity encompasses criterion-related validity (both predictive and concurrent validity) and congruent validity (both convergent and discriminant validity). Other types of validity include face validity and factorial validity. Each of these will be briefly explained.

Logical Validity   Logical validity includes content validity and construct validity. Both are derived through reasoning logically and deciding whether the measures conform to accepted logic or logical theories.

Content Validity   Content validity refers to a representative sampling of a whole set of items that could measure the concept. This validity basically refers to how well we have delineated the dimensions and elements of a concept.

Construct Validity   Construct validity is based on a determination of the degree to which the test result fits the theory around which the test was designed. This method of determining validity is useful in situations where no definitive criterion is available. Construct validity can be tested through nomological nets, a discussion of which is beyond the scope of this book. The interested student is referred to Cronbach (1970), and Selltiz, Wrightsman, and Cook (1976).

Empirical Validity   This validity is pragmatic and can be tested through assessing the correlations among certain variables in the data set. There are two types of empirical validity: criterion-related and congruent. These can be briefly explained.

Criterion-Related Validity   Criterion-related validity refers to establishing the validity of a test or an instrument that measures a concept by correlating the scores on the concept as measured by the instrument with a criterion or dependent variable. For instance, if we have developed a measure to tap job characteristics, and correlate the scores with, say, job satisfaction, then we are trying to establish criterion-related validity. If the criterion—a variable considered to provide a direct measure of the expected behavior—occurs at the same time the test is taken, we would have established concurrent validity; if it occurs in the future, we try to establish predictive validity. For example, if, on the one hand, we were to measure job characteristics and job satisfaction simultaneously, and to find a high correlation between the two, we would establish concurrent validity. On the other hand, if we measure the job characteristics now (say after a new job design), and then measure the job satisfaction of employees six months from now, we would be trying to establish predictive validity for our job characteristic measure.

Congruent Validity   Congruent validity is based on the correlations between a test and another test that have been established as measures of the same attribute, or two opposing attributes. Two derivations of the congruence test are convergent validity and discriminant validity. When two different measures measuring the same concept are highly correlated, we have *convergent validity*. When two measures tapping two opposite or two different traits such as self-esteem and self-hate are negatively correlated, then we have *discriminant validity*. In other words, two measures expected to measure the same concept should converge, and two measures intended to tap two opposite or two different concepts should discriminate each other. When high positive correlations between the first two measures and high negative correlations between the latter two measures are found, we can be reasonably sure that the measures developed are measuring what they are supposed to measure.

Other Uses of the Term "Validity"   *Face validity* is a term sometimes used to designate content validity. That is, a question, on the face of it, reads as if it is measuring what it is supposed to measure. The question "To what extent are you satisfied with the work you do?" looks as if it is measuring work satisfaction, and not work involvement. This item obviously has face validity. This really is no test of validity in the true sense but indicates an appearance of validity.

Factorial validity is an indication, through the use of factor-analytic techniques, that a test is a pure measure of some specific factor or dimension. This test of factorial validity is also useful in reducing a great number of items developed to measure a concept at the operational definition stage to a manageable number of items.

Face validity and factorial validity are both components of content validity.

Validity thus could be established in several ways. Empirical validity is fairly convenient to establish, and content validity can be established through factor analysis and item analysis. Published measures for various concepts report the kinds of validity that have been established for the instrument, so that the reader or user can determine whether the measure is validly measuring what it is supposed to measure.

Reliability

The reliability of a measure indicates the accuracy with which the instrument is measuring the concept. It helps to assess the "goodness" of a measure, regardless of what it measures (validity), by assessing the "consistency" or "stability" of the measure.

Stability of Measures   The ability of a measure to maintain stability over time, despite uncontrollable testing conditions and the state of the respondents themselves, is indicative of its stability and low vulnerability to changes in the situation. This attests to the goodness of the measure, inasmuch as it is accurately measuring the concepts no matter when they are measured. Two tests of stability are test-retest reliability and parallel-form reliability.

Test-Retest Reliability　The reliability coefficient obtained with repetition of an identical measure on a second occasion is called test-retest reliability. That is, when a questionnaire containing some items that are supposed to measure a concept is administered to a set of respondents now, and again to the same respondents, say several weeks to six months later, then the correlation between the scores obtained at the two different times from the same set of respondents is called the test-retest coefficient. The higher it is, the better the test-retest reliability, and hence the stability of the measure across time.

Parallel-Form Reliability　When responses on two comparable sets of measures tapping the same construct are highly correlated, we have parallel-form reliability. Both forms have the same number of items and the same response format with only the wordings and the ordering of questions changed. What we try to establish here is the error variability resulting from wording and ordering of the questions. If two such comparable forms are highly correlated (say .8 and above), we can be fairly certain that the measures are reasonably reliable, with minimal error variance caused by wording, ordering, or other factors.

Internal Consistency of Measures　The internal consistency of measures is indicative of the homogeneity of the items in the measure that tap the construct. In other words, the items should "hang together as a set" and be capable of independently measuring the same concept such that the respondents attach the same overall meaning to each of the items. Consistency could be tested through split-half reliability and interitem consistency reliability.

Split-Half Reliability　The split-half reliability is the correlation coefficient between one-half of the items measuring a concept and the other half of the items measuring the same concept. Suppose that 12 items measure a concept; the responses to these 12 items are separated into two randomly selected halves, and then compared. If the responses to these two halves are highly similar, the split-half reliability will be high. Thus the reliability coefficient between these halves is a test of the split-half reliability. The higher the coefficient, the better the reliability of the measure.

Interitem Consistency Reliability　This is a test of the consistency of respondents' responses to all the items in a measure. To the degree that items are independent measures of the same concept, they will be correlated with one another. The most popular test of interitem consistency reliability is the Cronbach's coefficient alpha (Cronbach's alpha; Cronbach, 1946), which is used for multipoint-scaled items, and the Kuder-Richardson formulas, used for dichotomous items.

Interrater Reliability   The consistency of the judgment of several raters on how they see a phenomenon or interpret some responses is also a measure of reliability. This interrater reliability is especially relevant when the data are obtained through observations, projective tests, or unstructured interviews, all of which are liable to be subjectively interpreted. More confidence in the measure is obtained when there is a high interrater reliability.

Goodness of Measures   In sum, the goodness of measures is established through different kinds of validity and reliability tests depicted in Figure 5.5. The results of any research can only be as good as the measures that tap the concepts in the theoretical framework. In order for research to be scientific, we need to use well-validated and reliable measures. Fortunately, measures have been developed for many important concepts in organizational research, and the psychometric properties of these measures (i.e., the reliability and validity) have been established by the developers of these instruments in most cases. Thus researchers can use the instruments that have already been reputed to be ''good,'' rather than develop their own measures. When using these measures, however, researchers should cite the source (i.e., the author and reference) so that the reader can seek more information if necessary.

Categorization

All responses on the nominal variables and closed-ended questions must be organized and grouped into categories in order to answer the research questions. In other words, it should be possible to place every response in some category, and the classification system should be determined before the data are collected. Categorization involves delineating the set of alternative responses applicable to each question. The nominally scaled variable, nationality, in Example 5.4, for instance, had seven categories of responses: African, Asian, Australian, European, North American, South American, and others. Categories set up must be mutually exclusive and collectively exhaustive. That is, the respondent should not be confused by overlapping categories, or unable to respond because a category is missing. For example, the seven categories provided for the nationality concept are mutually exclusive (e.g., an African cannot be an Australian or any other nationality) and collectively exhaustive. The category ''others'' allows a person to choose this category in the unlikely event that that person's national origin is different from one of the six specified categories. Thus all the possible categories are covered exhaustively.

Coding

Coding can be automatic in the case of some questionnaire items and structured interviews, as in the case of Likert-type scale responses, in which the respondent circles a number. Data are not automatically coded when responses to unstructured interviews or observational studies are obtained. Here the responses have first to be categorized (post hoc), and then coded, if possible.

General Appearance or "Getup" of the Questionnaire

Not only is it important to address issues of wording and measurement in questionnaire design; it is also necessary to pay attention to how the questionnaire looks. An attractive and neat questionnaire with appropriate introduction, instructions, and a well-arrayed set of questions and response alternatives will make it easier for the respondents to answer the items in the questionnaire. A good introduction, well-organized instructions, and neat alignment of the questions are all important. These elements are briefly discussed with examples.

A Good Introduction

A proper introduction that clearly discloses the identity of the researcher and the purpose of the survey is absolutely necessary. It is also essential to establish some rapport with the respondent and motivate him to respond to the questions in the questionnaire willingly and enthusiastically. Assuring confidentiality of the information provided by respondents will ensure less biased answers. The introduction section should end with a courteous note thanking the respondent for taking the time to respond to the survey. The following is an example of an appropriate introduction.

Example 5.8

Southern Illinois University at Carbondale
Carbondale, Illinois 62901
Department of Administrative Sciences

Dear Participant

This questionnaire is designed to study aspects of life at work. The information you provide will help us better understand the quality of our work life. Because *you* are the one who can give us a correct picture of how you experience your work life, we ask you to respond to the questions frankly and honestly.

Your response will be kept **strictly confidential.** Only members of the research team will have access to the information you give. In order to ensure the utmost privacy, we have provided an identification number for each participant. This number will be used by us only for follow-up procedures. The numbers, names, and questionnaires will not be made available to anyone other than the researchers.

A summary of the results will be mailed to you after the data are analyzed.

Thank you very much for your time and cooperation. We greatly appreciate your organization's and your help in furthering this research endeavor.

Cordially,

Uma Sekaran, Ph.D.

Uma Sekaran, Ph.D.
Associate Professor
of Administrative Sciences

Organizing Questions, Giving Instructions and Guidance, and Good Alignment

Organizing the questions logically and neatly in appropriate sections and providing instructions on how to complete the items in each section will help the respondents to answer the questions without difficulty. Questions should also be neatly and conveniently organized in such a way that the respondent can read and answer the questionnaire without eyestrain, and with a minimum of time and effort.

A specimen of a portion of a questionnaire incorporating the above points follows.

Example 5.9

Section Two: About Work Life

> The questions below provide descriptions about how you experience your work life. Think in terms of your everyday experience and accomplishments on the job and *circle* the most appropriate response for you.

Strongly Agree	Agree	Slightly Agree	Neutral	Slightly Disagree	Disagree	Strongly Disagree
1	2	3	4	5	6	7

1. I do my best work when my job assignments are fairly difficult.   1 2 3 4 5 6 7
2. When I have a choice, I try to work in a group instead of by myself.   1 2 3 4 5 6 7
3. In my work assignments, I try to be my own boss.   1 2 3 4 5 6 7
4. I seek an active role in the leadership of a group.   1 2 3 4 5 6 7
5. I try very hard to improve on my past performance at work.   1 2 3 4 5 6 7
6. I pay a good deal of attention to the feelings of others at work.   1 2 3 4 5 6 7
7. I go on my own way at work, regardless of the opinion of others.   1 2 3 4 5 6 7
8. I avoid trying to influence those around me to see things my way.   1 2 3 4 5 6 7
9. I take moderate risks and stick my neck out to get ahead at work.   1 2 3 4 5 6 7
10. I prefer to do my own work and let others do theirs.   1 2 3 4 5 6 7
11. I disregard rules and regulations that hamper my personal freedom.   1 2 3 4 5 6 7

Personal Data Demographic or personal data could be organized as in the specimen below. Note the scaling of the age variable.

Example 5.10

Section One: About Yourself

> Please *circle* the numbers representing appropriate responses for the following items.

1. Your Age (years)

1 Under 20
2 20–29
3 30–39
4 40–49
5 Over 49

2. Your Highest Completed Level of Education

1 Elementary school
2 High school
3 College degree
4 Graduate degree
5 Other (specify)

3. Your Sex

1 Female
2 Male

4. **Marital Status**

1 Married
2 Single
3 Widowed
4 Divorced or separated
5 Other (specify)

5. **Number of Pre-school Children (under 5 Years of Age)**

1 None
2 One
3 Two or more

6. **Age of the Eldest Child in Your Care (years)**

1 Under 5
2 5–12
3 13–19
4 Over 19
5 Not applicable

7. **Number of Years Worked in the Organization**

1 Less than 1
2 1–2
3 3–5
4 6–10
5 Over 10

8. **Number of Other Organizations Worked for before Joining this Organization**

1 None
2 One
3 Two
4 Three
5 Four or more

9. **Present Work Shift**

1 First
2 Second
3 Third

10. **Job Status**

1 Top management
2 Middle management
3 First-level supervisor
4 Nonmanagerial

Information on Income and Other Personal Data

Though demographic information can be asked either at the beginning or at the end of the questionnaire, information of a very private and personal nature such as income, if considered absolutely necessary for the survey, should be asked at the end of the questionnaire rather than at the beginning. Also, such questions should be justified by explaining why this information might contribute to knowledge and problem solving, so that respondents do not perceive the questions to be of a prying nature. Shifting such questions to the end would help reduce respondent bias in case the respondent gets irritated by the personal nature of the question. See the example below.

Example 5.11

> Because many people believe that income is a significant factor in explaining employment decisions, the following two questions are very important. Like all other items in this questionnaire, the responses to these two questions will be kept confidential. Please check the most appropriate box that describes your position.

Roughly, my *total yearly* income before taxes and other deductions is

- ☐ Less than $5,000
- ☐ $5,000–$7,999
- ☐ $8,000–$12,999
- ☐ $13,000–$16,999
- ☐ $17,000–$19,999
- ☐ $20,000–$25,000
- ☐ Over $25,000

Roughly, the *total yearly income* before taxes and other deductions *of my immediate family*—including my own income, income from other sources, and the income of my spouse—is

- ☐ Less than $5,000
- ☐ $5,000–$10,000
- ☐ $10,001–$20,000
- ☐ $20,001–$30,000
- ☐ $30,001–$40,000
- ☐ $40,001–$60,000
- ☐ Over $60,000

The end of the questionnaire could include an open-ended question allowing respondents to comment on any aspect they choose. The questionnaire would end with sincere thanks to respondents. The last page of the questionnaire could look like the following.

Example 5.12

We know that our questions have not allowed you to report some things you may want to say about your job and organization and yourself. Please make additional comments in the space provided.

We sincerely appreciate your time and cooperation. Please check to make sure that you have not skipped any questions, and then return the questionnaire.

How did you feel about completing this questionnaire? Check the face in the following diagram that truly reflects your feelings.

Thank you!

Review of Questionnaire Design

We have devoted a lot of attention to questionnaire design because it is one of the most common methods of collecting data. Managers who administer questionnaires or comment on questionnaires to be administered by consultants to members of the organization, as well as those who might be asked to participate in several organizational surveys by other researchers, will find that it is important to know the difference between good and bad questionnaires. The principles of questionnaire design relate to how the questions are worded and measured, and how the entire questionnaire is organized. To minimize respondent biases and measurement errors, all the principles have to be followed carefully.

Questionnaires are most useful as a data-collection method, especially when large numbers of people are to be reached in different geographical regions. Questionnaires are a popular method of collecting data because researchers can obtain data fairly easily, and the questionnaire responses are easily coded. When well-validated instruments are used, the findings of the study benefit the scientific community through replicated results and additions to the theory base.

Do Exercise 5.8.

OTHER METHODS OF DATA COLLECTION

Observational Surveys

Whereas interviews and questionnaires elicit responses from the subjects, it is possible to gather data without asking questions of the respondents by observing people in their natural work environment or in the lab setting, and recording their behaviors. The researcher can play one of two roles while gathering field observational data: nonparticipant observer or participant observer.

Nonparticipant Observer

The researcher can collect the data in the role of a pure researcher without trying to become an integral part of the organizational system. For example, a researcher might sit in the corner of an office, and see and record how the manager spends her time. These activities, carried out over a period of time and including observation of several managers, can allow the researcher to make some generalizations on how managers typically spend their time. By merely observing the activities and recording them on paper, the researcher comes up with some findings. Observers must naturally be physically present at the workplace for extended periods of time; thus observational studies are time consuming.

Participant Observer

Another observational role that the researcher can play is that of the participant observer. Here, the researcher enters the organization or the research setting actually becoming a part of the work team. For instance, if a researcher wants to study group dynamics in work organizations, then she may enter the organization in the role of an employee, and observe the dynamics in groups while being a part of the work organization and work groups. Most anthropological research is conducted in this manner, where the researcher becomes a part of the alien culture about which he is interested in knowing more.

Structured versus Unstructured
Observational Studies

Thus, observational studies could be of either the nonparticipant observer or the participant observer type. Both of these, again, could be either structured or unstructured. Where the observer has a predetermined set of categories of activities or phenomena that she plans to study, it is a structured observational study. Observation forms for the purpose could be specially designed. If, however, the observer has no definite ideas of the particular aspects that she wants to focus on in the observation, but records practically everything that is observed, it is an unstructured observational study.

Biases in Observational Studies

Data observed from the researcher's point of view are likely to be prone to observer biases. Moreover, where several observers are involved, interobserver reliability has to be established before the data can be accepted.

Observer fatigue could also be a source of bias. Observing the happenings day in and day out over extended periods of time could fatigue or bore the observers and introduce biases in the recording of the observations. To minimize observer bias, observers are usually given training on how to observe and what to record. Good observational studies would also establish interobserver reliability.

Respondent bias could also be a threat to the validity of the results of observational studies, because those who are observed may behave differently during the period the study is conducted, especially if the observations are done for a short period of time. However, in studies of longer duration, as the study progresses, the employees become more relaxed and tend to behave more normally. For these reasons, researchers doing observational studies discount the data recorded in the initial few days, if they seem to be quite different from what is observed later.

Motivational Research

Certain ideas and thoughts that cannot be easily verbalized or that remain on unconscious levels in the respondents' minds can usually be brought to the surface through motivational research. This is typically done by trained professionals who apply different probing techniques in order to surface deep-rooted ideas and thoughts in the respondents. Familiar techniques for gathering such data are word associations, sentence completion, thematic apperception tests (TAT), inkblot tests, and the like.

Word-association techniques, such as asking the respondent to quickly associate a word—say, *work*—with the first thing that comes to mind, are often used. The reply is an indication of what work means to the individual. Similarly, sentence completion would have the respondent quickly complete a sentence, such as "Work is _____." One respondent might say, "Work is a lot of fun," whereas another might say "Work is a drudgery." These responses may provide some insights into individuals' feelings and attitudes toward work.

Thematic apperception tests ask the respondent to develop a story around a picture or a drawing that is shown. Several need patterns and personality characteristics in employees could be traced through these tests. Inkblot tests, another form of motivational research, use colored inkblots that are interpreted by the respondents, who explain what they see in the various patterns and colors.

Although these types of motivational studies are useful for tapping attitudes and feelings that are difficult to obtain otherwise, they cannot be engaged in by researchers who are not trained to do such research.

Panel Studies

Where the effects of certain interventions or changes are to be studied over a period of time, panel studies are very useful. Several individuals are chosen to serve as panel members for a research study. For instance, if the effects of a proposed advertisement for a certain brand of coffee are to be assessed quickly, the panel members can be exposed to the advertisement and their intentions of purchasing the brand can be assessed. This can be taken as the response that could be expected of consumers if, in fact, they were exposed to the advertisement. Six months later, the product manager might think of changing the flavor of the same product, and might explore the effects of it on this panel. Thus, a continuing set of "experts" will provide the sample base, or serve as the sounding board for assessing the effects of change—that is, the introduction of a new variable. Such members are called a panel, and research that uses this panel is called a panel study. Nielsen ratings result from a panel study.

Panels can be either static (i.e., the same members serve on the panel over extended periods of time), or dynamic (i.e., the members are changed from time to time in order to test the effects of different changes). The main advantages of the static panel is that it offers a good and sensitive measurement of the changes that take place between two points in time— a much better measure than using two different groups at two different times. The disadvantage, however, lies in the fact that the panel members could become so sensitive to the changes as a result of being continuously interviewed, that their opinions might no longer be representative of what the others in the population might think. Members could also drop out of the panel from time to time for various reasons. The advantages and disadvantages of the dynamic panel are the reverse of the ones discussed for the static panel.

Unobtrusive Measures

Another important source of data consists of sources that are not people. For instance, the wear and tear on journals in a university library could be a good indication of their popularity, their usage, or both. The number of different brands of soft drink cans found in trashbags could be a measure of the consumption levels of different brands of soft drinks. Signatures on checks exposed to ultraviolet rays could be indicative of the extent of forgery and frauds; actuarial records are good sources for determining the births, marriages, and deaths in a community; company records disclose a lot of personal information about employees, the extent of company efficiency, and other data as well. Thus these unobtrusive sources of data and their use are also important in research.

MULTIMETHODS OF DATA COLLECTION

Because almost all data-collection methods have some biases associated with them, collecting data through multimethods and from multisources lends rigor to research. For instance, if the responses collected through interviews, questionnaires, and observation are strongly correlated with each other, then we will have more confidence about the goodness of the data that are being collected. If there are discrepancies in how the respondent answers the same question when interviewed, as opposed to how she answers the question in a questionnaire, then we would be inclined to discard the data as being biased.

Likewise, if data obtained from several sources are highly similar, we would have more faith in the goodness of the data. For example, if an employee rates his performance as four on a five-point scale, and his supervisor rates him the same way, we may be inclined to think that he is perhaps a better than average worker. In contrast, if he gives himself a five on the five-point scale, and his supervisor gives him a rating of two, then we will not know to what extent there is a bias and from which source. Therefore, high correlations among data obtained regarding the same variable from different sources lend more credibility to the research instruments and to the data obtained through these instruments. Good researchers try to obtain data from multiple sources and through multiple data-collection methods. Such research, though, would be more costly and time consuming.

SUMMARY

In this unit we learned about measuring concepts and collecting data for research. We discussed operational definition, scaling, reliability, and validity, and several ways in which data can be collected. Because bias exists in all forms of data collection, multimethods of data collection, as well as obtaining data from multiple sources, are recommended for rigorous research. Such plans however, must be made in the context of available resources, and the extent of rigor needed for a given research objective.

The next unit concentrates on the sample from which the data will be collected and the types of sampling designs that are appropriate for various research studies.

SUPPLEMENTAL READINGS

The following topic references will guide you to seek more information.

Topic	Reference	Chapter	Pages
Measurement of variables	Coombs (1966)	11	471–535
	Selltiz, Jahoda, Deutsch, & Cook (1959)	5	146–198

Topic	Reference	Chapter	Pages
Operational definition	Emory (1980)	2	28–30
	Runkel & McGrath (1972)	6	150–152
	Selltiz et al. (1959)	2	41–44
Scales and scaling	Bendig (1954)	(journal article)	
	Emory (1980)	5	117–126
		9	256–289
	Likert (excerpted in Fishbein, 1967)		90–95
	Selltiz et al. (1959)	10	343–384
Reliability and validity	Cook & Campbell (1979)	6	77–101
	Emory (1980)	5	128–135
	Kerlinger (1973)	26, 27	442–476
	Selltiz et al. (1959)	5	154–186
	Stone (1978)	3	43–60
Data-collection methods Interviewing	Cannell & Kahn (1966)	8	327–380
	Clover & Balsley (1979)	5	100–108
	Emory (1980)	10	293–307
	Kornhauser & Sheatsley (1959)	Appendix C	574–587
	Merton & Kendall (1955)		476–491
Questionnaires	Clover & Balsley (1979)	5	95–100
	Emory (1980)	10	307–312
	Selltiz et al. (1959)	7	236–268
Motivational research	Clover & Balsley (1979)	5	113–116
	Kerlinger (1973)	30	514–535
	Selltiz et al. (1959)	8	280–311
Observational studies	Emory (1980)	10	312–319
	Peak (1966)	6	243–299
	Riley & Nelson (1974)	Part III	117–120
Panel studies	Clover & Balsley (1979)	5	116–121
	Emory (1980)	4	86

Topic	Reference	Chapter	Pages
Unobtrusive measures	Angell & Freedman (1966)	7	300–326
	Emory (1980)	10	320
	Webb, Campbell, Schwartz, & Sechrest (1966)	A good reference book	
Questionnaire design	Clover & Balsley (1979)	6	128–148
	Emory (1980)	8	223–254
	Kornhauser & Sheatsley (1959)	Appendix C	546–574

REFERENCES

Angell, R. C., & Freedman, R. The use of documents, records, census materials, and indices. In L. Festinger & D. Katz (Eds.), *Research methods in the behavioral sciences.* New York: Holt, Rinehart and Winston, 1966.

Bendig, A. W. Transmitted information and the length of rating scales. *Journal of Experimental Psychology,* 1954, *47,* 303–308.

Cannell, C. F., & Kahn, R. L. The collection of data by interviewing. In L. Festinger & D. Katz (Eds.), *Research methods in the behavioral sciences.* New York: Holt, Rinehart and Winston, 1966.

Clover, V. T., & Balsley, H. L. *Business research methods* (2nd ed.). Columbus, Ohio: Grid Publishing Co., 1979.

Cook, T. D., & Campbell, D. T. Four kinds of validity. In R. T. Mowday & R. M. Steers (Eds.), *Research in organizations: Issues and controversies.* Santa Monica, Calif.: Goodyear Publishing Co., 1979.

Coombs, C. H. Theory and methods of social measurement. In L. Festinger & D. Katz (Eds.), *Research methods in the behavioral sciences.* New York: Holt, Rinehart and Winston, 1966.

Cronbach, L. J. Response sets and test validating. *Educational and Psychological Measurement,* 1946, *6,* 475–494.

Cronbach, L. J. *Essentials of psychological testing* (3rd ed.). New York: Harper and Row, 1970.

Crowne, D., & Marlowe, D. *The approval motive.* New York: John Wiley and Sons, 1964.

Edwards, A. *The social desirability variable in personality assessment and research.* New York: The Dryden Press, 1957.

Elmore, P. E., & Beggs, D. L. Salience of concepts and commitment to extreme judgments in response pattern of teachers. *Education,* 1975, *95*(4), 325–334.

Emory, C. W. *Business research methods* (Rev. ed.). Homewood, Ill.: Richard D. Irwin, Inc., 1980.

Festinger, L., & Katz, D. (Eds.). *Research methods in the behavioral sciences.* New York: Holt, Rinehart and Winston, 1966.

Fishbein, M. (Ed.). *Readings in attitude theory and measurement,* New York: John Wiley and Sons, 1967.

Horst, P. *Personality: Measurement of dimensions.* San Francisco: Jossey-Bass, 1968.

Kanuk, L., & Berenson, C. Mail surveys and response rates: A literature review. *Journal of Marketing Research,* 1975, *12,* 440–453.

Kerlinger, F. N. *Foundations of behavioral research* (2nd ed.). New York: Holt, Rinehart and Winston, 1973.

Kornhauser, A., & Sheatsley, P. B. Questionnaire construction and interview procedure. In C. Selltiz, M. Jahoda, M. Deutsch, & S. W. Cook (Eds.), *Research methods in social relations* (Rev. ed.). New York: Holt, Rinehart and Winston, 1959.

Lazarsfeld, P. F. The art of asking why. *National Marketing Research,* 1935, *1,* 26–38.

Merton, R. K., & Kendall, P. L. The focused interview. In P. F. Lazarsfeld & M. Rosenberg (Eds.), *The language of social research.* New York: The Free Press, 1955.

Oppenheim, A. N. *Questionnaire design and attitude measurement.* New York: Basic Books, 1966.

Payne, S. L. *The art of asking questions.* Princeton, N.J.: Princeton University Press, 1951.

Peak, H. Problems of objective observation. In L. Festinger & D. Katz (Eds.), *Research methods in the behavioral sciences.* New York: Holt, Rinehart and Winston, 1966.

Riley, M. W., & Nelson, E. E. *Sociological observation: A strategy for new social knowledge.* New York: Basic Books, 1974.

Runkel, P. J., & McGrath, J. E. *Research on human behavior: A systematic guide to method.* New York: Holt, Rinehart and Winston, 1972.

Selltiz, C., Jahoda, M., Deutsch, M., & Cook, S. W. *Research methods in social relations* (Rev. ed.). New York: Holt, Rinehart and Winston, 1959.

Selltiz, C., Wrightsman, L. S., & Cook, S. W. *Research methods in social relations* (3rd ed.). New York: Holt, Rinehart and Winston, 1976.

Stone, E. *Research methods in organizational behavior.* Santa Monica, Calif.: Goodyear Publishing Co., 1978.

Webb, E. J., Campbell, D. T., Schwartz, R. D., & Sechrest, L. *Unobtrusive measures: Nonreactive research in the social sciences.* Chicago: Rand-McNally, 1966.

POINTS TO PONDER AND RESPOND TO

1. It is advisable to use instruments that have already been developed and repeatedly used in published studies, rather than developing our own measures.

2. A valid instrument is always reliable, but a reliable instrument is not always valid.

3. Every data-collection method has its own built-in biases. Therefore, resorting to multimethods of data collection is only going to compound the biases.

4. One way to deal with discrepancies found in the data obtained from multiple sources is to average the figures and take the mean as the value on the variable.

5. The fewer the biases in measurement and in the data-collection procedures, the more scientific the research.

EXERCISES

Exercise 5.1

Schematically depict the operational definition of the concept of **stress** and develop 10 questions that would measure stress. Use your own notebook for this.

Exercise 5.2

Schematically depict the operational definition of the concept of **enriched job** and develop 12 items to measure the concept. Use your own notebook.

Exercise 5.3

Think of two variables that would be natural candidates for nominal scales, and set up mutually exclusive and collectively exhaustive categories for each.

Exercise 5.4

Develop an ordinal scale for consumer preferences for different brands of beer.

Exercise 5.5

Mention three variables that could be tapped on an interval scale.

Exercise 5.6

Example 5.2 lists 14 items directed toward tapping achievement motivation. Take items 6 to 9 and item 14, and use an interval scale to measure them. Reword the questions if you wish, without changing their meaning.

Exercise 5.7

Mention one variable for each of the four scales in the context of a market survey, and explain how or why they would fit into the scale.

Exercise 5.8

The president of Serakan Co. suspects that most of the 500 male and female employees in her organization are somewhat alienated from work. She also suspects that those who are more involved (less alienated) are also the ones who are more satisfied with their work lives.

Design a questionnaire the president could use to test her hypotheses. Use your own notebook for this.

UNIT 6
SAMPLING

ISSUES DISCUSSED

Population, Element, Population Frame, Sample, Subject

Sampling

Reasons for Sampling

Representativeness of the Sample

Probability Sampling
- Simple Random Sampling
- Systematic Sampling
- Stratified Random Sampling: Proportionate and Disproportionate
- Cluster Sampling: Single-stage and Multistage Clusters
- Area Sampling
- Double Sampling

Nonprobability Sampling
- Convenience Sampling
- Judgment Sampling
- Quota Sampling

Issues of Precision and Accuracy in Determining Sample Size

Precision and Accuracy—Trade-offs

Sample Data and Hypothesis Testing

Sample Size

Efficiency in Sampling

UNIT OBJECTIVES

After completing Unit 6 you should be able to:

1. Define sampling, sample, population, element, subject, and population frame.
2. Describe and discuss the different sampling designs.
3. Identify the use of appropriate sampling designs for different research purposes.
4. Explain how to use sample data to test hypotheses.
5. Discuss precision and accuracy.
6. Estimate sample size using the appropriate formula.
7. Discuss the factors to be taken into consideration for determining sample size.

8. Discuss efficiency in sampling.
9. Discuss generalizability in the context of sampling designs.
10. Apply the material learned in this unit to class assignments and projects.

One of the important research design decisions pertains to sampling. Sampling design relates to both the methods used to select the sample from the population, and the size of the sample necessary to generalize the findings from the sample data to the total population. These issues will be discussed in this unit. Before we get into sampling design, however, we need to understand some terms that will be used in this unit.

POPULATION, ELEMENT, POPULATION FRAME, SAMPLE, AND SUBJECT

Population

Population refers to the entire group of people, events, or things of interest that the researcher wishes to investigate. If the researcher is interested in investigating the alienation of blue-collar workers in the plastics industry in the United States, then all blue-collar workers in the plastics industry throughout the country will form the population. If an organizational consultant is interested in studying the effects of a four-day workweek on the white-collar workers in a telephone company in southern Illinois, then all white-collar workers in the telephone company in southern Illinois will form the population. If a professor is interested in examining the learning abilities of freshmen in a university, then all freshmen in that particular university will be the population for study; if, however, the professor is interested only in the learning abilities of the freshmen in his class, then the freshmen in that particular class will form the population. Thus the term population refers to all members in the group that happen to be the focus of the study.

Element

An element is a single member of the population. If 1000 blue-collar workers in a particular organization happen to be the population of interest to a researcher, each single blue-collar worker in this population is an element. If 500 pieces of machinery are to be approved after inspecting a few, there would be 500 elements in this population.

Population Frame

The population frame is a listing of all the elements in the population from which the sample is to be drawn. The payroll of an organization could be the population frame, if members of the organization are to be studied. Likewise, the university registry containing a listing of all students, faculty, administrators, and support staff in the university during a particular academic year or semester could serve as the population frame for a study of the university population. Likewise, a roster of class students could be the population frame for the study of students in a class. The telephone directory is also frequently used as a population frame for some types of studies, even though it has an inherent bias inasmuch as some numbers are unlisted.

Although the population frame is useful in providing a listing of each element in the population, it may not always be a current, updated document. For instance, members who have just left the organization or dropped out of the university, as well as members who have just joined the organization or the university may not appear in the organization's payroll or the university registers on a given day. Telephones newly installed during the last few days or disconnected during that time, likewise will not be represented in the current telephone directory. Hence, though the population frame may be available in many cases, it may not always be current. The researcher might recognize this problem and may not be too concerned about it, because a few additions and deletions may not make much difference to the study. Even if the researcher is concerned about it, and spends time and effort trying to obtain an updated population frame, there is no guarantee that the new population frame will give an accurate listing of all the elements, for the reasons already discussed.

Sample

A sample is a subset of the population. It comprises some members selected from the population. In other words, some, but not all, elements of the population would form the sample. If 200 members are drawn from a population of 1000 blue-collar workers, these 200 members form the sample for the study. That is, by studying these 200 members, the researcher would draw conclusions about the entire population of the 1000 blue-collar workers considered in the study.

A sample is thus a subgroup or subset of the population. By studying the sample, the researcher would be able to draw conclusions that would be generalizable to the population of interest.

Subject

A subject is a single member of the sample, just as an element is a single member of the population. In the above example, 200 members from the total population of 1000 blue-collar workers formed the sample for the study; each blue-collar worker in the sample is a subject. If a sample of 50 machines from a total of 500 machines is to be inspected, then every one of the 50 machines is a subject, just as every single machine in the total population of 500 machines is an element.

SAMPLING

Sampling is the process of selecting a sufficient number of items from the population so that by studying the sample, and understanding the properties or the characteristics of the sample subjects, we will be able to generalize the properties or characteristics to the population elements. The central tendencies, the dispersions, and other statistics in the sample of interest to the research are treated as approximations of the central tendencies, dispersions, and other parameters of the population. All conclusions drawn about the sample being studied are generalized to the population. In other words, the sample statistics are used as estimates of the population parameters. Figure 6.1 shows the relationship between the sample and the population.

Reasons for Sampling

The reasons for using a sample rather than collecting data from the entire population are fairly obvious. In research investigations involving several hundreds and even thousands of elements, it would be practically impossible to collect data from, or to test, or to examine every element. Even if it

Figure 6.1

The relationship between sample and population.

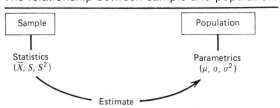

were possible, it would be prohibitive in terms of time, costs, and other human resources. Studying a sample rather than the entire population is also sometimes likely to lead to more reliable results, mostly because there will be less fatigue, and hence fewer errors in collecting data, especially when the elements involved are many in number. In a few cases, it would also be impossible to use the entire population to know or test something. Consider, for instance, the case of electric bulbs. In testing the life of a batch of bulbs, if we were to burn every bulb produced, there would be none to sell!

Representativeness of Samples

No single sample is going to be the exact replica of the population from which it is drawn. For instance, no sample mean ($\overline{X}$) is likely to be exactly equal to its population mean (μ). Nor is the standard deviation of the sample (S) going to be the same as the standard deviation of the population (σ). However, if we choose the sample in a scientific way, we can be reasonably sure that the sample statistic (e.g., $\overline{X}$, S, S^2) will be as close to the population parameters as possible (i.e., μ, σ, σ^2). To put it differently, we should be able to choose the sample in such a way that it is representative of the population it is expected to characterize.

Normality of Distributions

Almost every attribute or characteristic in the population is generally normally distributed. That is, attributes such as height and weight are such that most people will be clustered around the mean and there will be a few people at the extremes who are either very tall or very short, very heavy or very light, and so on, as indicated in Figure 6.2a. If we are to estimate the population characteristics reasonably precisely from the characteristics represented in a sample, the sample has to be chosen such that the distribution of the characteristics of interest follows the same type of normal

Figure 6.2a
Normal distribution in a population.

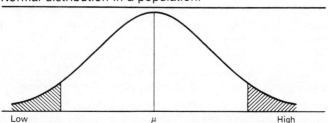

Low μ High

Figure 6.2b

Skewed distributions.

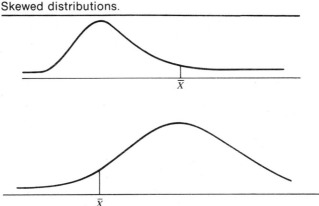

distribution in the sample as it does in the population. From the central limit theorem, we know that the sampling distribution of the sample mean is normally distributed. Irrespective of whether or not the attributes in the population are normally distributed, if we take *large enough* samples and *choose* the sample carefully, we will have a sampling distribution of the mean that has normality. This is the reason that the two important issues in sampling are the sample size (n) and the sampling design. When the properties of the population are not overrepresented or underrepresented in the sample, we will have a sample that is not skewed. When a sample consists of elements in the population that have extremely high values on the variable we are studying, it will be skewed to the right as shown on the top of Figure 6.2b, in which case the mean of the sample, $\overline{X}$, will be far higher than the population mean μ. If, in contrast, the sample subjects consist of elements in the population with extremely low values on the variable of interest, then the sample would be skewed to the left, which means that the sample mean $\overline{X}$ will be much lower than the true population mean μ. If our sampling design and sample size are right, however, the sample mean $\overline{X}$ will be within close range of the true population mean μ. Thus through appropriate sampling designs, we can ensure that the sample subjects are not chosen from the extremes, but are representative of the true properties of the population. The more representative the sample is of the population, the more generalizable are the findings of the research. Recall that generalizability is one of the hallmarks of scientific research, as we saw in Unit 1.

Though we may be concerned about generalizability, and hence be particular about choosing representative samples for most research, at some stages of research we may not be very concerned about generalizability. For instance, at the exploratory stages of fact finding, the researcher may be interested only in "getting a handle" on what is going on in the situation, for which purpose the most conveniently available people may be interviewed. The same is true when time is of the essence in getting some information rather than getting the most accurate information. For instance, a film agency might want to find out quickly the impact on the viewers of a newly released film exhibited the previous evening. The interviewer might ask questions of the first twenty people she can find. On the basis of their replies, the interviewer may form an opinion as to the possible success of the film. In such cases, having some quick information is more important than having the most representative facts. Thus, sampling designs are available that are useful for quick information gathering rather than being geared to getting the most accurate information. We will discuss the different types of sampling designs.

PROBABILITY AND NONPROBABILITY SAMPLING

There are two major types of sampling designs: probability and nonprobability sampling. In probability sampling, the elements in the population have some known chance or probability of being selected as sample subjects. In nonprobability sampling, the elements do not have a known or predetermined chance of being selected as subjects. Probability sampling designs are used when the representativeness of the sample is of importance for purposes of wider generalizability. When time rather than generalizability is the critical issue, nonprobability sampling is generally used.

Each of these two major designs has different sampling strategies. Depending on the extent of generalizability desired, the availability of time and other resources, and the purpose for which the study is done, different types of probability and nonprobability sampling designs will be chosen. The various types available are discussed next.

Probability Sampling

Probability sampling can be either unrestricted (or simple random sampling) or restricted (or complex probability sampling) in nature.

Unrestricted or Simple Random Sampling

In the unrestricted probability sampling design, more commonly known as simple random sampling, every element in the population has a *known* and *equal* chance of being selected as a subject. For instance, let us say there are 1000 elements in the population, and we need a sample of 100. Suppose we were to drop chits in a hat, each bearing the name of one of the elements, and we were to draw 100 of those names from the hat with our eyes closed. We know that each one of those elements has a 100/1000 chance of being drawn. In other words we know that the probability of any one of them being chosen as a subject is .1, and we also know that each single element in the hat has the same or equal probability of being chosen. When we thus draw the elements from the population, it is most likely that the distribution patterns of the characteristics we are interested in investigating in the population, are also likewise distributed in the subjects we draw for our sample. This sampling design, known as simple random sampling, has the least bias and offers the most generalizability. However, this sampling process could become cumbersome and expensive, in addition to the fact that an entirely updated listing of the population may not always be available, as discussed earlier. For these and other reasons, other probability sampling designs are often chosen instead.

Restricted or Complex Probability Sampling

As an alternative to the simple random (unrestricted) sampling design, several complex probability sampling (restricted probability) designs can be used. These probability sampling procedures offer a viable, and sometimes more efficient alternative to the cumbersome unrestricted design we just discussed. Efficiency is gained in that more information can be obtained for a given sample size using some of the complex probability sampling procedures than using the simple random sampling design. The five most common complex probability sampling designs—systematic sampling, stratified random sampling, cluster sampling, area sampling, and double sampling—will now be discussed.

Systematic Sampling The systematic sampling design involves drawing every nth element in the population starting with a randomly chosen element between 1 and n. The procedure follows the example cited below.

If we want a sample of 35 households from a total population of 260 houses in a particular locality, then we could sample every seventh house starting from a random number from 1 to 7. Let us say that the random number is 7, then houses numbered 7, 14, 21, 28, and so on, would be sampled until the 35 houses are obtained for the sample.

The one problem that the researcher has to be aware of in the systematic sampling design is the probability of a systematic bias creeping into the sample. In the above example, for instance, let us say that every seventh house happens to be a corner house. Residents of corner houses have been shown through previous research to have life-styles different from the residents of the rest of the houses in the street. When information is gathered from corner house dwellers, it may not be representative of the population that is being surveyed. The results of the survey may thus become quite biased. Thus the scope for systematic bias is present in systematic sampling, and the researcher must consider his plans carefully and make sure that the systematic sampling plan is appropriate for the study before making the decision to use it. For market surveys, consumer attitude surveys, and the like, the telephone directory—which, as stated before, has its inherent biases—frequently serves as the population frame for systematic sampling plans.

Stratified Random Sampling   Stratified random sampling, as its name implies, involves a process of stratification or segregation, followed by random selection of subjects from the strata. In stratified random sampling the population is first divided into mutually exclusive groups that are relevant, appropriate, and meaningful in the context of the study. For instance, if the president of a company is concerned about low motivational levels or high absenteeism rates among the employees, it makes sense to stratify the population of organizational members according to their job levels. Contrary to expectation, it may be the middle level managers who are not motivated; hence studying the employees at lower levels alone would not indicate where the real problem lies. It may also be interesting to determine whether there are significant differences in the motivational levels of employees at various levels in the organization, or with different job classifications. For example, are the clerical employees less or more motivated than the secretaries or the blue-collar workers? When we wish to answer such types of research questions, it is a lot more efficient to stratify the population according to job level, and to obtain and analyze the data on this basis. Significant information can be gathered this way. In the instance above, this kind of stratification would also give the president a better idea of the level at which changes, if any, need to be made in the organization. If instead of stratifying in this manner, a researcher simply collected data based on a simple random sampling procedure or through systematic sampling, then the high motivation at some job levels and the low motivation at other levels will nullify each other, thus masking the real problems that exist at particular levels.

Stratification is thus an efficient research design; that is, it provides more information with a given sample size. Stratification should follow the lines that are appropriate to the research question. If we are studying consumer preferences for a product, stratification of the population could be by geographical areas, market segments, consumer age, consumer gender, or various combinations of these. If an organization is contemplating budget cuts, the effects of these cuts on employee attitudes can be studied with stratification by department, function, or region. Stratification ensures homogeneity within each stratum (i.e., very few differences or dispersions on the variable of interest within each stratum), but heterogeneity between strata. In other words, there will be more between-group differences than within-group differences.

Proportionate and Disproportionate Stratified Random Sampling Once the population has been stratified in some meaningful way, a sample

Table 6.1

Proportionate and Disproportionate Stratified Random Sampling

Job Level	Number of Elements	Number of Subjects in the Sample	
		Proportionate Sampling (20% of the elements)	Disproportionate Sampling
Top management	10	2	7
Middle level management	30	6	15
Lower level management	50	10	20
Supervisors	100	20	30
Clerks	500	100	60
Secretaries	20	4	10
Total	710	142	142

of members from each stratum can be drawn using either a simple random sampling or a systematic sampling procedure. The subjects drawn from each stratum can be either proportionate or disproportionate to the number of elements in the stratum. For instance, if an organization consists of 10 top managers, 30 middle managers, 50 lower level managers, 100 supervisors, 500 clerks, and 20 secretaries, and a stratified sample of about 140 people is needed for a survey, the researcher might decide that 20 percent of members from each stratum will be included in the sample. That is, members represented in the sample from each stratum will be proportionate to the total number of elements in the respective strata. This would mean that 2 from the top, 6 from the middle, and 10 from the lower levels of management will be included in the sample. In addition, 20 supervisors, 100 clerks, and 4 secretaries will be represented in the sample, as shown in the third column of Table 6.1. This type of sampling is called a proportionate stratified random sampling design.

In situations like the one above, researchers might sometimes be concerned that obtaining information from just 2 members at the top and 6 from the middle levels would not be representative of how members at those levels would respond. Therefore, a researcher might decide to use a disproportionate stratified random sampling procedure instead. Keeping the sample size the same, the number of subjects from each stratum will now be altered. Such a sampling design is illustrated in the far right-hand column in Table 6.1. The idea here is that the 60 clerks might be considered adequate to represent the population of 500 clerks; 7 out of 10 managers at the top level would also be considered an adequate representation of the top managers, and likewise 15 out of the 30 managers at the middle level. This redistribution of the numbers in the strata would be considered more appropriate and representative for the study than the previous sampling design.

Disproportionate sampling decisions are made either when some stratum or strata are too small or too large, or when there is more variability suspected within a particular stratum—for example, the educational levels among supervisors may range from elementary school to master's degrees, and educational level might be expected to influence perceptions, in which case more people will be sampled at this level. Disproportionate sampling is sometimes done when it is easier, simpler, and less expensive to collect data from one or more strata than from others.

In summary, stratified random sampling involves stratifying the elements along meaningful lines, and taking proportionate or disproportionate samples from the strata. This sampling design is more efficient than the simple random sampling design because, for the same sample size, we get more representativeness from each important segment of the population and obtain more valuable and differentiated information with respect to each group.

Cluster Sampling   Groups or chunks of elements that, ideally, would have heterogeneity among the members within each group are chosen for study in cluster sampling. This is in contrast to choosing some elements from the population as in simple random sampling, or stratifying and then choosing members from the strata as in stratified random sampling, or choosing every nth element in the population as in systematic sampling. When several groups with intragroup heterogeneity and intergroup homogeneity are found, then a random sampling of the clusters or groups can ideally be done with information gathered from each of the members in the randomly chosen clusters.

Universitywide committees provide a good example of clusters qualifying for cluster sampling. These committees usually consist of members drawn from faculty among various disciplines, having different philosophies, values, attitudes, perceptions, and orientations. Because virtually all university committees are drawn in this way, there is likely to be more heterogeneity among the members within each committee, and more homogeneity among the various committees themselves. If a researcher wants to study decision-making styles and processes in university committees, a random sample of perhaps 10 of a total of 28 clusters could be drawn, and all the members in each of these 10 clusters could be interviewed.

Naturally occurring clusters, such as clusters of residents, buyers, students, or shops, do not have much heterogeneity among the elements. In fact, there is more intracluster homogeneity than heterogeneity in such clusters. Hence, cluster sampling, though less costly, does not offer much efficiency in terms of accuracy (i.e., absence of bias) and precision (i.e., confidence in the results). In many cases, though, cluster sampling offers convenience. For example it is easier to inspect all units packed inside, say, 4 boxes (i.e., all the elements in four clusters) than to open 30 boxes in a shipment in order to inspect a few units at random.

Single-stage and Multistage Cluster Sampling   We have thus far been discussing single-stage cluster sampling, which involves the division of the population into convenient clusters, randomly choosing the required number of clusters as sample subjects, and investigating all the elements in each of the randomly chosen clusters. Cluster sampling can also be done in several stages, and is then called multistage cluster sampling. If we were to do a national survey of the average monthly bank deposits, for instance, cluster sampling would first be used to select the urban, semiurban, and rural geographical locations for study. At the next stage, particular areas in each of these locations would be chosen. At the third stage, banks within each area would be chosen. In other words, multistage cluster sampling involves a probability sampling of the primary sampling units; from each of these primary units, a probability sample of the secondary sampling units is then drawn; in turn, a third level of probability sampling is done from each of these secondary units, and so on, until we have reached the final stage of breakdown for the sample units, when we will sample every member in those units.

Area Sampling   When the research pertains to populations within identifiable geographical areas such as counties, city blocks, or particular boundaries within a locality, area sampling can be done. Area sampling is a form of cluster sampling within an area. Sampling the needs of consumers before opening a 24-hour store in a particular part of the town would involve area sampling. Area sampling is less expensive than most other probability sampling designs, and it is not dependent on a population frame. A city map showing the blocks of the city would be adequate information to allow a researcher to take a sample of the blocks and obtain data from the residents therein.

Double Sampling   When a sample is used in a study to collect some preliminary information of interest, and later a subsample of this primary sample is used to examine the matter in more detail, such a sampling design is called double sampling. For example, a structured interview might indicate that a subgroup of the respondents have more insight into the problems of the organization. These respondents might be interviewed again with additional questions. This research would have adopted a double sampling procedure.

Review of Probability Sampling Designs

There are two basic probability sampling plans: the unrestricted or simple random sampling, and the restricted or complex probability sampling plans. In the simple random sampling design, every element in the population has a known and equal chance of being selected as a subject. The complex probability plan consists of five different sampling designs. Of these five, the cluster sampling design is probably the least expensive as well as the least dependable. The stratified random sampling design is probably the most efficient in the sense that for the same number of sample subjects it offers more precise and detailed information. The systematic sampling design has the built-in hazard of possible systematic bias. Area sampling is a form of cluster sampling, and double sampling takes place when a subgroup of a sample is used a second time to obtain more information.

Nonprobability Sampling

In nonprobability sampling designs, the elements in the population do not have any probabilities attached to their being chosen as sample subjects. This means that the findings from the study of the sample cannot be confidently generalized to the population. As stated earlier, however, researchers may at times be less concerned about generalizability than they are about obtaining some preliminary information in a quick and inexpensive way. They would then resort to nonprobability sampling. Some of the nonprobability sampling plans are more dependable than others and could offer some important leads to potential useful information with regard to the population. The nonprobability sampling designs, which fit into the broad categories of convenience and purposive sampling, will be discussed next.

Convenience Sampling

As its name implies, convenience sampling involves collecting information from members of the population who are conveniently available to provide this information. One would expect that the "Pepsi Challenge" contest was administered on a convenience sampling basis. Such a contest, with the purpose of determining whether people prefer one product over another, might be set up at a shopping mall visited by many shoppers. Those who would be inclined to take the test might form the sample for the study of how many people prefer Pepsi over Coke or product X over product Y. Such a sample is a convenience sample.

Consider another example. A convenience sample of 20 students who have attended a lecture on yoga may be interviewed as they walk out of the lecture hall, with the purpose of deciding whether or not the same lecturer should be invited the next week to deliver another lecture. A probability sampling design in this case is impossible because of the lack of a population frame, and besides, it is perhaps not really necessary. A decision based on the responses of the 20 students who were interviewed might be just as good and valid as one made with a probability sampling design!

Purposive Sampling

Instead of obtaining information from those who are most conveniently available, it might sometimes become necessary to obtain information from specific targets—that is, specific types of people who will be able to provide the desired information, either because they are the only ones who can give the needed information, or because they conform to some criteria set by the researcher. Such types of sampling designs are called purposive sampling, and the two major types—judgment sampling and quota sampling—will now be explained.

Judgment Sampling Judgment sampling involves the choice of subjects who are in the best position to provide the information required. For instance, if a researcher wants to find out what it takes for women managers to make it to the top, the only people who can give firsthand information are the women managers who are the presidents, vice-presidents, and important top-level executives in work organizations. Having themselves gone through the experiences and processes, they might be expected to have expert knowledge, and perhaps be able to provide good data or information to the researcher. Thus, the judgment sampling design is used when a limited category of people have the information that is sought. In such cases, any type of probability sampling across a cross section of people is purposeless and not useful. Although judgment sampling may curtail the generalizability of the findings due to the fact that we are using a sample of experts who are conveniently available to us, it is the only viable sampling method for obtaining the type of information that is required from very specific pockets of people who possess the knowledge and can give the information sought.

Quota Sampling Quota sampling is a form of proportionate stratified sampling, in which a predetermined proportion of people are sampled from different groups, but on a convenience basis. For instance, it may be surmised that the work attitudes of blue-collar workers in an organization are quite different from those of white-collar workers. If there are 60 percent blue-collar workers and 40 percent white-collar workers in this organization, and if a total of 30 people are to be interviewed to find the answer to the research question, then a quota of 18 blue-collar workers and 12 white-collar workers will form the sample, because these numbers represent 60 and 40 percent of the sample size. The first 18 conveniently available blue-collar workers and 12 white-collar workers will be sampled according to this quota. Needless to say, the sample may not be totally representative of the population; hence the generalizability of the findings will be restricted. However, the convenience it offers in terms of effort, costs, and time makes quota sampling attractive for some research efforts. Quota sampling also becomes a necessity when a subset of the population is underrepresented in the organization—for example, minority groups, foremen, etc.

Review of Nonprobability
Sampling Designs

There are two main types of nonprobability sampling designs: convenience sampling and purposive sampling. Convenience sampling is the least reliable of all sampling designs in terms of generalizability, but sometimes it may be the only viable alternative when quick and timely information is needed. Purposive sampling plans fall into two categories: judgment and quota sampling designs. Judgment sampling, though restricted in generalizability, may sometimes be the best sampling design choice, especially when there is a limited population that can supply the information needed. Quota sampling, though not very reliable for generalization, is often used for cost and time considerations. The generalizability of all nonprobability sampling designs is very restricted, but they have other advantages and are sometimes the only viable alternative for the researcher.

ISSUES OF PRECISION
AND ACCURACY IN
DETERMINING SAMPLE SIZE

Having discussed the various probability and nonprobability sampling designs, we now need to focus attention on the second aspect of the sampling design issue—sample size. Suppose we select 30 people from a population of 3000 through a simple random sampling procedure. Will we be able to generalize our findings to the population with accuracy, having chosen a probability design that has the most generalizability? What is the sample size that would be required to make reasonably precise and accurate generalizations? What do precision and accuracy mean? These issues will be considered now.

A reliable and valid sample should enable us to generalize the findings from the sample to the population we are investigating. In other words, the sample statistics should be good estimates and reflect the population parameters as closely as possible within a narrow range. No sample statistic ($\overline{X}$, for instance), is going to be exactly the same as the population parameter (μ, for instance), no matter how sophisticated the probability sampling design. Remember that the very reason for a probability design is to increase the probability that the sample statistics will be as close as possible to the population parameters! Though the point estimate $\overline{X}$ may not accurately reflect the population mean μ, an interval estimate can be made within which μ will lie, and this estimate can be made with probabilities attached—that is, at particular confidence levels. The issues of confidence interval and confidence level are addressed in our discussions of precision and accuracy.

Precision

Precision refers to the extent of the variability of the sampling distribution of the sample mean. That is, if we take a number of different samples from a population, and take the mean of each of these, we will usually find that they are all different, are normally distributed, and have a dispersion associated with them. The smaller this dispersion or variability, the greater the probability that the sample mean will be closer to the population mean. We need not necessarily take several different samples to estimate this variability. For instance, even if we take only one sample of 30 subjects from the population, we will still be able to estimate the variability of the sampling distribution of the sample mean. This variability is called the standard error of estimate of the mean, or simply the standard error, denoted by $S_{\bar{x}}$. The standard error is calculated by the following formula:

$$S_{\bar{x}} = \frac{S}{\sqrt{n-1}}$$

where S is the standard deviation of the sample, n is the sample size, and $S_{\bar{x}}$ indicates the standard error or the extent of precision offered by the sample.

Note that the standard error varies inversely with the square root of the sample size. Hence, if we want to reduce the standard error given a particular standard deviation in the sample, we need to increase the sample size. Another noteworthy point is that the smaller the variation in the population, the smaller the standard error of estimate of the sample mean, which in turn implies that the sample size need not necessarily be large when there is very low variability in the population.

Thus, the closer we want our sample results to reflect the population characteristics, the greater will be the precision we would be aiming for. The greater the precision required, the larger will be the sample size needed, especially when the variability in the population itself is large.

Accuracy

Accuracy of the sample refers to the absence of bias in the sample. In other words, accuracy reflects the extent to which underestimation or overestimation of the population properties is not present in the sample. We know from the laws of normal distribution that the range of properties in the population are covered within three standard deviations of the mean. Hence, if we want to have a high level of confidence in our estimates, it is necessary to have a bigger sample size. This is further discussed and illustrated in the following section.

SAMPLE DATA, PRECISION, AND ACCURACY IN ESTIMATION

Precision and accuracy are important issues in sampling because when we use sample data to draw inferences about the population, we hope to be fairly "on target," and have some idea of the amount of possible error. Because a point estimate provides no measure of possible error, we do an interval estimation to ensure a *relatively accurate* estimation of the population parameter. Statistics that have the same distribution as the sampling distribution of the mean are used in this procedure, usually a z or a t statistic.

For example, we may want to estimate the mean IQ of all the college of business students and use a random sample of 50 students. We may find that the sample mean $\bar{X} = 105$, and the sample standard deviation $S = 10$. $\bar{X}$, the sample mean, is a point estimate of μ, the population mean. To determine the relative accuracy, we could construct a confidence interval around $\bar{X}$. The standard error $S_{\bar{x}}$ and the percentage confidence we require will determine the width of the interval, which can be represented by the following formula, where K is the z statistic for the level of confidence desired.

$$\mu = \bar{X} \pm KS_{\bar{x}}$$

$$S_{\bar{x}} = \frac{S}{\sqrt{n-1}} = \frac{10}{\sqrt{49}} = 1.43$$

From the table of critical values for t in any statistics book, we know the following:

For 90 percent confidence level, the K value is 1.645.

For 95 percent confidence level, the K value is 1.96.

For 99 percent confidence level, the K value is 2.576.

If we desire a 90 percent confidence level in the above case, $\mu = 105 \pm 1.645(1.43)$ (i.e., $\mu = 105 \pm 2.352$), and μ would thus fall between 102.648 and 107.352. These results indicate that using a sample size of 50, we could state with 90 percent confidence that the true population mean IQ for all the college of business students would lie anywhere between 102.65 and 107.35. If we now want to be 99 percent confident of our results without increasing the sample size, we would necessarily have to sacrifice our precision, as can be seen from the following calculation: $\mu = 105 \pm 2.576(1.43)$. The value for μ now falls between 101.317 and 108.683. In other words, the width of the confidence interval has increased and we are now less precise in estimating the population mean, though we are a lot more confident about our estimation. It is not difficult to see that if we want

Figure 6.3

Illustration of the trade-off between precision and accuracy. (a) More precision but less accuracy. (b) More accuracy but less precision.

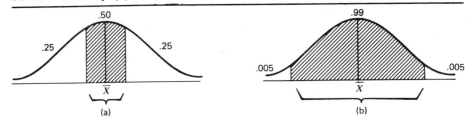

to maintain our original precision while increasing the confidence, or we want to increase the confidence while maintaining the same precision, or we want to increase both the accuracy and the precision, we need a bigger or larger sample size.

The Trade-off Between Accuracy and Precision

From the foregoing it is clear that if we want more precision, or more accuracy, or both, the sample size needs to be increased—unless, of course, there is very little variability in the population itself. However, if the sample size (*n*) cannot be increased, for whatever reason—say, we cannot afford the costs of increased sampling—then, with the same *n*, the only way to maintain the same level of precision would be by forsaking the confidence with which we can predict that our estimates will be precise (i.e., be close to the target μ). That is, we are reducing the confidence level or the accuracy of our estimate. This trade-off between precision and accuracy is illustrated in Figures 6.3a and b. Figure 6.3a indicates that 50 percent of the time the true mean μ will fall within the narrow range indicated in the figure, the .25 in each tail representing the 25 percent nonconfidence or the probability of making errors in our estimation on either side. Figure 6.3b indicates that 99 percent of the time we would expect the true mean μ to fall within the much wider range indicated in the figure and there is only a .005 percent chance that we would be making an error in this estimation. That is, in Figure 6.3a, we have more precision but less accuracy (our confidence level is only 50 percent). In Figure 6.3b, we have high confidence (99 percent), but then we are far from being precise—that is, our estimate falls within a long interval range.

It thus becomes necessary for researchers to consider at least four aspects while making decisions on the sample size needed to do the research: (1) How much precision is really needed in estimating the population characteristics of interest—that is, what is the *margin* of error we can make? (2) How much accuracy is really needed—that is, how much *chance* can we take of making errors in estimating the population parameters? (3) To what extent is there a *variability* in the population on the characteristics investigated? (4) What is the *cost-benefit* analysis of increasing the sample size?

SAMPLE DATA AND HYPOTHESIS TESTING

So far we have talked about sample data as a means of estimating the population parameters, but sample data can also be used to test hypotheses about population values rather than simply to estimate population values. The procedure for this testing incorporates the same information as in interval estimation, but the goals behind the two methods are somewhat different.

Using the same data as before, instead of trying to estimate the average IQ of college of business students with a certain degree of accuracy, let us say that we wish to determine if the college of business (COB) students have the same average IQ as the college of liberal arts (COLA) students—a different population. Following what we learned in Unit 3, we would set up the null hypothesis to state that there would be no difference in the IQ of the two populations, which would be expressed thus:

H_0: $\mu_{COB} - \mu_{COLA} = 0$

The alternate hypothesis of differences would be stated thus:

H_A: $\mu_{COB} - \mu_{COLA} \neq 0$

Let us assume that we take a sample of 20 students from each of the two colleges and find that the mean IQ of the college of business students is 105, with a standard deviation of 10, and the mean and standard deviation for the COLA students are 100 and 15, respectively. From this information we can see that

$\bar{X}_{COB} - \bar{X}_{COLA} = 105 - 100 = 5$

Our null hypothesis was $\mu_{COB} - \mu_{COLA} = 0$. Because there is a difference of 5 in the sample means, would we conclude that our null hypothesis is wrong? No! To determine this, however, we should first find the probability or likelihood of the two group mean IQs having a difference of 5, if we hypothesize a difference of 0. This can be done by converting the difference in the sample means to a statistic where we know the probabilities of all values in the distribution. One such statistic is *z* and the other is the *t* statistic. The t statistic can be calculated for testing our hypothesis as follows:

$$t = \frac{(\bar{X}_1 - \bar{X}_2) - (\mu_1 - \mu_2)}{S_{\bar{X}_1} - S_{\bar{X}_2}}$$

$$S_{\bar{X}_1} - S_{\bar{X}_2} = \sqrt{\frac{n_1 s_1{}^2 + n_2 s_2{}^2}{n_1 + n_2 - 2}\left(\frac{1}{n_1} + \frac{1}{n_2}\right)}$$

$$= \sqrt{\frac{(20 \times 10^2) + (20 \times 15^2)}{(20 + 20 - 2)}\left(\frac{1}{20} + \frac{1}{20}\right)}$$

$$= 4.136$$

We already know that $\mu_1 - \mu_2 = 0$. So $t = [(5 - 0)/4.136]$. Thus, applying the formula, we find that the t value is 1.209. If our null hypothesis is true, K would be 0. Now, we can use the table of t values to find the probability of 1.209 when we have two samples of size 20. We find that the probability is greater than .10. Generally, a probability of .05 or less would lead the researcher to reject the null hypothesis. So, in this case, we would retain the null and conclude that the two populations are not significantly different in their IQs. The results can be visually depicted as in Figure 6.4.

Thus the sample data can be used not only for estimating the population parameters, but also for testing hypotheses about population values, population correlations, and so forth, as we will see more fully later in Unit 7.

DETERMINING THE SAMPLE SIZE

Now that we are aware of the fact that the sample size is governed by the extent of precision and accuracy desired, how do we determine the sample

Figure 6.4
Hypothesis testing through sample data.

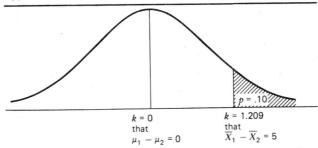

size required for our research? The procedure can be illustrated through an example.

Suppose that we want to be 95 percent confident what the expected monthly withdrawals in a bank will be within an interval of $\pm\$500$. Let us say that a study of a sample of clients indicates that the average withdrawals made by them has a standard deviation of $3500. The interval estimate of $\pm\$500$ has to encompass a dispersion of ±1.96 standard error of the mean. Hence, one standard error of the mean equals $500/1.96 or $255.10. With these data, we can calculate the sample size needed to have a precision level of $\pm\$500$ with a 95 percent confidence level.

$$S_{\bar{x}} = \frac{S}{\sqrt{n-1}}$$

$$255.10 = \frac{3500}{\sqrt{n-1}}$$

$$n = 187$$

Another way of stating the formula for determining the sample size is as follows:

$$n = \left(\frac{S^2}{S_{\bar{x}}^2}\right) + 1$$

The sample size needed in the above was 187. Let us say that this bank has a total clientele of only 185. This means we cannot sample 187 clients. We can in this case apply the correction formula and see what sample size would be needed to have the same level of accuracy and precision, given the fact that we have a total of only 185 clients. The correction formula is as follows:

$$S_{\bar{x}} = \frac{S}{\sqrt{n-1}} \times \sqrt{\frac{N-n}{N-1}}$$

where N is the total number of elements in the population, n is the sample size to be estimated, $S_{\bar{x}}$ is the standard error of estimate of the mean, and S is the standard deviation of the sample mean.

Applying the correlation formula, we find that

$$255.10 = \frac{3500}{\sqrt{n-1}} \times \sqrt{\frac{185-n}{184}}$$

$$n = 94$$

We would now sample 94 of the total 185 clients.

IMPORTANCE OF SAMPLING DESIGN AND SAMPLE SIZE

It is now possible to see how both sampling design and sample size are important to establish the representativeness of the sample for generalizability. If the appropriate sampling design is not used, a large sample size will not, in itself, allow the findings to be generalized to the population. Likewise, unless the sample size is adequate for the desired level of precision and accuracy, no sampling design, however sophisticated, can be useful to the researcher in meeting the objectives of the study. Hence, sampling decisions should consider both the sampling design and the sample size. Too large a sample size, however (say, over 500) could also become a problem inasmuch as we would be prone to committing Type II errors. That is, we would be accepting the findings of our research, when in fact we should be rejecting them. In other words, with too large a sample size, even small numbers (say a correlation of .10 between two variables) reach significance levels, and we would be inclined to believe that these significant relationships found in the sample are indeed true of the population, when in fact they may not be. Thus, too large a size is not likely to be good.

Roscoe (1975) proposes the following rules of thumb for determining sample size:

1. Sample sizes larger than 30 and less than 500 are appropriate for most research.

2. Where samples are to be broken into subsamples (males/females, juniors/seniors, etc.), a minimum sample size of 30 for each category is necessary.

3. In multivariate research (including multiple regression analyses), the sample size should be several times (preferably 10 times or more) as large as the number of variables in the study.

4. For simple experimental research with tight experimental controls (matched pairs, etc.), successful research is possible with samples as small as 10 to 20 in size.

EFFICIENCY IN SAMPLING

Efficiency in sampling is attained when for a given level of precision (standard error), the sample size could be reduced, or for a given sample size (n), the level of precision could be increased. Some probability sampling designs are more efficient than others. The simple random sampling procedure is not always the most efficient plan to adopt; some other probability designs are often more efficient. A stratified random sampling plan is often the most efficient, and a disproportionate stratified random sampling design has been shown to be more efficient than a proportionate sampling design in many cases. Cluster sampling is less efficient than simple random sampling because there is more homogeneity among the elements in the clusters than is found in the population. Multistage cluster sampling is more efficient than single-stage cluster sampling when there is more heterogeneity found in the earlier stages. There is often a trade-off between time and cost efficiencies (as achieved in nonprobability sampling designs) and precision efficiencies (as achieved in many probability sampling plans). The choice of a sampling plan thus depends on the objectives of the research, as well as on the extent and nature of efficiency desired.

Review of Sample Size Decisions

We can summarize the factors affecting decisions on sample size as (1) the extent of precision desired (the confidence interval); (2) the amount of risk allowable in predicting that level of precision (confidence level); (3) the amount of variability in the population itself; (4) the cost and time constraints; and, in some cases, (5) the size of the population itself. As a rule of thumb, sample sizes between 30 and 500 could be effective depending on the type of research question investigated.

SUMMARY

Decisions regarding sampling are important aspects of research design. Sampling design decisions include both the sampling plan to be used and the sample size that will be needed. Probability sampling plans lend themselves to greater generalizability than nonprobability sampling designs. Some probability plans are more efficient than others. Though nonprobability sampling designs are not readily generalizable, they are often useful for obtaining certain types of information quickly and relatively inexpensively. The sample size is determined by the level of precision and accuracy desired in estimating the population parameters, as well as the variability in the population itself. The generalizability of the findings from a study of the sample to the population is dependent on the sophistication of the sampling designs used, which includes the sample size used in the study. In all research, care should also be taken not to overgeneralize the results of the study to populations that are not represented by the sample. This is a common problem in many research studies. Sample data are used both for estimating population parameters and hypothesis testing.

In the next unit, we will see how the data that are gathered from a sample of respondents in the population will be analyzed to test the hypothesis and answer the research questions.

SUPPLEMENTAL READINGS

The following topic references will guide you to seek more information.

Topic	Reference	Chapter	Page
Sampling	Campbell & Katona (1966)	2	15–55
	Chein (1959)	Appendix B	509–545
	Clover & Balsley (1979)	10	221–247
	Emory (1980)	6	146–188
	Kish (1965)		
	Kish (1966)	5	175–240
	Stone (1978)	5	77–86
Representativeness of sample	Clover & Balsley (1979)	10	234–237
	Emory (1980)	6	148–149
Probability and nonprobability sampling designs	Emory (1980)	6	150–179
Sample size	Clover & Balsley (1979)	10	·222–232
	Emory (1980)	6	160–183
	Roscoe (1975)	20	182–186
Efficiency in sampling	Emory (1980)	6	167, 172, 173
Selection of the sample	Kish (1966)	5	175–239

REFERENCES

Campbell, A. A., & Katona, G. The sample survey: A technique for social science research. In L. Festinger & D. Katz (Eds.), *Research methods in the behavioral sciences.* New York: Holt, Rinehart and Winston, 1966.

Chein, I. An introduction to sampling. In C. Selltiz, M. Jahoda, M. Deutsch, & S. W. Cook (Eds.). *Research methods in social relations* (Rev. ed.). New York: Holt, Rinehart and Winston, 1959.

Clover, V. T., & Balsley, H. L. *Business research methods* (2nd ed.). Columbus, Ohio: Grid Publishing Co., 1979.

Emory, C. W. *Business research methods* (Rev. ed.). Homewood, Ill.: Richard D. Irwin, Inc., 1980.

Kish, L. *Survey sampling.* New York: John Wiley and Sons, 1965.

Kish, L. Selection of the sample. In L. Festinger & D. Katz (Eds.), *Research methods in the behavioral sciences.* New York: Holt, Rinehart and Winston, 1966.

Roscoe, J. T. *Fundamental research statistics for the behavioral sciences* (2nd ed.). New York: Holt, Rinehart and Winston, 1975.

Stone, E. *Research methods in organizational behavior.* Santa Monica, Calif.: Goodyear Publishing Co., 1978.

POINTS TO PONDER AND RESPOND TO

1. A convenience sample used in organizational research is alright because all members share the same organizational stimuli and go through almost the same kinds of experiences in their organizational lives.

2. Having a sample of 5000 is not necessarily better than having a sample of 500.

3. Nonprobability sampling designs ought to be preferred to probability sampling designs in some cases.

4. Because there seems to be a trade-off between accuracy and precision for any given sample size, accuracy should be always considered more important than precision.

5. Overgeneralizations give rise to a lot of confusion and other problems for researchers who try to replicate the findings.

6. Double sampling is probably the least used of all sampling designs in organizational research.

UNIT 7
DATA ANALYSIS AND INTERPRETATION

ISSUES DISCUSSED

Getting Data Ready for Analysis
- Editing Data
- Handling Blank Responses
- Coding
- Categorizing

The SPSS Program

Data Analysis
- Feel for the Data
- Testing Goodness of Data
- Hypothesis Testing
- Use of Several Data-Analytic Techniques

Interpretation of Results

UNIT OBJECTIVES

After completing Unit 7 you should be able to:

1. Edit questionnaire and interview responses.
2. Be able to handle blank responses.
3. Set up the coding key for the data set and code the data.
4. Categorize data.
5. Punch the data on to IBM cards or create a disk file using a CRT terminal.
6. Do SPSS programming.
7. Get a feel for the data.
8. Test the goodness of data.
9. Interpret the computer results.
10. Deal with any data set given to you or collected by you.

After data have been collected from a representative sample of the population, the next step is to analyze the data so that the research hypotheses

Figure 7.1

Flow diagram of data analysis process.

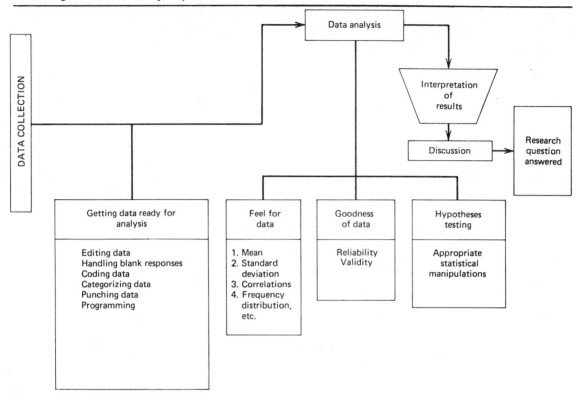

can be tested. Before we can do this, however, some preliminary steps need to be completed. These steps help to prepare the data for analysis, ensure that the data obtained are reasonably good and allow the results to be meaningfully interpreted. Figure 7.1 shows these steps and identifies the four steps in data analysis as (1) getting data ready for analysis, (2) getting a feel for the data, (3) testing the goodness of data, and (4) testing the hypotheses. Each of these steps can now be examined.

GETTING DATA
READY FOR ANALYSIS

After the questionnaire or interview responses, or the observational data have been obtained, the data need to be edited. The blank responses, if any, have to be handled in some way; the data then have to be coded, categorized, and punched; and decisions need to be made as to how they will be submitted for computer analysis. Each of these stages of data preparation will be briefly discussed.

Editing Data

Especially when the data come from interviews, observations, and questionnaires containing open-ended questions, the data have often to be edited. In other words, information that may have been written by the interviewer, observer, or respondent in a hurry, must now be clearly deciphered so that all of it can be coded systematically. Lack of such clarification at this stage will result in confusion when the coding starts and the data have to be categorized under broad heads, and errors in categorization may result from misinterpretation. Also, if there are some inconsistencies in the responses that can be logically corrected, they should be rectified and edited at this stage. For instance, the respondent might have inadvertently not answered the question whether or not she is married. In the column asking for the number of years married, she might have responded 12 years; in the number of children column, she might have marked 2 and for ages of children, she might have answered 8 and 4. The latter three responses would indicate that the respondent is married. The first response could then be edited by the researcher to read "YES." However, it is possible that the respondent deliberately omitted responding to the item because she is either a widow or has just been separated or widowed. If such is the case, we would be introducing a bias in the data by editing the data to read "yes." Hence, whenever possible, it would be better to follow up with the respondent and get the correct data while editing. The example we saw is a clear case for editing, but some others may not be so simple, and biases could be left unnoticed and not rectified. Thus some respondent biases could affect the goodness of the data, and the researcher may have no control over them. The validity and the replicability of the study could thus be impaired.

Handling Blank Responses

Not all respondents answer every item in the questionnaire. Questions may have been left blank because the respondent did not understand the question, was not willing to answer them, or was simply indifferent to responding to the entire questionnaire. If the latter is the case, the respondent may have left many of the items blank. If more than a third of the questionnaire has been left blank, it may be a good idea to throw out the questionnaire and not include it in the data set for analysis. If, however, only two or three items are left blank in a questionnaire with, say, 30 or more items, we need to decide how these blank responses should be handled.

One way to handle a blank response to an interval-scaled item with a midpoint would be to assign the midpoint in the scale for that particular item. Another way of handling it is to allow the computer to ignore the blank responses when the analyses are done. A third way is to assign the item the mean value of the responses of all those who have responded to that particular item. A fourth way is to give the item the mean of the responses of this particular respondent to all other questions. A fifth way of dealing with it is to give the missing response a random number within the range of numbers that could occur. As can be seen, there are several ways of handling blank responses; a common way of dealing with it, however, is either to give the midpoint in the scale as the value or to ignore the particular item during the analysis. The computer can be programmed to do this. The latter is probably the best way to handle missing data to enhance the validity of the study.

Where items have a "do not know" response, they can be treated as a missing value and ignored in the analysis. If many of the respondents have answered "do not know" to a particular item or items, however, it might be worth further investigation to find out whether the question was not clear or something else is happening in the organization that might need further probing.

Coding

The next step is to code the responses. A coding system has to be set up for this purpose. The easiest way to illustrate a coding scheme is through an example. Let us take the correct answer provided for Exercise 5.8, the questionnaire design exercise to test the job involvement—job satisfaction hypothesis in the Serakan Co. case and set up a coding key (coding system) for it.

Coding Key for the Serakan Co. Data

In the Serakan Co. questionnaire, we have five demographic variables and 16 items measuring involvement and satisfaction. To follow the points being made here, refer frequently to the code key in Table 7.1. The responses for the demographic variables can be coded from 1 to 5 for the variables age, education, and number of years in the organization, depending on which box in the columns was checked by the respondent. Sex can be coded as 1 or 2 depending on whether the response was from a male or a female. The job levels can be coded from 1 to 6 depending on the actual job level of the respondent as in the numbers given in the boxes in the table. Item numbers 1 to 16 on the questionnaire can be coded by using the actual number circled by the respondents. If, for instance, 3 has been circled for the first question, then the response will be coded as 3; if it was circled 4, we would code it as 4, and so on, for each of the next 15 items. Note that in this questionnaire, every item can have only a single-digit response. Contrast this with asking the *actual* age without giving a range. In this case, one would expect to find double-digit number responses from organizational members (age is 35, 46, etc.). If only a one-digit number is to be coded on the code sheet, it is enough to give one column for the variable; if, however, some variables are likely to have

Table 7.1

Setup of Coding Key for the Serakan Co. Questionnaire

Age (years)	Education	Job Level	Sex
1 Under 25	1 High school	1 Manager	1 M
2 25–35	2 Some college	2 Supervisor	2 F
3 36–45	3 Bachelor's degree	3 Clerk	
4 46–55	4 Master's degree	4 Secretary	
5 Over 55	5 Doctoral degree	5 Technician	
		6 Other (specify)	

Number of Years in this Organization

1 Less than 1
2 1–3
3 4–8
4 9–15
5 More than 15

Coding Demographic Variables

Variable	Column No.	Variable No.
1. Age	7	001
2. Education	8	002
3. Job level	9	003
4. Sex	10	004
5. # of years in organization	11	005

> Here are some questions that ask you to tell us how you experience your worklife in general. Please circle the appropriate number on the scales below.

To what extent would you agree with the following statements, on a scale of 1 to 7, 1 denoting very low agreement, and 7 denoting very high agreement?

									Column No.	Variable No.
1.	The major happiness of my life comes from my job.	1	2	③	4	5	6	7	12	006
2.	Time at work flies by quickly.	1	2	3	4	5	6	7	13	007
3.	Working here is a drag.	1	2	3	4	5	6	7	14	008
4.	Most things in life are more important than work.	1	2	3	4	5	6	7	15	009
5.	I live, eat, and breathe my job.	1	2	3	4	5	6	7	16	010
6.	My work is not the most important part of my life.	1	2	3	4	5	6	7	17	011

Table 7.1—(Continued)

									Column No.	Variable No.
7.	My work is fascinating.	1	2	3	4	5	6	7	18	012
8.	My work gives me a sense of accomplishment.	1	2	3	4	5	6	7	19	013
9.	My supervisor praises good work.	1	2	3	4	5	6	7	20	014
10.	My supervisor is not very capable.	1	2	3	4	5	6	7	21	015
11.	My coworkers are very stimulating.	1	2	3	4	5	6	7	22	016
12.	I get a lot of cooperation at the workplace.	1	2	3	4	5	6	7	23	017
13.	My pay is barely adequate to take care of my expenses.	1	2	3	4	5	6	7	24	018
14.	People can live comfortably with their pay in this organization.	1	2	3	4	5	6	7	25	019
15.	The opportunities for advancement are very good here.	1	2	3	4	5	6	7	26	020
16.	The promotion policies here are very unfair.	1	2	3	4	5	6	7	27	021
	Respondent no. (questionnaire no.)								76–80	

either single- or double-digit numbers (e.g., age 9 or 90), then we need to allocate two columns on the code sheets for coding such variables. The 9 will be coded in the second column, and the 90 in columns 1 and 2 as 9 and 0. Age 9 can also be coded as 09 in columns 1 and 2.

Every code sheet (which is a replica of the punched card) has 80 columns. Coding could start from any column. You could start coding from column 1, or you could leave, say, the first six columns blank and start coding from column 7. The last four of the 80 columns can be kept for coding the number of the questionnaire. This may prove useful later to identify errors in coding and rectifying them. As the questionnaires are received, they could be sequentially numbered. We do not normally expect to administer more than 9999 questionnaires, so the last four of the 80 columns are considered more than adequate to record the questionnaire number.

Taking the Serakan Co. questionnaire, we could start coding from column 7 and end the coding of the five demographic variables and the other 16 items in column 27 of the code sheet. See the column number specified to the immediate right of the items in Table 7.1. This questionnaire is fairly short and hence a simple one to code. What if one had a questionnaire with 120 items in it for coding? In this case, instead of only one card, we may need to code three cards for each questionnaire. If you consider each row of the Fortran statement to represent an IBM card, then each questionnaire response will be coded in the first three rows of the Fortran coding form; that is, for each questionnaire response, three cards will be punched. In other words, there will be three cards per case. The cards can bear the numbers 1, 2, and 3, and this can be coded (and punched) in column 2 of the first three cards. Because there is a likelihood of the cards falling on the floor and getting mixed up during the course of data analysis, it is a good idea also to sequentially number each of the cards that has been coded. That is, if there are three cards per case, and a total of 200 questionnaires are coded, then 600 lines on the Fortran sheet would have been coded, with each line representing a card. These 600 cards can be sequentially numbered. This can be done in columns 73 to 76. That is, the first card will be coded 1 in column 76, the second one will be coded 2, and so on, until card number 9999 is coded from columns 73 to 76. Thus, if a card gets shuffled (and it is not unusual for this to happen), it can be immediately replaced in the right order. Table 7.2 exemplifies the setup for coding on the Fortran coding sheet from which the data cards can be punched.

Note that coding could start from column 1 of each card, if necessary. Each subject could also be given an identification number, in addition to every card being given a running serial number.

Variables Listing

Now that the variables have been coded, they need to be given sequential variable numbers starting with VAR001 (for variable 1, which is the age variable). Because we have a total of 21 variables (five demographic plus 16 to measure involvement and satisfaction), we will number them as VAR001 to VAR021. See the variable numbers so identified to the extreme right of the items in Table 7.1. The variables can also be numbered V1 to V21 instead of VAR001 to VAR021. Identifying the variables thus will help in setting up the computer program to analyze the data.

Categorization

At this point it is useful to categorize the variables such that the several items measuring the concept are all grouped together for feeding into the computer later. Some of the negatively worded questions have to be re-

Table 7.2

Code Setup for the Serakan Co. Responses

FORTRAN Coding Form

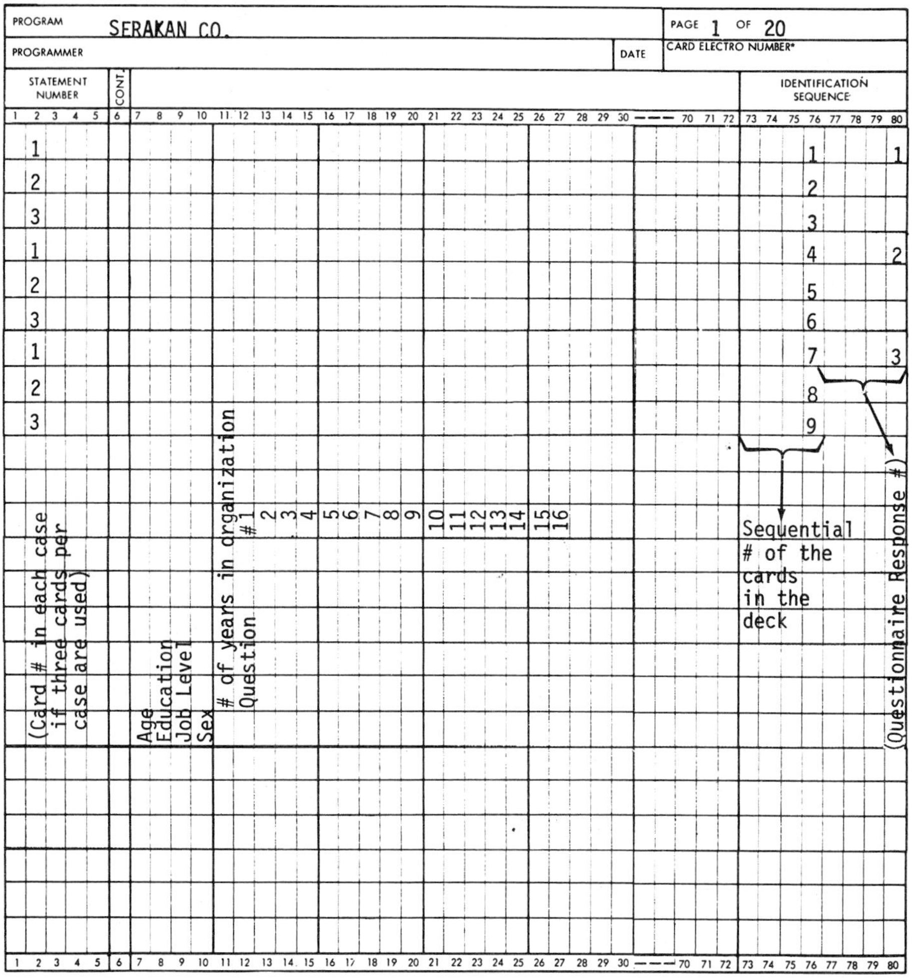
PROGRAM SERAKAN CO.
PAGE 1 OF 20
PROGRAMMER
DATE
CARD ELECTRO NUMBER*
STATEMENT NUMBER
CONT.
IDENTIFICATION SEQUENCE
(Card # in each case if three cards per case are used)
Age
Education
Job Level
Sex
# of years in organization
Question #1 2 3 4 5 6 7 8 9 10 11 12 13 14 15 16
Sequential # of the cards in the deck
(Questionnaire Response #)

versed so that all answers are in the same direction. Note that with respect to negatively worded questions, a response of 7 on a seven-point scale, with 7 denoting "strongly agree," really means "strongly disagree," which actually is a 1 on the seven-point scale. Thus the item has to be reversed so as to be in the same direction as the positively worded questions. The procedure for reversing is to add 1 to the highest point on the Likert-type scale used (i.e., 7 + 1 = 8 if it is a seven-point scale, 6 if it is a five-point scale, etc.), and then subtract the actual response on the negatively worded item. That is, if an individual has circled 3 on a negatively worded question, even though the actual score is coded as 3, it will be (8 − 3 =) 5. The computer run can later be programmed for this. In the meantime, all the raw variables will have to be clearly identified under the correct categories so that we know how they will be programmed later.

In the Serakan Co. coding, the final *job involvement* score will be arrived at by the following categorization:

$$VAR\ 006 + VAR\ 007 + (8-VAR\ 008) + (8-VAR\ 009) + VAR\ 010 + (8-VAR\ 011)$$

The *job satisfaction* variable will be categorized and calculated as follows:

$$VAR\ 012 + VAR\ 013 + VAR\ 014 + (8-VAR\ 015) + VAR\ 016 + VAR\ 017 + (8-VAR\ 018) + VAR\ 019 + VAR\ 020 + (8-VAR\ 021).$$

If the questions measuring a concept are not contiguous but are scattered over various parts of the questionnaire, care has to be taken to include all the items without any omissions or wrong inclusions. The reversal of the appropriate items is also important. This categorization will be used when the computer programs are to be run.

Because coding can become monotonous if the number of questionnaires to be coded is large and the number of questions in the questionnaire are also many, human errors can occur while coding. Therefore, at least 10 percent of the coded questionnaires should be checked for coding accuracy. Questionnaires may be selected using a systematic sampling procedure for this purpose. That is, every nth form coded will be verified for accuracy.

Punching Data on Computer Cards

The data from the code sheets need to be punched on to the IBM cards exactly as they have been coded. Instructions for keypunching are available at all computer centers. Keypunching is fairly easy, but many keypunching mistakes can occur, such as punching the wrong numbers or punching them in the wrong columns. In order to ensure that errors in keypunching do not bias the results, at least 10 percent of the punched cards need to be verified for accuracy. If there are too many errors detected during verification, all cards may have to be verified by another person. Because the results obtained while testing the hypotheses can be only as good as the data punched on to the cards, we should ensure that the keypunching errors are minimal.

For convenience in handling and accessing the data, the data can be put on tapes or disks. A disk file can also be created by entering the data using a CRT terminal in your computer system. Creating a disk or putting the data on tape avoids the cumbersome handling of cards everytime the data are submitted for analysis. Instructions on how to create disks and tapes will be available from the computer departments in universities.

We will now discuss one of the canned statistical packages in detail to prepare you for data analysis.

Programming

The *Statistical Package for the Social Sciences* (SPSS) is a commonly used computer program for data analysis in management research. We will discuss this program in some detail. The *Statistical Analysis System* (SAS) is also used for data analysis in management research. Manuals are available for all canned programs and are useful for setting up the computer cards for data analysis. We will discuss SPSS here in sufficient detail to familiarize you with its use.

SPSS Cards

The Job Control Cards   The first three cards of the SPSS program are called the job control cards (JCL or job control language cards). The first card is called a JOB card and is usually a colored card. Your instructor will give you the computer number that should be punched in the card to do your data analysis. Table 7.3 shows the model for SPSS programming for the Serakan Co. example. Note that the first card in Table 7.3 is the job card for a run submitted at a midwestern university, where there are two computer buildings. This is how the instructor at this university described the job card to the students.

*The first card (job card) starts with: //FA and the number 1235. The FA indicates that you expect your computer output to come to WHAM computer building. If you would rather have it at FANER, you need to punch the letter FB. You can have any four-digit number after this. The last two digits indicate the **bin** number in which you can find your **output**. For instance, if you had //FB6058, you can expect to find your computer output in bin 58 in Faner. For //FA1235, you will find your output in WHAM in bin 35.*

The symbol ▲ denotes a blank space. You should leave that column blank and not punch anything there. The word ''DICK'' could be replaced by your first name, for example, ''GREGORY.'' You could leave the rest of the first card as it is.

Your instructor will explain the job card to you as would be appropriate at your university.

Table 7.3

Guide to SPSS Programming

```
Col
 1
                        @
//FA1235▲JOB▲(1,C101025), 'DICK', TIME=(0,29), REGION=256K
//▲EXEC▲SPSS
//SPSS.SYSIN▲DD▲*

                                        Col
                                         16

VARIABLE▲LIST                   VAR001▲TO▲VAR021
INPUT▲MEDIUM                     CARD
N▲OF▲CASES                      35

INPUT▲FORMAT                    FIXED (6X,21F1.0)

COMPUTE                         VAR100=(VAR006+VAR007+(8-VAR008)+
                                (8-VAR009)+VAR010+(8-VAR011))/6

COMPUTE                         VAR101=(VAR012+VAR013+VAR014+(8-VAR015)+
                                VAR016+VAR017+(8-VAR018)+VAR019+VAR020+
                                (8-VAR021))/10

VAR▲LABELS                      VAR001,AGE/VAR002,EDUCATION/VAR003,JOB
                                LEVEL/VAR004,SEX/VAR005,YRS IN
                                ORG/VAR100,INVOLVEMENT/VAR101,
                                SATISFACTION

READ▲INPUT▲DATA
                   { PLACE PUNCHED CARDS DECK }

FREQUENCIES                     GENERAL=VAR001▲TO▲VAR005
STATISTICS                      ALL

OPTIONS                         8

CONDESCRIPTIVE                  VAR100,VAR101

PEARSON▲CORR                    VAR100,VAR101,VAR001▲TO▲VAR005

T-TEST                          GROUPS=VAR004(1,2)/VARIABLES=VAR100,VAR101

REGRESSION                      VARIABLES=VAR100,VAR101,VAR001▲TO▲VAR005/
                                REGRESSION=VAR100 WITH VAR101,▲VAR001▲TO▲
                                VAR005 (2) /

FINISH
/*
//
              @ Use appropriate number given to you by instructor
```

Program Cards Immediately after the JCL cards, you could have a RUN NAME card, which would identify your program by any name you want. An example of a run name is as follows:

RUN NAME   TESTING DIFFERENCES IN ROOM TEMPERATURES AND THEIR EFFECTS

The punching will start in column 1 with a blank between RUN and NAME. The other words can go in any column that you may choose to have after a blank after NAME.

All the rest of the cards shown in Table 7.3, up to and including the READ INPUT DATA card, are called *program* cards. Note that the columns 1 and 16 are identified for these in the table. These column numbers have to be adhered to. The explanation of the program cards follows:

1. The VARIABLE LIST card refers to the variables you have in your study. In the Serakan Co. study we had 21 variables; so we have listed our variables as VAR001 to VAR021. Note again that from now on until the READ INPUT DATA card, columns 1 and 16 of the cards become important and the format should be strictly adhered to.

2. The N OF CASES refers to the number of questionnaires that have been coded. If we had received 35 questionnaires from the Serakan Co. and coded them all, the N OF CASES here would be 35.

3. The INPUT FORMAT refers to the columns on the card in which the variables can be found by the computer. In the Serakan Co. coding, the first variable (VAR001) would be found in column 7, because the first six columns were left blank. Note that even if we had coded the card number or something else there, it is still not the variable in the questionnaire; the first variable will still be found in column 7 only. Therefore, we are asking the computer to skip the first six columns (6X, then we are telling the computer to read 21 variables, each of which occupies one column. This is indicated by 21F1.0). The closing parenthesis after 21F1.0 indicates to the computer that we have no more variables in the data set for the computer to read.

Further Clarification of the Input Format Now, let us assume that you have 50 variables in your questionnaire, and variables 010 to 013 were two-digit numbers occupying two columns each. Let us also presume that such was the case with variables 018 to 025 also. This means the following:

The first 6 columns are blank.	(6X,
The first 9 variables occupied one column each.	9F1.0,

The next 4 variables occupied two columns each.	4F2.0,
The next 4 variables occupied one column each.	4F1.0,
The next 8 variables occupied two columns each.	8F2.0,
The last 25 variables occupied one column each.	25F1.0)

Therefore, the input format statement would read as follows:

```
INPUT  FORMAT   FIXED(6X,9F1.0,4F2.0,4F1.0,8F2.0,25F1.0)
```

Now, let us say that you had punched data on three cards for each questionnaire, and for the sake of convenience, let us presume that these three cards also had 50 variables each coded in exactly the same way we have described above; the input format will then read as follows:

```
Column                Column
1                     16
INPUT  FORMAT   FIXED(6X,9F1.0,4F2.0,4F1.0,8F2.0,25F1.0/
                6X,9F1.0,4F2.0,4F1.0,8F2.0,25F1.0/
                6X,9F1.0,4F2.0,4F1.0,8F2.0,25F1.0)
```

Note that the instruction to the computer to read the next card in the case has been given by a slash (/) at the end of the data on the first and the second cards. The closing parenthesis at the end of the third card indicates to the computer that there are no further data for the computer to read for each case. Note that when the keypunching has to be continued on to the next card, the column to start is column 16 on the next card as shown above—not column 1.

4. The COMPUTE cards tell the computer to combine the responses to the various questions that measure a concept. This is the same as the categorization of the variables we had discussed earlier. The only additional decision now to be made is whether we would like a summated scale, in which the responses to all the items measuring a concept are added up, or we would prefer that they be averaged over the number of items. In the example COMPUTE statements set up for the Serakan Co. in Table 7.3, the score is averaged over the 6 items for involvement and over the 10 items for satisfaction. If a summated scale is to be used instead of an averaged scale as shown in the format in Table 7.3, then the /6 and the /10 would be ignored. All the 6 items

for involvement, and the 10 items for satisfaction, will then be added and a summated scale will be used for all further analysis.

5. VAR LABELS identifies the variable numbers by the actual variable name. This is useful when the computer outputs are received and the data are to be interpreted, because both the label and the variable number will be printed on the computer outputs, making the interpretations easier. If the VAR LABELS are not identified (and this card is not absolutely necessary), then we need to go through the coding key to remember what VAR001 means, and so on. Though it may be tedious and cumbersome to identify every single variable in the questionnaire, it may be useful to identify the demographic variables, the computed variables, and any other variable that might be expected to be used in the analysis. In the Serakan study, the demographic, involvement, and satisfaction variables are labeled, as shown in Table 7.3.

6. The next card is the READ INPUT DATA card, after which the data deck of punched cards will be placed.

Procedure Cards   The procedure cards are inserted after the data deck. Table 7.3 shows how some of the procedures can be run to get (1) frequency distributions; (2) mean, standard deviation, and other statistics of the variables; (3) Pearson correlation among variables; (4) a *t* test; and (5) regression analysis. These are included to give you an idea of the setup of the procedure cards. After the last procedure card comes the FINISH card. The FINISH card is important and without it the computer will not process the other procedure cards. That is, the computer will be looking for the FINISH card in order to do all the calculations necessary to give you the results asked for in your procedure cards.

Note again how each command starts in column 1 of the card, and the variables and other data are listed starting in column 16.

Computer Time

The computer turnaround time is a function of the time you specify on the job card. Most of the jobs you run for class work could be completed in twenty-nine seconds or less as indicated in Table 7.3. Some jobs may not need more than ten seconds of computer time, in which case you can specify, TIME=(0,10). If, however, more time is needed, you could change the time to make it TIME=(0,59), TIME=(1,30), and the like. The more computer time asked for, the slower will be the turnaround time and hence the greater the delay in receiving the output.

Error Messages

Even simple errors in the job, control, or program cards such as a missing comma will give error messages. The format of the SPSS language must be strictly followed. Make sure that the parentheses in a COMPUTE state-ment match and the cards in the deck are not out of sequence. The *SPSS Manual* is fairly comprehensive; in case of doubt, it is useful to consult it for both programming and for interpretation of error messages on the computer outputs.

The data should now be ready to be submitted to the computer for analysis.

DATA ANALYSIS

In data analysis we have three objectives: getting a feel for the data, testing the goodness of data, and testing the hypotheses developed for the re-search. The feel for the data will give preliminary ideas of how good the scales are, how well the coding and punching have been done, and so on. Suppose an item tapped on a seven-point scale has been improperly coded and/or punched as 8; this will be highlighted, and can be corrected by repunching the card and resubmitting the program for analysis. The second objective—testing the goodness of data—can be accomplished by submitting the data for factor analysis, obtaining the Cronbach's alpha and the split-half reliability of the measures, and so on. The third objec-tive—hypotheses testing—is achieved by programming the computer to test each of the hypothesis with the appropriate statistical test, the results of which will determine whether or not the hypotheses are substantiated. The data analysis with respect to each of these three objectives will now be discussed in detail.

Feel for the Data

A feel for the data is acquired by checking the central tendency, the dis-persion, and the skewness of the data. The mean, the range, standard deviation, and the variance in the data will give the researcher a good idea of how the respondents reacted to the items in the questionnaire and how good the items and measures are. If the responses do not range over all points in the scale and show very little variance, then the researcher would suspect that the question was probably not properly worded and the re-spondents did not quite understand what was intended to be asked. Halo effects, if any, could also be detected if the respondents have stuck to the end points in the scale with very little variance in the answers. The mean, standard deviation, maximum and minimum scores, the range and other statistics can be easily obtained through the CONDESCRIPTIVE command discussed later. It is important to obtain these statistics. There are tests to determine whether the responses are normally distributed, but we will not go into the details here.

Researchers go to great lengths obtaining the central tendency, the range, the dispersion, and other statistics for every single item measuring the variables, especially when the measures are being developed and tested.

It is also important to get a feel for the demographic characteristics of the respondents. A frequency distribution can be obtained by the FRE-QUENCIES command shown in the same table. STATISTICS ALL will give a variety of statistics, including the median, mode, skewness and kurtosis. The histograms could also be plotted by the OPTIONS 8 card. Note that the command starts on column 1 (i.e., the **words** STATISTICS, OPTIONS), and the actual requirements (ALL, 8, etc.) are on column 16.

In addition to the frequency distributions and the means and standard deviations, it is good to know how the dependent and independent variables are related to each other. An intercorrelation matrix of these variables can be obtained through the PEARSON CORR command shown in the table. Irrespective of whether the hypotheses are directly related to the following analyses or not, it is always prudent to obtain the frequency distributions with all the statistics for the demographic variables, get the mean and standard deviation, range, and variance on the other dependent and independent variables, and obtain an intercorrelation matrix of the variables. These statistics give a feel for the data. In other words, looking at the results of these analyses, we would know how the respondents perceive the work environment or any other variable that is assessed—obtained through the mean, median, or mode—and how clustered or dispersed these perceptions happen to be. The correlations would also give an indication of how closely related or unrelated the variables under investigation are. If the correlation between two variables happens to be high—say, over .65—we might start wondering whether there are really two different concepts, or whether they are measuring the same concept. If two variables that are theoretically stated to be related do not seem to be significantly correlated to each other in our sample, we would begin to wonder if we have measured the concepts validly and reliably. Recall our discussions on convergent and discriminant validity in Unit 5. Such concerns for goodness of our data surface even as we go through the preliminary steps discussed here. Hence, getting a feel for the data becomes the necessary first step in all data analysis. Based on this initial feel, further detailed analyses can be done to test the goodness of the data.

Testing Goodness of Data

The reliability and validity of the measures can now be tested. The Cronbach's alpha and the split-half reliabilities can be obtained from the computer, the program card for which is shown later in the unit. Discussions on establishing different types of validity are beyond the scope of this book. Interested students can read the other references detailed at the end of this unit to obtain more information on the subject.

Hypotheses Testing

Different types of statistical tests are necessary to test different types of hypotheses. For instance, the difference in the means of two groups on a continuous (interval-scaled) variable can be tested through a t test. Significant differences among the means of several groups can be tested through an analysis of variance, or **ANOVA** procedure, as it is called. The extent to which the variance in a dependent variable is explained by several independent variables influencing it simultaneously can be determined through a multiple regression analysis.

All the statistical tests mentioned thus far are mainly relevant to variables that have been measured on an interval or ratio scale. These statistical tests are also known as parametric statistics. The statistical procedures intended for use with nominal and ordinal data are known as nonparametric statistics. Nonparametric statistics are used to test hypotheses that do not involve specific values of parameters such as the population mean (Roscoe, 1975). Whereas the mean is the measure of central tendency for interval- and ratio-scaled data, the mode is the measure of central tendency for nominal and ordinal data. Likewise, just as the Pearson product moment correlation coefficient indicates the relationship between two variables that are interval or ratio scaled, the Spearman rank correlation coefficient and the Kendall's tau indicate the correlation between two variables that are ordinally scaled. Although a complete discussion of these various statistical tests will not be attempted here, Table 7.4 provides a classification of the types of tests that would be appropriate for the kinds of data collected. It will also now become clear why a more powerfully scaled instrument—wherever appropriate and feasible—would be preferable to a less powerfully scaled instrument as discussed in Unit 5. Variables measured on the interval or ratio scale lend themselves to the more powerful parametric statistical analysis.

The computer is so versatile that almost any test can be made and the results obtained in a matter of minutes, but unless the appropriate tests are made, the results will be biased. It is important to know what kinds of tests should be performed on the data we have, to test each of the hypotheses.

DATA ANALYSIS AND INTERPRETATION

Data analysis and interpretation of the data from the results of the computer printouts can be most meaningfully explained by referring to an actual research project done by a professor teaching research methods. After a very brief description of the background and the sample for the research, we will discuss the data analysis done for testing each hypothesis and how the computer results were interpreted.

Table 7.4

Statistical Techniques and Tests Classified According to Type, Number, and Measurement Scale of Variables[a]

Variates		Criterion Variables					
		One			Two or More		
		Nominal	Ordinal	Interval	Nominal	Ordinal	Interval
One	Nominal	Chi-square test for independence Contingency coefficient Cochran Q test Fisher extract probability Test for 2 × 2 tables	Sign test Median test Mann-Whitney U test Kruskal-Wallis one-way analysis of variance	Analysis of variance			Multiple discriminant analysis
One	Ordinal		Spearman's rank correlation Kendall's rank correlation	Analysis of variance with trend analysis			
One	Interval	Analysis of variance		Regression analysis (multiple coefficient) correlation	Analysis of variance		Multiple regression analysis
Two or More	Nominal		Friedman two-way analysis of variance	Analysis of variance (factorial design)			Analysis of variance
Two or More	Ordinal						
Two or More	Interval	Multiple discriminant analysis		Multiple regression analysis	Multiple discriminant analysis		Canonical correlation

[a] Taken from R. L. Baker, & R. E. Schutz (Eds.). *Instructional product research*. New York: Van Nostrand Co., 1972, p. 110.

RESEARCH ON RESEARCH METHODS COURSE

The professor, who did extensive course development work for the research methods course that she has been teaching for some time, wanted to know some of the attitudinal and behavioral responses of the students to the course. A previous literature survey indicated that some demographic variables, some personality characteristics and predispositions, some course characteristics, and some outcome variables were important for the study. The professor collected longitudinal data on the important variables from 88 students who had taken the course during two fall semesters and a spring semester.

On the first day of each semester, information on the gender and the current GPA of the students who had enrolled for the class was obtained. The students were also asked to indicate their grade aspirations for the course. When the semester was two-thirds over, the same students were asked to indicate their grade expectations in the course, how they experienced the course in terms of specific course characteristics (challenge, variety, etc.), how much stress they experienced in the course, their need patterns (i.e., need for achievement, affiliation, autonomy, and dominance), and the extent to which they valued the protestant work ethic. On the last day of class they were asked the extent of their involvement in the course, the sense of competence they derived from the course, their satisfaction with the course, and the feelings of self-esteem they derived from the course. The professor also had a score on their actual performance in the course based on the several assignments and tests that they had done during the semester. Thus, longitudinal data, as well as both same-source and other-source performance data, were utilized.

The professor wanted to find answers to several questions and to test some specific hypotheses. The research questions were as follows:

1. Were there significant differences between the male and female students with respect to the extent of their involvement, competence, experienced stress, self-esteem, need patterns, protestant work ethic values, perceived course characteristics, and performance? (Some gender differences were expected for at least some of these factors.)

2. The professor wanted to know whether (a) grade aspiration was independent of gender, and whether (b) grade expectation at the end of the semester was independent of students' grade aspirations at the beginning of the course. (In both cases she thought they would not be independent.)

3. Would the correlation of satisfaction and performance for male and for female students be significantly different? (The professor hypothesized that the correlations would be significantly different.)

4. Would students with different levels of grade expectations experience satisfaction differentially? (The hypothesis was that they would.)

5. To what extent would the performance and satisfaction of the students be influenced by their starting GPA, work ethic values, extent of their involvement in the course, experienced stress in the course, and the perceived course characteristics? What would be the importance of these variables for their performance?

Apart from the feeling that many of the variables in item (5) would significantly influence performance and satisfaction, the professor had no other specific research hypothesis.

To examine these five questions, the professor submitted the data for computer analysis using the SPSS program. Let us now proceed step by step with the computer printout received so that we understand how the SPSS program works. We will first see how the computer processes the control cards; next we will see how the professor programmed for and interpreted the results of the computer outputs with respect to the following:

1. Checking for the reliability of the measures.
2. Obtaining the frequency distributions.
3. Obtaining the means, standard deviations, and other statistics for the dependent and independent variables.
4. Obtaining a Pearson correlation matrix.
5. Testing the five research questions stated earlier.

The five questions were examined through the use of (1) t test, (2) chi-square (χ^2) test, (3) r to z transformations, (4) ANOVA, and (5) stepwise and simple multiple regression analysis.

Each of the steps in computer analysis will now be detailed.

The Processing of the Control Cards by the Computer

Computer Output Part 7A shows how the control cards in the data deck were processed by the computer. Note that immediately after the INPUT FORMAT card, the computer specifies the columns in which the variables were found. To make sure that there are no mistakes in the INPUT FORMAT submitted to the computer, it would be a good idea to check the columns printed by the computer to make sure that the variables are where they are supposed to be. If there are any mistakes, the input format should be immediately corrected so that we are not later surprised by meaningless results from the data analysis done.

Computer Output Part 7A

Processing of the Control Cards by the Computer

1	RUN NAME	ADSC 361 RESEARCH	
2	VARIABLE LIST	VAR001 TO VAR126	
3	INPUT MEDIUM	CARD	
4	N OF CASES	88	
5	INPUT FORMAT	FIXED(X,2F2.0,67F1.0/X,51F1.0,F2.0,2F1.0,F2.0,2F1.0)	

ACCORDING TO YOUR INPUT FORMAT, VARIABLES ARE TO BE READ AS FOLLOWS

VARIABLE	FORMAT	RECORD	COLUMNS	
VAR001	F 2. 0	1	2-	3
VAR002	F 2. 0	1	4-	5
VAR003	F 1. 0	1	6-	6
VAR004	F 1. 0	1	7-	7
VAR005	F 1. 0	1	8-	8
VAR006	F 1. 0	1	9-	9
VAR007	F 1. 0	1	10-	10
VAR008	F 1. 0	1	11-	11
VAR009	F 1. 0	1	12-	12
VAR010	F 1. 0	1	13-	13
VAR011	F 1. 0	1	14-	14
VAR012	F 1. 0	1	15-	15
VAR013	F 1. 0	1	16-	16
VAR014	F 1. 0	1	17-	17
VAR015	F 1. 0	1	18-	18
VAR016	F 1. 0	1	19-	19
VAR017	F 1. 0	1	20-	20
VAR018	F 1. 0	1	21-	21
VAR019	F 1. 0	1	22-	22
VAR020	F 1. 0	1	23-	23
VAR021	F 1. 0	1	24-	24
VAR022	F 1. 0	1	25-	25
VAR023	F 1. 0	1	26-	26
VAR024	F 1. 0	1	27-	27
VAR025	F 1. 0	1	28-	28
VAR026	F 1. 0	1	29-	29
VAR027	F 1. 0	1	30-	30
VAR028	F 1. 0	1	31-	31
VAR029	F 1. 0	1	32-	32
VAR030	F 1. 0	1	33-	33
VAR031	F 1. 0	1	34-	34
VAR032	F 1. 0	1	35-	35
VAR033	F 1. 0	1	36-	36
VAR034	F 1. 0	1	37-	37
VAR035	F 1. 0	1	38-	38
VAR036	F 1. 0	1	39-	39
VAR037	F 1. 0	1	40-	40
VAR038	F 1. 0	1	41-	41
VAR039	F 1. 0	1	42-	42
VAR040	F 1. 0	1	43-	43
VAR041	F 1. 0	1	44-	44
VAR042	F 1. 0	1	45-	45
VAR043	F 1. 0	1	46-	46
VAR044	F 1. 0	1	47-	47
VAR045	F 1. 0	1	48-	48
VAR046	F 1. 0	1	49-	49
VAR047	F 1. 0	1	50-	50
VAR048	F 1. 0	1	51-	51
VAR049	F 1. 0	1	52-	52
VAR050	F 1. 0	1	53-	53
VAR051	F 1. 0	1	54-	54

Computer Output Part 7A—(Continued)

VARIABLE	FORMAT	RECORD	COLUMNS	
VAR066	F 1. 0	1	69-	69
VAR067	F 1. 0	1	70-	70
VAR068	F 1. 0	1	71-	71
VAR069	F 1. 0	1	72-	72
VAR070	F 1. 0	2	2-	2
VAR071	F 1. 0	2	3-	3
VAR072	F 1. 0	2	4-	4
VAR073	F 1. 0	2	5-	5
VAR074	F 1. 0	2	6-	6
VAR075	F 1. 0	2	7-	7
VAR076	F 1. 0	2	8-	8
VAR077	F 1. 0	2	9-	9
VAR078	F 1. 0	2	10-	10
VAR079	F 1. 0	2	11-	11
VAR080	F 1. 0	2	12-	12
VAR081	F 1. 0	2	13-	13
VAR082	F 1. 0	2	14-	14
VAR083	F 1. 0	2	15-	15
VAR084	F 1. 0	2	16-	16
VAR085	F 1. 0	2	17-	17
VAR086	F 1. 0	2	18-	18
VAR087	F 1. 0	2	19-	19
VAR088	F 1. 0	2	20-	20
VAR089	F 1. 0	2	21-	21
VAR090	F 1. 0	2	22-	22
VAR091	F 1. 0	2	23-	23
VAR092	F 1. 0	2	24-	24
VAR093	F 1. 0	2	25-	25
VAR094	F 1. 0	2	26-	26
VAR095	F 1. 0	2	27-	27
VAR096	F 1. 0	2	28-	28
VAR097	F 1. 0	2	29-	29
VAR098	F 1. 0	2	30-	30
VAR099	F 1. 0	2	31-	31
VAR100	F 1. 0	2	32-	32
VAR101	F 1. 0	2	33-	33
VAR102	F 1. 0	2	34-	34
VAR103	F 1. 0	2	35-	35
VAR104	F 1. 0	2	36-	36
VAR105	F 1. 0	2	37-	37
VAR106	F 1. 0	2	38-	38
VAR052	F 1. 0	1	55-	55
VAR053	F 1. 0	1	56-	56
VAR054	F 1. 0	1	57-	57
VAR055	F 1. 0	1	58-	58
VAR056	F 1. 0	1	59-	59
VAR057	F 1. 0	1	60-	60
VAR058	F 1. 0	1	61-	61
VAR059	F 1. 0	1	62-	62
VAR060	F 1. 0	1	63-	63
VAR061	F 1. 0	1	64-	64
VAR062	F 1. 0	1	65-	65
VAR063	F 1. 0	1	66-	66
VAR064	F 1. 0	1	67-	67
VAR065	F 1. 0	1	68-	68

Computer Output Part 7A—(Continued)

```
VARIABLE   FORMAT   RECORD    COLUMNS

VAR114     F 1. 0      2      45-   46
VAR115     F 1. 0      2      47-   47
VAR116     F 1. 0      2      48-   48
VAR117     F 1. 0      2      49-   49
VAR118     F 1. 0      2      50-   50
VAR119     F 1. 0      2      51-   51
VAR120     F 1. 0      2      52-   52
VAR121     F 2. 0      2      53-   54
VAR122     F 1. 0      2      55-   55
VAR123     F 1. 0      2      56-   56
VAR124     F 2. 0      2      57-   58
VAR125     F 1. 0      2      59-   59
VAR126     F 1. 0      2      60-   60
```

THE INPUT FORMAT PROVIDES FOR 126 VARIABLES. 125 WILL BE READ
IT PROVIDES FOR 2 RECORDS ('CARDS') PER CASE. A MAXIMUM OF   72 'COLUMNS' ARE USED ON A RECORD.

```
    6 COMPUTE      VAR201=(VAR003+VAR004+VAR006+VAR008+VAR011+VAR013)/6
    7 COMPUTE      VAR202=(VAR005+VAR007+VAR009+VAR010+VAR012)/5
    8 COMPUTE      VAR203=(VAR014+VAR018+VAR022+VAR023+VAR024+VAR025+VAR026+
    9              VAR027)/8
   10 COMPUTE      VAR204=(VAR015+VAR019+VAR020+VAR021+VAR028)/5
   11 COMPUTE      VAR205=(VAR017+VAR029+VAR030+VAR031)/4
   12 COMPUTE      VAR206=(VAR032+VAR033+VAR034)/3
   13 COMPUTE      VAR207=(VAR203+VAR204+VAR205+VAR206+VAR016)/5
   14 COMPUTE      VAR209=(VAR045+VAR046+VAR047+VAR048+VAR049+VAR050+VAR051+
   15              VAR052+VAR053+VAR054+VAR055+VAR056+(8-VAR057)+VAR058+
   16              (8-VAR059)+VAR060+VAR061+VAR062+VAR063)/19
   17 COMPUTE      VAR211=(VAR078+VAR079+VAR080+VAR081+VAR082+VAR083)/6
   18 COMPUTE      VAR214=((8-VAR086)+(8-VAR090)+(8-VAR094)+VAR098+(8-VAR102))/5
   19 COMPUTE      VAR217=((8-VAR089)+VAR093+(8-VAR097)+(8-VAR101)+(8-VAR105))/5
   20 COMPUTE      VAR218=(VAR106+VAR107+VAR108+VAR109+VAR110+VAR111+VAR112+
   21              VAR113+VAR114)/9
   22 COMPUTE      VAR219=(32-(VAR115+VAR116+VAR117+VAR118))/4
   23 COMPUTE      VAR220=(5-VAR119)
   24 COMPUTE      VAR221=(5-VAR120)
   25 VAR LABELS   VAR121,COURSE PERFORMANCE/VAR122,STARTING GRADE POINT AVERAGE/
   26              VAR125,SEX/VAR201,COURSE INVOLVEMENT/
   27              VAR202,SENSE OF COMPETENCE/VAR207,GLOBAL SATISFACTION/
   28              VAR209,PROTESTANT ETHIC/VAR211,COURSE JOB CHARACTERISTICS/
   29 VAR LABELS   VAR214,NEED FOR ACHIEVEMENT/
   30              VAR217,NEED FOR DOMINANCE/
   31 VAR LABELS   VAR218,COURSE STRESS/VAR219,SELF ESTEEM/
   32              VAR220,GRADE ASPIRATION/VAR221,GRADE EXPECTATION
   33 FREQUENCIES  GENERAL=VAR125,VAR122
   34 STATISTICS   ALL
   35 OPTIONS      8
```

GIVEN WORKSPACE ALLOWS FOR   4608 VALUES AND   1382 LABELS PER VARIABLE FOR 'FREQUENCIES'

```
   36 READ INPUT DATA
```

Checking the Reliability of the Measures

Even though she was using well-validated measures to tap the variables in the study with only minor adaptations in some cases to suit the classroom situation, the professor still wanted to see if the measures had sufficient interitem consistency reliability (Cronbach's alpha) and split-half reliability for this population of research methods students. On testing for these reliabilities, she found that but for two measures (the items measuring

Computer Output Part 7B

Checking Reliability of Measures

```
     RELIABILITY      VARIABLES=VAR003 TO VAR034/
                      SCALE(JI)=VAR003,VAR004,VAR006,VAR008,VAR011,VAR013/
                      SCALE(JI)=VAR003,VAR004,VAR006,VAR008,VAR011,VAR013/
                      MODEL=SPLIT/

* * * * R E L I A B I L I T Y   A N A L Y S I S   F O R   S C A L E   ( J I )

        1.      VAR003
        2.      VAR004
        3.      VAR006
        4.      VAR008
        5.      VAR011
        6.      VAR013


RELIABILITY COEFFICIENTS

N OF CASES =       88.0          N OF ITEMS =  6

ALPHA =   0.83754

* * * * R E L I A B I L I T Y   A N A L Y S I S   F O R   S C A L E   ( J I )

        1.      VAR003
        2.      VAR004
        3.      VAR006
        4.      VAR008
        5.      VAR011
        6.      VAR013


RELIABILITY COEFFICIENTS

N OF CASES =       88.0          N OF ITEMS =  6

CORRELATION BETWEEN FORMS =  0.74812         EQUAL-LENGTH SPEARMAN-BROWN =  0.85591

UNEQUAL-LENGTH SPEARMAN-BROWN =  0.85591      GUTTMAN SPLIT-HALF =  0.35591

     3 ITEMS IN PART 1                           3 ITEMS IN PART 2

ALPHA FOR PART 1 =   0.70042                  ALPHA FOR PART 2 =   0.71547
```

need for affiliation and need for dominance), all other measures had Cronbach's alpha and split-half reliabilities of over .80. The two variables that had low reliability (less than .60) were excluded from all further analyses, since the results of the study would be biased if measures with low internal consistency are used, and the scientific quality of the study will be adversely affected.

An example of one of the reliabilities programmed for and processed can be seen in Computer Output Part 7B. Note that the first card lists all the variables comprising the measure (more variables can be added if reliabilities for more than one measure are needed to be programmed); the next reliability card, starting on column 16, produces the Cronbach's alpha; and the third reliability card generates the split-half reliability. Several other reliabilities for different measures can follow the third card, each starting on column 16, provided all the raw variables are listed on the first reliability card, which starts in column 1. At the end of all the program cards, will of course, come the FINISH card. Note that if there are some items to be reversed, this is done through a RECODE card, which should be placed immediately after the COMPUTE cards and before the VAR LABELS card. An example RECODE statement would look like this:

Column 1   **Column 16**

```
RECODE          VAR122, VAR126, VAR115 to VAR118 (1=7)
                (2=6) (3=5) (5=3) (6=2) (7=1)
```

This statement will reverse the items so that all items measuring a variable are in the same direction. The reliabilities obtained would then be correct.

The results of the output indicate that the Cronbach's alphas for the six-item involvement measure (JI) is .83754 (i.e., .84), and the Spearman-Brown split-half reliability is .85591, or about .86. Both of these reliabilities are fairly good. Reliabilities of less than .60 would be considered poor. It is for this reason that the need for affiliation and need for dominance measures were eliminated from further analysis in this study.

Frequency Distributions

Having established the reliability of the measures, the professor next wanted to see the demographic characteristics of the sample. Frequency distributions for the four demographic variables of gender, starting GPA, grade aspiration for the course, and the final grade expectation were obtained.

Computer programming and results in respect to gender and starting GPA are shown in Computer Output Part 7C. Note the FREQUENCIES card, the STATISTICS card, and the OPTIONS card, which gave the frequency distributions, the various statistics, and also the histograms with respect to the variables.

Interpretation of Results

Based on the frequency distribution results, the professor found that 66 of the students were males and constituted 75 percent of the respondents. Twenty-two (i.e., 25 percent) of the respondents were females. The most frequent starting GPA (the mode) was between 2.51 and 3.00 (category 3 in the computer results), and 30 students, constituting 34 percent of the respondents, fell into this category. The frequency distributions on the grade aspiration at the beginning of the semester, and grade expectations

Computer Output Part 7C

Frequency Distributions

ADSC 361 RESEARCH

FILE   NONAME   (CREATION DATE = 05/28/82)

VAR125   SEX

CATEGORY LABEL	CODE	ABSOLUTE FREQ	RELATIVE FREQ (PCT)	ADJUSTED FREQ (PCT)	CUM FREQ (PCT)
	1.	66	75.0	75.0	75.0
	2.	22	25.0	25.0	100.0
	TOTAL	88	100.0	100.0	

VAR125   SEX

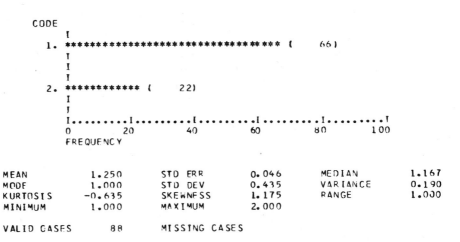

MEAN	1.250	STD ERR	0.046	MEDIAN	1.167
MODE	1.000	STD DEV	0.435	VARIANCE	0.190
KURTOSIS	−0.635	SKEWNESS	1.175	RANGE	1.000
MINIMUM	1.000	MAXIMUM	2.000		

VALID CASES   88   MISSING CASES

Computer Output Part 7C—(Continued)

VAR122   STARTING GRADE POINT AVERAGE

CATEGORY LABEL	CODE	ABSOLUTE FREQ	RELATIVE FREQ (PCT)	ADJUSTED FREQ (PCT)	CUM FREQ (PCT)
	1.	7	8.0	8.0	8.0
	2.	21	23.9	23.9	31.8
	3.	30	34.1	34.1	65.9
	4.	23	26.1	26.1	92.0
	5.	5	5.7	5.7	97.7
	6.	2	2.3	2.3	100.0
	TOTAL	88	100.0	100.0	

VAR122   STARTING GRADE POINT AVERAGE

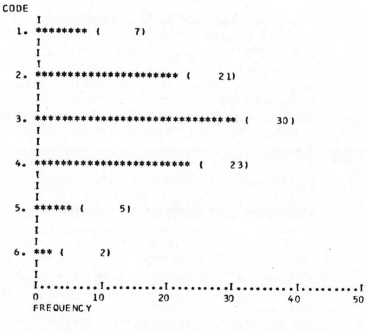

MEAN	3.045	STD ERR	0.120	MEDIAN	3.033
MODE	3.000	STD DEV	1.124	VARIANCE	1.262
KURTOSIS	-0.076	SKEWNESS	0.207	RANGE	5.000
MINIMUM	1.000	MAXIMUM	6.000		

toward the end of the semester (results not shown here in Computer Output Part 7B) indicated that about 53 percent of the students aspired for a B in the course at the beginning, and about 52 percent of the students actually expected to get a B toward the end of the semester.

Means, Standard Deviation, Variance, and Range for the Dependent and Independent Variables

By using a CONDESCRIPTIVE card, the professor obtained all important statistics such as the mean, range, standard deviation, and variance on all the dependent and independent variables in the study.

The programming and results of these statistics are shown for a few variables in Computer Output Part 7D.

Interpretation of Results

Statistics Relating to Involvement in and Overall Satisfaction with the Course As can be seen from the results, the average involvement (VAR201) and overall satisfaction (VAR207) of the students were reasonably high (a mean of 5.16 and 5.33 on a seven-point scale), and the spread for involvement was more than that for satisfaction. In other words, whereas some were more involved than others, the satisfaction among the students was not very different from one another (see the standard deviation and variance for the two variables). The minimum and maximum were 1.5 and 7.0 for involvement, whereas they were 3.2 and 6.7 for satisfaction. To put it differently, although no one had low satisfaction, at least some had low levels of involvement in the course.

Perceptions of Course Characteristics (VAR211) The course was perceived by students as fairly challenging, and as utilizing a variety of skills (5.89 on a seven-point scale); however, there was dispersion on these perceptions (standard deviation 1.08, variance 1.16). A few students obviously perceived the course as very low in challenge (minimum 1.00), whereas many seem to have perceived the course as quite challenging (maximum 7.0). We can conclude that only a few must have perceived it as low in challenge because the mean is fairly high. This kind of information is useful, because in a case like this, the professor need not be concerned too much about the minimum perceived challenge of 1.00, because the mean is high. However, if the mean was also low, there would be cause for anxiety and a need to think about course redesigning.

Stress (VAR218) The mean stress level experienced by students also seems to be appropriate (3.14 on a five-point scale), and there is very little variance in the amount of experienced stress (standard deviation .53, vari-

Computer Output Part 7D

CONDESCRIPTIVE: Mean, Standard Deviation, and Other Statistics

VARIABLE   VAR 201   COURSE INVOLVEMENT

MEAN	5.163	STD ERROR	0.124	STD DEV	1.166
VARIANCE	1.360	KURTOSIS	0.834	SKEWNESS	-1.058
RANGE	5.500	MINIMUM	1.500	MAXIMUM	7.000
SUM	454.333				

VALID OBSERVATIONS -   88   MISSING OBSERVATIONS -   0

- -

VARIABLE   VAR207   GLOBAL SATISFACTION

MEAN	5.330	STD ERROR	0.082	STD DEV	0.768
VARIANCE	0.590	KURTOSIS	0.245	SKEWNESS	-0.732
RANGE	3.527	MINIMUM	3.215	MAXIMUM	6.742
SUM	469.045				

VALID OBSERVATIONS -   88   MISSING OBSERVATIONS -   0

- -

VARIABLE   VAR211   COURSE JOB CHARACTERISTICS

MEAN	5.892	STD ERROR	0.115	STD DEV	1.076
VARIANCE	1.157	KURTOSIS	9.032	SKEWNESS	-2.739
RANGE	6.000	MINIMUM	1.000	MAXIMUM	7.000
SUM	518.500				

VALID OBSERVATIONS -   88   MISSING OBSERVATIONS -   0

- -

VARIABLE   VAR218   COURSE STRESS

MEAN	3.141	STD ERROR	0.056	STD DEV	0.528
VARIANCE	0.278	KURTOSIS	0.703	SKEWNESS	0.052
RANGE	2.778	MINIMUM	1.778	MAXIMUM	4.556
SUM	276.444				

VALID OBSERVATIONS -   88   MISSING OBSERVATIONS -   0

- -

ADSC 361 RESEARCH   05/28/82   PAGE   12

FILE   NONAME   (CREATION DATE = 05/28/82)

VARIABLE   VAR121   COURSE PERFORMANCE

MEAN	77.761	STD ERROR	0.819	STD DEV	7.680
VARIANCE	58.988	KURTOSIS	2.227	SKEWNESS	-1.225
RANGE	43.000	MINIMUM	48.000	MAXIMUM	91.000
SUM	6843.000				

VALID OBSERVATIONS -   88   MISSING OBSERVATIONS -   0

ance .28). In other words, the students do not seem to be experiencing either very high or very low levels of stress. Earlier research by others in the stress area indicates that optimal levels of stress (i.e., neither high nor low) are good for a high level of performance (Lazarus, 1966). Hence the instructor may continue to demand the same levels of effort, attention, and so on, from the students.

Performance (VAR121) The performance scores indicate that the mean for the class is 77.76 (for a total of 100), with a standard deviation of 7.7. The maximum score is 91 percent (an A) and the minimum score is 48 (an F). The mean grade for the class is a C+. If the professor would like to bring the mean to a B, several strategies to accomplish the goal would have to be considered.

Pearson Correlation Among the Variables

Next, the instructor wanted to see the intercorrelations among the several variables in the study. Hence a Pearson correlation matrix was obtained. The programming and results can be seen in Computer Output Part 7E. The PEARSON CORR card gives the matrix. Note that by having a STATIS-TICS card next to it, the means and standard deviations of the variables can also be obtained at the top of the computer printout.

Observe that the upper half of the matrix (all figures above the top diagonal line) is a mirror-image of the bottom half (all figures below the bottom diagonal line). Each of the correlations has three pieces of information. The first figure is the correlation between two variables. The second figure, in parentheses, shows the sample size. The third figure ($p = .$) shows the significance level. By convention a 95 percent level of significance (confidence) is an acceptable level. Hence any $p \leq .05$ is significant.

Interpretation of Results

The correlation matrix seems rather unusual in that most of the correlations are significant, and only 11 of the total of 45 correlations (roughly 25

Computer Output Part 7E

Pearson Correlation Matrix

```
              38 PEARSON CORR      VAR201,VAR202,VAR207,VAR209,VAR121,VAR211,
              39                   VAR218,VAR214,VAR217,VAR219
              40 STATISTICS        1

    *****  PEARSON CORR PROBLEM REQUIRES      2160 BYTES WORKSPACE *****


ADSC 361 RESEARCH

FILE   NONAME   (CREATION DATE = 05/28/82)

          VARIABLE        CASES             MEAN          STD DEV

          VAR201            88            5.1629           1.1662
          VAR202            88            5.4523           0.9630
          VAR207            88            5.3301           0.7681
          VAR209            88            4.6310           0.5929
          VAR121            88           77.7614           7.6804
          VAR211            88            5.8920           1.0757
          VAR218            88            3.1414           0.5276
          VAR214            88            5.0068           1.0014
          VAR217            88            4.6705           1.1191
          VAR219            88            5.4347           0.9203
```

Computer Output Part 7E—(Continued)

- - - - - - - P E A R S O N   C O R R E L A T I O N   C O E F F I C I E N T S - - - - - - - -

Each cell: COEFFICIENT / (CASES) / SIGNIFICANCE

	VAR201	VAR202	VAR207	VAR209	VAR121	VAR211	VAR213	VAR214	VAR217	VAR219
VAR201	1.0000 (88) P=*****	0.7882 (88) P=0.000	0.5256 (88) P=0.000	0.2886 (88) P=0.003	0.3812 (88) P=0.000	0.4524 (88) P=0.000	-0.1039 (88) P=0.168	0.2969 (88) P=0.002	0.1608 (88) P=0.067	0.3862 (88) P=0.000
VAR202	0.7882 (88) P=0.000	1.0000 (88) P=*****	0.6259 (88) P=0.000	0.3688 (88) P=0.000	0.3100 (88) P=0.002	0.5477 (88) P=0.000	-0.3023 (88) P=0.002	0.2476 (88) P=0.010	0.1753 (88) P=0.051	0.5013 (88) P=0.000
VAR207	0.5256 (88) P=0.000	0.6259 (88) P=0.000	1.0000 (88) P=*****	0.3137 (88) P=0.001	0.3229 (88) P=0.001	0.5157 (88) P=0.000	-0.4953 (88) P=0.000	0.0910 (88) P=0.200	0.0193 (88) P=0.429	0.5018 (88) P=0.000
VAR209	0.2886 (88) P=0.003	0.3688 (88) P=0.000	0.3137 (88) P=0.001	1.0000 (88) P=*****	0.0582 (88) P=0.295	0.4535 (88) P=0.000	-0.2002 (88) P=0.031	0.2925 (88) P=0.003	0.0320 (88) P=0.384	0.2780 (88) P=0.004
VAR121	0.3812 (88) P=0.000	0.3100 (88) P=0.002	0.3229 (88) P=0.001	0.0582 (88) P=0.295	1.0000 (88) P=*****	0.2714 (88) P=0.005	-0.1306 (88) P=0.113	0.2791 (88) P=0.004	0.1804 (88) P=0.046	0.3828 (88) P=0.000
VAR211	0.4524 (88) P=0.000	0.5477 (88) P=0.000	0.5157 (88) P=0.000	0.4535 (88) P=0.000	0.2714 (88) P=0.005	1.0000 (88) P=*****	-0.3415 (88) P=0.001	0.1768 (88) P=0.050	0.0554 (88) P=0.304	0.3295 (88) P=0.001
VAR218	-0.1039 (88) P=0.168	-0.3023 (88) P=0.002	-0.4953 (88) P=0.000	-0.2002 (88) P=0.031	-0.1306 (88) P=0.113	-0.3415 (88) P=0.001	1.0000 (88) P=*****	-0.1421 (88) P=0.093	-0.0634 (88) P=0.279	-0.4772 (88) P=0.000
VAR214	0.2969 (88) P=0.002	0.2476 (88) P=0.010	0.0910 (88) P=0.200	0.2925 (88) P=0.003	0.2791 (88) P=0.004	0.1768 (88) P=0.050	-0.1421 (88) P=0.093	1.0000 (88) P=*****	0.6745 (88) P=0.000	0.3447 (88) P=0.001
VAR217	0.1608 (88) P=0.067	0.1753 (88) P=0.051	0.0193 (88) P=0.429	0.0320 (88) P=0.384	0.1804 (88) P=0.046	0.0554 (88) P=0.304	-0.0634 (88) P=0.279	0.6745 (88) P=0.000	1.0000 (88) P=*****	0.2355 (88) P=0.014
VAR219	0.3862 (88) P=0.000	0.5013 (88) P=0.000	0.5018 (88) P=0.000	0.2780 (88) P=0.004	0.3828 (88) P=0.000	0.3295 (88) P=0.001	-0.4772 (88) P=0.000	0.3447 (88) P=0.001	0.2355 (88) P=0.014	1.0000 (88) P=*****

(COEFFICIENT / (CASES) / SIGNIFICANCE)

(A VALUE OF 99.0000 IS PRINTED IF A COEFFICIENT CANNOT BE COMPUTED)

233

percent) are not significant. Eight of the correlations are $>.50$, and the correlation between involvement (VAR201) and competence (VAR202) is as high as .79. The correlation between competence and satisfaction (VAR202 and VAR207) is .63. These rather high correlations among the three outcome variables (involvement, competence, and satisfaction) introduce some doubts as to whether these variables are perceived by the students to be so similar that they are not distinct concepts. In other words, we are now concerned about the validity of the measures; are the questions intended to measure the three distinct concepts of involvement, competence, and satisfaction, indeed measuring three distinct concepts, or are they all measuring just one concept? This doubt certainly needs to be clarified by doing some discriminant and convergent validity tests on the measures.

The performance variable (VAR121) is only modestly correlated to involvement ($r = .38$), competence ($r = .31$), and satisfaction ($r = .32$). It correlates .27 with course characteristics, .28 with need for achievement, .18 with the need for dominance, and .38 with self-esteem derived from the course. Performance is not significantly correlated with protestant work ethic ($r = .06$).

Need for dominance (VAR217) and need for achievement (VAR214) are also correlated rather highly ($r = .67$). Although there is no extreme multicollinearity (i.e., very high correlations, usually over .80 between independent variables), it would be advisable to test the factorial validity and the convergent and discriminant validity of some of the measures at least—particularly the three outcome variables and the two need variables.

Having had a good feel for the data and feeling reasonably satisfied with the reliability but not the validity of the measures, the professor set out to test the several hypotheses. Let us see how this was done and how the results were interpreted.

Hypotheses Testing

Hypothesis 1: Use of t Test

Hypothesis 1 can be stated in the null and the alternate as follows:

H_0: There will be no differences between male and female students in their mean course involvement, competence, experienced stress, self-esteem derived from the course, need for achievement, need for dominance, protestant work ethic values, perceived course characteristics, and performance in the course.

H_0: $\mu_1 = \mu_2$

where μ_1 represents the mean on each variable for the male students and μ_2 represents the mean on each variable for the female students.

H_A: There will be significant differences between male and female students with respect to their involvement, competence, experienced stress, self-esteem derived from the course, need for achievement, need for dominance, protestant work ethic, the perceived course characteristics, and performance in the course.

Note that a two-tailed test is involved here because the direction of the difference is not stated.

H_A: $\mu_1 \neq \mu_2$

The use of a t test is appropriate to examine whether or not there is a significant difference in the mean for two groups, with regard to a quantitative (or continuous) dependent variable. If the t statistic is significant, then we would decide that there are significant differences for the two groups; if the t statistic is not significant, then we would conclude that there are no significant mean differences between two groups on that variable.

The programming and the results are as in Computer Output Part 7F.

Interpretation of Results   The computer results show the number of men and women in the two groups, the mean and standard deviations for each of the variables for men and women, and the t values and associated probabilities or p values for each of the t values. It is the p value that indicates whether the mean values for men and women for each of the variables are significantly different. Note that there are significant differences ($p \leq .05$) in the means for only two variables: need for achievement and self-esteem derived from the course. The p values for these are .008 and .013, respectively, with the t values being -2.74 and -2.56. That is, these two t statistics show that there is a significant difference in the mean value of need for achievement and the derived self-esteem from the course, with women being higher on both the mean values as compared to men. We know this because men were coded as 1 and women as 2 in the gender variable. There were no other significant differences in the male and female students. So, with respect to this hypothesis, only two of the nine hypothesized differences were substantiated. Women have a higher need for achievement and derive more self-esteem from the course.

Hypothesis 2a and 2b: Use of χ^2 (Chi-Square) Tests

a.   Gender and grade aspirations will not be independent of each other; they will be related.

b.   Grade aspiration and grade expectation will also be related to each other; they will not be independent of each other.

Computer Output Part 7F

Use of t Test

GROUP 1 - VAR125 EQ 1.
GROUP 2 - VAR125 EQ 2.

T-TEST

VARIABLE	NUMBER OF CASES	MEAN	STANDARD DEVIATION	STANDARD ERROR	F VALUE	2-TAIL PROB.	POOLED VARIANCE ESTIMATE T VALUE	DEGREES OF FREEDOM	2-TAIL PROB.	SEPARATE VARIANCE ESTIMATE T VALUE	DEGREES OF FREEDOM	2-TAIL PROB.
VAR201 COURSE INVOLVEMENT												
GROUP 1	66	5.0934	1.232	0.152	1.74	0.157	-0.97	86	0.336	-1.11	47.29	0.273
GROUP 2	22	5.3712	0.934	0.199								
VAR202 SENSE OF COMPETENCE												
GROUP 1	66	5.4364	1.022	0.126	1.71	0.169	-0.27	86	0.790	-0.31	46.92	0.762
GROUP 2	22	5.5000	0.780	0.166								
VAR218 COURSE STRESS												
GROUP 1	66	3.1599	0.570	0.070	2.27	0.039	0.57	86	0.571	0.69	54.63	0.491
GROUP 2	22	3.0859	0.379	0.081								
VAR219 SELF ESTEEM												
GROUP 1	66	5.3220	0.982	0.121	2.66	0.015	-2.02	86	0.046	-2.56	59.63	0.013
GROUP 2	22	5.7727	0.602	0.128								
VAR214 NEED FOR ACHIEVEMENT												
GROUP 1	66	4.8758	1.065	0.131	2.63	0.016	-2.17	86	0.033	-2.74	59.28	0.008
GROUP 2	22	5.4000	0.656	0.140								
VAR217 NEED FOR DOMINANCE												
GROUP 1	66	4.7091	1.088	0.134	1.27	0.451	0.56	86	0.578	0.53	32.69	0.603
GROUP 2	22	4.5545	1.228	0.262								

ADSC 361 RESEARCH

FILE   NONAME   (CREATION DATE = 05/28/82)

GROUP 1 - VAR125   EQ   1.
GROUP 2 - VAR125   EQ   2.

- T- TEST - - - - - - - - - - - - - - - - -

VARIABLE	NUMBER OF CASES	MEAN	STANDARD DEVIATION	STANDARD ERROR	*	F VALUE	2-TAIL PROB.	* POOLED VARIANCE ESTIMATE *	T VALUE	DEGREES OF FREEDOM	2-TAIL PROB.	* SEPARATE VARIANCE ESTIMATE	T VALUE	DEGREES OF FREEDOM	2-TAIL PROB.
VAR211 COURSE JOB CHARACTERISTICS					*			*							
GROUP 1	66	5.8182	1.110	0.137	*	1.35	0.446	*	-1.12	86	0.267	*	-1.21	41.48	0.235
GROUP 2	22	6.1136	0.955	0.204	*			*				*			
VAR121 COURSE PERFORMANCE					*			*							
GROUP 1	66	77.1515	7.782	0.958	*	1.16	0.729	*	-1.30	86	0.199	*	-1.34	38.50	0.187
GROUP 2	22	79.5909	7.229	1.541	*			*				*			
VAR209 PROTESTANT ETHIC					*			*							
GROUP 1	66	4.6069	0.559	0.069	*	1.54	0.189	*	-0.66	86	0.512	*	-0.59	30.60	0.559
GROUP 2	22	4.7033	0.694	0.148	*			*				*			

Computer Output Part 7G

Use of χ^2 Test: Two Levels of One Nominal Variable and Multilevels of Another Nominal Variable

```
        43 CROSSTABS      TABLES=VAR125 BY VAR220
        44 STATISTICS     1


ADSC 361 RESEARCH

FILE   NONAME   (CREATION DATE = 05/28/82)

* * * * * * * * * * * * * * * * *  C R O S S T A B U L A T I O N  O F  * * * * * * *
    VAR125    SEX                               BY   VAR220    GRADE ASPIRATION
* * * * * * * * * * * * * * * * * * * * * * * * * * * * * * * * * * * * * * * * * * * *

                     VAR220
           COUNT   I
           ROW PCT I                                                        ROW
           COL PCT I                                                        TOTAL
           TOT PCT I     1.I      2.I      3.I      4.I      5.I
   VAR125  --------I--------I--------I--------I--------I--------I
              1.  I     2  I     2  I    28  I    33  I     1  I     66
                  I   3.0  I   3.0  I  42.4  I  50.0  I   1.5  I   75.0
                  I 100.0  I  66.7  I  80.0  I  70.2  I 100.0  I
                  I   2.3  I   2.3  I  31.8  I  37.5  I   1.1  I
                 -I--------I--------I--------I--------I--------I
              2.  I     0  I     1  I     7  I    14  I     0  I     22
                  I   0.0  I   4.5  I  31.8  I  63.6  I   0.0  I   25.0
                  I   0.0  I  33.3  I  20.0  I  29.8  I   0.0  I
                  I   0.0  I   1.1  I   8.0  I  15.9  I   0.0  I
                 -I--------I--------I--------I--------I--------I
           COLUMN       2        3       35       47        1       88
           TOTAL      2.3      3.4     39.8     53.4      1.1    100.0

      6 OUT OF    10 ( 60.0%) OF THE VALID CELLS HAVE EXPECTED CELL FREQUENCY LESS THAN 5.0.
MINIMUM EXPECTED CELL FREQUENCY =  0.250
CHI SQUARE =      2.15224 WITH   4 DEGREES OF FREEDOM   SIGNIFICANCE =   0.7078
```

Because the variables in both (a) and (b) above are nominally scaled, the χ^2 test of independence—a nonparametric statistic—will be most appropriate to test the hypotheses. Let us take each hypothesis separately and examine it.

Hypothesis 2a The hypothesis can be stated in the null and in the alternate as follows:

H_0: Gender and grade aspiration are not related; that is, they are independent of each other.

H_A: Gender and grade aspiration are related; that is, they are not independent of each other.

The programming for and results of the χ^2 test are as in Computer Output Part 7G. Note that both the CROSSTABS and the STATISTICS cards are necessary for this test. The STATISTICS 1 card is the one that gives the results of the χ^2 test.

Interpretation of Results (CROSSTABS) The CROSSTABS tabulates how many male and female students (denoted by 1 and 2 at the extreme left column) were distributed across the five levels of grade aspiration for the course—A+, A, B+, B, and C (denoted by 1. 2. 3. 4. and 5. on the top row). The table shows the frequency distributions in terms of (1) the number of individuals in each cell; (2) this number as a percentage of the total number of the gender to which they belong; (3) as a percentage of the total number of both males and females responding to that particular grade description; and (4) as a percentage of all the respondents in the survey. Thus the first square contains a 2, which is the number of male respondents who aspired for an A+ grade. The next figure in that square, 3.0, denotes that these two males constituted 3 percent of all males; the figure 100.0 indicates that they formed 100 percent of all respondents (both males and females) who aspired for an A+; and the last figure, 2.3, means that these two males formed 2.3 percent of all the respondents (i.e., all 88 students). If you want to know how many aspired to a B in the course, look at column 4, which shows that this grade was desired by 33 men and 14 women (50 percent of the men and 63.6 percent of the women, respectively).

Interpretation of Results (χ^2 *Statistic*) The chi-square value is printed at the bottom of the computer output. It is 2.152, with 4 degrees of freedom. The significance level is .71. The degrees of freedom are arrived at by subtracting 1 from both the number of rows (R) and the number of columns (C), and multiplying the results, that is: $[(R - 1) \times (C - 1)]$. In this case, the figures are $(2 - 1) \times (5 - 1) = 4$ (the two rows represent the two genders and the five columns represent the grade levels). The chi-square value with 4 degrees of freedom has a probability or significance level of .71; this is far above the accepted level of significance (i.e., $p = .05$). Hence, we would accept the null hypothesis that they are independent. In other words, gender and grade aspiration are independent; there is no relationship between the two variables.

Hypothesis 2b The hypothesis that is being tested here, stated in the null and the alternate, is as follows:

H_0: Grade expectation (an ordinal-scale variable) is not related to grade aspiration (another ordinal-scale variable); that is, they are independent of each other.

H_A: Grade expectation and grade aspiration are related; that is, they are not independent of each other.

Computer Output Part 7H

Use of χ^2 Test: Multiple Levels of Two Variables

```
              45 CROSSTABS       TABLES=VAR220 BY VAR221
              46 STATISTICS      1
```

```
* * * * * * * * * * * * * * * *   C R O S S T A B U L A T I O N   O F   * * * * * * *
    VAR220    GRADE ASPIRATION                           BY  VAR221    GRADE EXPECTATION
* * * * * * * * * * * * * * * * * * * * * * * * * * * * * * * * * * * * * * * * * * *
```

	VAR221						
COUNT I ROW PCT I COL PCT I TOT PCT I	-2.I	1.I	2.I	3.I	4.I	5.I	ROW TOTAL
VAR220							
1. I I I I	0 I 0.0 I 0.0 I 0.0 I	0 I 0.0 I 0.0 I 0.0 I	1 I 50.0 I 5.0 I 1.1 I	1 I 50.0 I 2.2 I 1.1 I	0 I 0.0 I 0.0 I 0.0 I	0 I 0.0 I 0.0 I 0.0 I	2 2.3
2. I I I I	0 I 0.0 I 0.0 I 0.0 I	0 I 0.0 I 0.0 I 0.0 I	2 I 66.7 I 10.0 I 2.3 I	1 I 33.3 I 2.2 I 1.1 I	0 I 0.0 I 0.0 I 0.0 I	0 I 0.0 I 0.0 I 0.0 I	3 3.4
3. I I I I	1 I 2.9 I 100.0 I 1.1 I	1 I 2.9 I 100.0 I 1.1 I	14 I 40.0 I 70.0 I 15.9 I	18 I 51.4 I 39.1 I 20.5 I	1 I 2.9 I 5.6 I 1.1 I	0 I 0.0 I 0.0 I 0.0 I	35 39.8
4. I I I I	0 I 0.0 I 0.0 I 0.0 I	0 I 0.0 I 0.0 I 0.0 I	3 I 6.4 I 15.0 I 3.4 I	26 I 55.3 I 56.5 I 29.5 I	17 I 36.2 I 94.4 I 19.3 I	1 I 2.1 I 50.0 I 1.1 I	47 53.4
5. I I I I	0 I 0.0 I 0.0 I 0.0 I	0 I 0.0 I 0.0 I 0.0 I	0 I 0.0 I 0.0 I 0.0 I	0 I 0.0 I 0.0 I 0.0 I	0 I 0.0 I 0.0 I 0.0 I	1 I 100.0 I 50.0 I 1.1 I	1 1.1
COLUMN TOTAL	1 1.1	1 1.1	20 22.7	46 52.3	18 20.5	2 2.3	88 100.0

```
   24 OUT OF     30 ( 80.0%) OF THE VALID CELLS HAVE EXPECTED CELL FREQUENCY LESS THAN 5.0.
MINIMUM EXPECTED CELL FREQUENCY =  0.011
CHI SQUARE =    72.53378 WITH  20 DEGREES OF FREEDOM    SIGNIFICANCE =   0.0000
```

The programming for and results of this analysis are as shown in Computer Output Part 7H.

Interpretation of Results (χ^2 *Statistic*)   Note that the chi-square value of 72.53, with 20 degrees of freedom, is highly significant (p = .00001). This shows that grade aspirations at the beginning of the course and grade expectations near the end of the course are not independent of each other. In other words, we would reject the null, retain the alternate, and conclude that grade aspirations do influence grade expectations. Note also that one of the respondents who had not answered the grade expectation question has been assigned a value of -2 by the computer (preprogrammed).

Hypothesis 3: *r* to *z* Transformations of the Two Correlations

The next hypothesis stated in the null and alternate would be as follows:

H_0: The correlations of satisfaction and performance for the male students and the female students will not be significantly different.

H_A: There will be a significant difference in the correlation of performance and satisfaction for male as opposed to female students.

To do this, the computer was programmed to split the sample into two groups (i.e., males and females) through the use of a SELECT IF statement, as can be seen in Computer Output Part 7I. A Pearson correlation between satisfaction and performance for each of the two groups was then obtained. The sample correlations were transformed to *z* values using Fisher's logarithmic-transformation formula, and the *z* values were used to test for the significant differences in the correlations.

The programming for and the results of the correlation analysis for the two subgroups is as shown in Computer Output Part 7I.

Interpretation of Results   As can be seen, the correlation between satisfaction and performance for the male students ($n = 66$) is .277 ($p = .01$), and for the female students it is .478 ($p = .012$). Though there is a numerical difference in the two correlation coefficients (.277 and .478), are they really significantly different? In other words, what is the true probability of their being different? The Fisher's *r* to *z* formula will help us determine this. The formula is as follows:

$$z = \frac{r_1 - r_2}{\sqrt{\frac{1}{n_1 - 3} + \frac{1}{n_2 - 3}}}$$

where r_1 and r_2 are the two correlations, n_1 is the sample size relating to the first correlation, and n_2 is the sample size relating to the second correlation.

$$z = \frac{.277 - .478}{\sqrt{\frac{1}{66 - 3} + \frac{1}{22 - 3}}}$$

$$z = .776$$

For a .05 level of significance, the critical *z* value is 1.96. Because the *z* value obtained here (.776) is much lower than the critical value of 1.96, we

Computer Output Part 7I

Correlation Between Two Variables for Two Subgroups

```
                    55 *SELECT IF      (VAR 125=1)
                    56 PEARSON CORR    VAR121 WITH VAR207

   ***** PEARSON CORR PROBLEM REQUIRES      48 BYTES WORKSPACE *****


ADSC 361 RESEARCH

FILE   NONAME   (CREATION DATE = 05/28/82)

- - - - - - - - - - - P E A R S O N   C O R R E L A T I O N   C O E F F I C I E N T S


            VAR207

VAR121       0.2771
            (   66)
            P=0.012


(COEFFICIENT / (CASES) / SIGNIFICANCE)




                    57 *SELECT IF      (VAR 125=2)
                    58 PEARSON CORR    VAR121 WITH VAR207

   ***** PEARSON CORR PROBLEM REQUIRES      48 BYTES WORKSPACE *****


ADSC 361 RESEARCH

FILE   NONAME   (CREATION DATE = 05/28/82)

- - - - - - - - - - - P E A R S O N   C O R R E L A T I O N   C O E F F I C I E N T S


            VAR207

VAR121       0.4782
            (   22)
            P=0.012


(COEFFICIENT / (CASES) / SIGNIFICANCE)
```

would accept the null hypothesis that there are no differences in how performance and satisfaction are correlated for male as opposed to female students.

Hypothesis 4: Use of ANOVA

The professor's fourth hypothesis can be stated in the null and alternate as follows:

H_0: Student satisfactions with the course will not differ for students who have different grade expectations.

H_A: Students who have different grade expectations will differ in their experienced satisfaction with the course.

In this case, grade expectations is a qualitative or discrete variable (can be treated as being an ordinal scale), but the satisfaction variable is measured on a Likert-type scale and is a quantitative or continuous variable. Where this is the case, we could use the analysis of variance procedure, or ANOVA as it is called, and use the F statistic produced by this test to determine whether or not the hypothesis is substantiated.

The F statistic is actually the ratio of variances between groups and within groups. If between-group differences are greater than within-group differences for the variable under consideration, a significant F statistic is produced. This would imply that there is a significant difference in the means of the groups on the variable of interest. Note that a t test is used when we are interested in finding whether there is a significant difference in the means of two groups. The ANOVA procedure is also a test of mean differences, but it is used when we are interested in testing for significant differences in the means of more than two groups. The null hypothesis in the case of ANOVA where, say, six groups are involved is as follows:

H_0: $\mu_1 = \mu_2 = \mu_3 = \mu_4 = \mu_5 = \mu_6$

where μ_1 to μ_6 represent the means of six groups (at six different job levels, or six different educational levels, etc.), on a quantitative dependent variable of interest such as involvement or satisfaction.

The programming for and results of the ANOVA procedure to test hypothesis 4 are shown in Computer Output Part 7J. Note that the professor tried to examine if there were any significant differences in the extent of satisfaction experienced with the course among the four groups of students who had different grade expectations toward the end of the semester—those expecting to get A, B, C, and D. This is signified by VAR221(1,4). If we had six groups, we would have specified the lowest and highest numbers for these groups, that is (1,6).

Interpretation of Results The first column, SOURCE OF VARIATION, has MAIN EFFECTS, VAR221, and EXPLAINED printed. All three refer to the independent variable, grade expectation. The term RESIDUAL in the same column refers to the effects not explained by the independent variable.

The second column, SUM OF SQUARES, is a measure of variation. The total variation in the dependent variable, satisfaction, is 46.966, which is derived from two sources:

1. Between-group variation, or that which is explained by the independent variable—grade expectation—which is 4.886.
2. Within-group variation, or that which we cannot explain, called the residual or error sum of squares, which is 42.08.

Computer Output Part 7J

The ANOVA Procedure

```
                    47 ANOVA          VAR207 BY VAR221(1,4)/

'ANOVA' PROBLEM REQUIRES      268 BYTES OF SPACE.


ADSC 361 RESEARCH

FILE   NONAME   (CREATION DATE = 05/28/82)

* * * * * * * * * * A N A L Y S I S   O F   V A R I A N C E * * * * * * * * * * *
            VAR207    GLOBAL SATISFACTION
         BY VAR221    GRADE EXPECTATION
* * * * * * * * * * * * * * * * * * * * * * * * * * * * * * * * * * * * * * * * *
```

SOURCE OF VARIATION	SUM OF SQUARES	DF	MEAN SQUARE	F	SIGNIF OF F
MAIN EFFECTS	4.886	3	1.629	3.135	0.030
VAR221	4.886	3	1.629	3.135	0.030
EXPLAINED	4.886	3	1.629	3.135	0.030
RESIDUAL	42.080	81	0.520		
TOTAL	46.966	84	0.559		

```
      88 CASES WERE PROCESSED.
      3 CASES (  3.4 PCT) WERE MISSING.
```

DF in the third column refers to the degrees of freedom, and each source of variation has associated degrees of freedom. For the EXPLAINED variance, $DF = (k - 1)$, where k is the number of groups or levels. Because there were four different levels of grade expectations, we have $(4 - 1) = 3$ DF for the independent variable. The degrees of freedom for residual sum of squares equals $N - K$, where N is the total number of respondents and K is the total number of groups. Whereas the actual degrees of freedom for the residual should have been $(88 - 4) = 84$, there were three cases that had missing values because of the reduction in the number of categories for grade expectations in this analysis. The value for residual degrees of freedom thus becomes $(85 - 4) = 81$.

The mean square for each source of variation (column 4 of the results) is derived by dividing the sum of squares by its associated DF. Finally, the F value itself equals the explained mean square divided by the residual mean square.

$$F = \frac{MS \text{ explained}}{MS \text{ residual}}$$

For this hypothesis, $F = 3.135$. This F value is significant at the .03 level. This implies that there are significant differences in the mean satisfaction levels of the four groups with different grade expectations, and that the null hypothesis can be *rejected* with 97 percent confidence. We can thus conclude that students with the four different levels of grade expectations do not have the same average level of satisfaction with the class. In other words, hypothesis 4 is substantiated.

The *F* test used here is called the overall or omnibus *F* test. To determine among which groups the true differences lie, separate *t* tests taking two groups at a time could be done. This would reveal which particular groups tend to feel differential satisfaction. The difference could lie between those who expected an A and those who expected to get a D, between those who expected A and those who expected B, or between some other pair. Doing multiple *t* tests when there are several group comparisons introduces Type I error problems. To avoid this, several other types of tests can be done post hoc to detect which groups have significant mean differences. Among such are the Newman-Kuels test, Duncan Multiple-Range test, and the Bonferonni Inequality test.

Research Question 5: Use of Stepwise and Simple Multiple Regression Analysis

Recall that the last research question had two subparts as follows:

1. To what extent would the five independent variables of starting GPA, work ethic values, extent of involvement, experienced stress, and perceived course characteristics influence student performance, and what would be their order of importance in explaining the variance in performance?

2. To what extent would the same five independent variables explain the variance in student satisfaction with the course? The professor did not necessarily seem to be interested in determining the order of importance of these variables.

Multiple Regression Analysis

When we want to assess the amount of variance explained in the dependent variable by a number of predictors (more than one), and/or we want to know which variable(s) contribute more to the variance, we can do a multiple regression analysis to answer these questions, provided we have a large enough sample. As a rule of thumb, we should have at least 10 times the number of people (sample size) as we have predictors. For example, if we have six predictors, the sample size should be, at the very least, 60 and more would be better.

Multiple regression analysis helps to predict the variance in the criterion variable taking into account the joint linear influences of the several predictors. Recall from Unit 3 that the criterion variable is the same as the dependent variable and the predictors are none other than the indepen-

Computer Output Part 7K

Programming for Stepwise and Simple Multiple Regression Analysis

```
48  REGRESSION      VARIABLES=VAR121,VAR207,VAR122,VAR201,VAR209,
49                  VAR211,VAR218/
50                  REGRESSION=VAR121 WITH VAR122,VAR201,VAR209,
51                  VAR211,VAR218(3)/
52                  REGRESSION=VAR207 WITH VAR122,VAR201,VAR209,
53                  VAR211,VAR218(2)/
54  STATISTICS      1,2
```

ADSC 361 RESEARCH

FILE   NONAME   (CREATION DATE = 05/28/82)

VARIABLE	MEAN	STANDARD DEV	CASES
VAR121	77.7614	7.6804	88
VAR207	5.3301	0.7681	88
VAR122	3.0455	1.1235	88
VAR201	5.1629	1.1662	88
VAR209	4.6310	0.5929	88
VAR211	5.8920	1.0757	88
VAR218	3.1414	0.5276	88

CORRELATION COEFFICIENTS

	VAR121	VAR207	VAR122	VAR201	VAR209	VAR211	VAR218
VAR121	1.00000	0.32295	0.54741	0.38123	0.05816	0.27139	-0.13057
VAR207	0.32295	1.00000	0.01578	0.52555	0.31370	0.51566	-0.49528
VAR122	0.54741	0.01578	1.00000	0.01914	0.22438	0.07702	-0.02174
VAR201	0.38123	0.52555	0.01914	1.00000	0.28858	0.45244	-0.10394
VAR209	0.05816	0.31370	0.22438	0.28858	1.00000	0.45349	-0.20023
VAR211	0.27139	0.51566	0.07702	0.45244	0.45349	1.00000	-0.34148
VAR218	-0.13057	-0.49528	-0.02174	-0.10394	-0.20023	-0.34148	1.00000

dent variables. A stepwise multiple regression analysis would help to determine the order of importance of the predictors because the variables will enter the regression model one at a time, in the order in which they exert influence on the criterion variable after the effects of the previously entered variables have been accounted for. Hence, to answer research question (1), a stepwise multiple regression analysis was done, and for research question (2), a simple multiple regression analysis, where all the predictors enter the model simultaneously, was done.

The programming for multiple regression analysis is as in Computer Output Part 7K. Note that by asking for statistics 1 and 2, we are also able to get the means and standard deviations and the Pearson correlation among all the variables in the analysis, if needed.

The first REGRESSION card specifies all the variables included in the analysis (dependent and independent), and ends with a slash /. The second

REGRESSION card, which starts in column 16, first specifies the dependent variable and then lists the independent variables after the word WITH. The odd number (3) at the end of the card indicates to the computer that a stepwise regression analysis should be done. Any other odd number such as 9, 7, 5, would do the same. The card ends with a slash / as shown in Part 7K.

Note that the next REGRESSION card, which regresses satisfaction (VAR207) with the independent variables ends with a (2)—an even number—before the ending slash. This indicates that a stepwise regression is not called for. Any other even number would do as well. If no number is put at all, the computer would perform a simple regression analysis.

Note also that once all the variables that could possibly be used in the regression lists are entered in the very first REGRESSION card, several REGRESSION program statements beginning in column 16 can be done.

Some Important Points to Understand in Multiple Regression Analysis Outputs

In order to explain a few key issues in regression analysis, a small section of the computer results of the analysis to our research question is shown in Computer Output Part 7L.

Let us first list and understand some of the important factors that we should be looking for in the results of a multiple regression analysis.

1. The variables (both dependent and independent) are labeled in the printout with the VAR number and the variable name. The label or the variable name will not be printed if we do not have a VAR LABELS card in our data deck.

2. In a stepwise multiple regression analysis, the most important variable that influences the dependent variable will enter the model at the first step; the second most influential variable will enter the model in the second step, and so on. If a stepwise analysis is not asked for, all the predictor variables will enter in one step.

3. The R SQUARE—the second item on the extreme left of the printout at each step—shows the proportion of variance explained in the dependent variable by the variables in the model. For instance, in step 1, the R^2 or the variance explained in performance by the starting GPA is 30 percent (R square, .29966).

4. The DF column in the printout contains two figures. The numerator indicates the number of predictors in the regression model at each step and the denominator denotes $(n - k - 1)$, where n is the sample size and k is the number of predictors in the model.

Computer Output Part 7L

Partial Results from a Regression Analysis to Explain Some Features

```
* * * * * * * * * * * * * * * * * * M U L T I P L E   R E G R E S S I O N * * * * * * * * * * * * * * * * * *
```

DEPENDENT VARIABLE.. VAR121   COURSE PERFORMANCE

VARIABLE LIST 1
REGRESSION LIST 1

VARIABLE(S) ENTERED ON STEP NUMBER 1.. VAR122   STARTING GRADE POINT AVERAGE

MULTIPLE R	0.54741		ANALYSIS OF VARIANCE	DF	SUM OF SQUARES	MEAN SQUARE	F
R SQUARE	0.29966		REGRESSION	1.	1537.84770	1537.84770	36.79736
ADJUSTED R SQUARE	0.29152		RESIDUAL	86.	3594.14094	41.79234	
STANDARD ERROR	6.46470						

```
-------------- VARIABLES IN THE EQUATION --------------      -------------- VARIABLES NOT IN THE EQUATION --------------
```

VARIABLE	B	BETA	STD ERROR B	F		VARIABLE	BETA IN	PARTIAL	TOLERANCE	F
VAR122	3.742136	0.54741	0.61689	36.797		VAR201	0.37089	0.44311	0.99963	20.767
(CONSTANT)	66.36486					VAR209	-0.06809	-0.07929	0.94966	0.538
						VAR211	0.23059	0.27473	0.99407	6.939
						VAR218	-0.11873	-0.14184	0.99953	1.745

```
* * * * * * * * * * * * * * * * * * * * * * * * * * * * * * * * * * * * * * * * * * * * * * * * * * * * * * * *
```

5. The *F* statistic at the extreme right of the printout indicates whether or not the explained variance is significant. The *p* value for the *F* statistic could be obtained from an *F*-distribution table (see end of this book) with the degrees of freedom shown for the step. For instance, with 1 and 86 degrees of freedom at the first step, the *F* value required for *p* = .05, is 3.96, as can be observed from the *F* tables. The *F* value of 36.797 at the first step is highly significant (*p* = .00001).

6. Under VARIABLES IN THE EQUATION section, the BETA values and the *F* value attached to each beta are important. The beta indicates the standardized regression weight of each variable as it influences the dependent variable. The BETA can be thought of as the pull or the influence a variable exerts on the dependent variable. The *F* value attached to it signifies whether or not the influence of the particular variable is significant. The degrees of freedom (DF) attached to each BETA would be (1,($n - 1 - 1$)). With 1, and 86 degrees of freedom for this sample, the *F* value required for significance is 3.96. Hence, any *F* value equal to or above 3.96 for this particular sample will be significant.

Having understood some of these important things to look for in a regression analysis, let us now interpret the results of the computer output.

The results of the stepwise multiple regression analysis to determine the importance of the independent variables in explaining the variance in student performance is as shown on Computer Output Part 7M.

Interpretation of Results:
Stepwise Multiple
Regression Analysis

As can be seen, the starting grade point average (VAR122), which entered the model at the first step, is the most important variable explaining the variance in student performance. This variable explains about 30 percent of the variance in students' course performance (*R* square, .29966). The *F* value of 36.79 with DF (1,86) is highly significant (*p* = .00001).

The next variable to enter the regression model is course involvement (VAR201). Starting GPA and course involvement together significantly explain 44 percent of the variance in the criterion variable (*R* square, .43717). Thus, course involvement explains 14 percent of the variance over and above that explained by starting GPA (.44 − .30).

The third variable to enter the regression equation is the protestant work ethic (VAR209), which explains an additional 3 percent in the variance in performance over and above that explained by the first two variables (.47 − .44).

Computer Output Part 7M

Results of Stepwise Regression Analysis with Performance as the Dependent Variable

* * * * * * * * * * M U L T I P L E   R E G R E S S I O N * * * * * * * * * * * * * * * * * *

DEPENDENT VARIABLE.. VAR121   COURSE PERFORMANCE

VARIABLE(S) ENTERED ON STEP NUMBER 1.. VAR122   STARTING GRADE POINT AVERAGE

MULTIPLE R	0.54741	
R SQUARE	0.29966	
ADJUSTED R SQUARE	0.29152	
STANDARD ERROR	6.46470	

ANALYSIS OF VARIANCE	DF	SUM OF SQUARES	MEAN SQUARE	F
REGRESSION	1.	1537.84770	1537.84770	36.79736
RESIDUAL	86.	3594.14094	41.79234	

------- VARIABLES IN THE EQUATION -------

VARIABLE	B	BETA	STD ERROR B	F
VAR122	3.742136	0.54741	0.61689	36.797
(CONSTANT)	66.36486			

------- VARIABLES NOT IN THE EQUATION -------

VARIABLE	BETA IN	PARTIAL	TOLERANCE	F
VAR201	0.37089	0.44311	0.99963	20.767
VAR209	-0.06809	-0.07929	0.94966	0.538
VAR211	0.23055	0.27473	0.99407	6.939
VAR218	-0.11873	-0.14184	0.99953	1.745

* *

VARIABLE(S) ENTERED ON STEP NUMBER 2.. VAR201   COURSE INVOLVEMENT

MULTIPLE R	0.66119	
R SQUARE	0.43717	
ADJUSTED R SQUARE	0.42393	
STANDARD ERROR	5.82938	

ANALYSIS OF VARIANCE	DF	SUM OF SQUARES	MEAN SQUARE	F
REGRESSION	2.	2243.54633	1121.77316	33.01112
RESIDUAL	85.	2888.44231	33.98167	

------- VARIABLES IN THE EQUATION -------

VARIABLE	B	BETA	STD ERROR B	F
VAR122	3.693609	0.54031	0.55637	44.073
VAR201	2.442519	0.37089	0.53598	20.767
(CONSTANT)	53.90222			

------- VARIABLES NOT IN THE EQUATION -------

VARIABLE	BETA IN	PARTIAL	TOLERANCE	F
VAR209	-0.19579	-0.24326	0.86880	5.283
VAR211	0.07838	0.09289	0.79063	0.731
VAR218	-0.08118	-0.10761	0.98881	0.984

```
* * * * * * * * * * * * * * * * * * * * *  M U L T I P L E   R E G R E S S I O N  * * * * * * * * * * * * * * * * * * * * *     VARIABLE LIST  1
                                                                                                                                 REGRESSION LIST  1
DEPENDENT VARIABLE..    VAR121     COURSE PERFORMANCE

VARIABLE(S) ENTERED ON STEP NUMBER  3..    VAR209      PROTESTANT ETHIC

MULTIPLE R          0.68591                      ANALYSIS OF VARIANCE      DF        SUM OF SQUARES       MEAN SQUARE           F
R SQUARE            0.47047                      REGRESSION                 3.          2414.46962         804.82321        24.87753
ADJUSTED R SQUARE   0.45156                      RESIDUAL                  84.          2717.51901          32.35142
STANDARD ERROR      5.68783

------------ VARIABLES IN THE EQUATION ------------                   ------ VARIABLES NOT IN THE EQUATION ------

VARIABLE         B          BETA       STD ERROR B       F              VARIABLE      BETA IN      PARTIAL     TOLERANCE      F

VAR122        3.986639     0.58318      0.55763       51.112            VAR211       0.17941       0.20353      0.68147      3.587
VAR201        2.809218     0.42657      0.54676       26.398            VAR218      -0.11781      -0.15839      0.95712      2.136
VAR209       -2.536463    -0.19579      1.10351        5.283
(CONSTANT)   62.86289

* * * * * * * * * * * * * * * * * * * * * * * * * * * * * * * * * * * * * * * * * * * * * * * * * * * * * * * * * * * * * * *

VARIABLE(S) ENTERED ON STEP NUMBER  4..    VAR211      COURSE JOB CHARACTERISTICS

MULTIPLE R          0.70172                      ANALYSIS OF VARIANCE      DF        SUM OF SQUARES       MEAN SQUARE           F
R SQUARE            0.49241                      REGRESSION                 4.          2527.04254         631.76064        20.12945
ADJUSTED R SQUARE   0.46795                      RESIDUAL                  83.          2604.94610          31.38489
STANDARD ERROR      5.60222

------------ VARIABLES IN THE EQUATION ------------                   ------ VARIABLES NOT IN THE EQUATION ------

VARIABLE         B          BETA       STD ERROR B       F              VARIABLE      BETA IN      PARTIAL     TOLERANCE      F

VAR122        3.997940     0.58483      0.54927       52.979            VAR218      -0.08068      -0.10603      0.87657      0.932
VAR201        2.395304     0.36372      0.58119       16.986
VAR209       -3.360321    -0.25939      1.17072        8.239
VAR211        1.280994     0.17941      0.67638        3.587
(CONSTANT)   61.23306
```

251

Computer Output Part 7M—(Continued)

ADSC 361 RESEARCH

* * * * * * * * * * * * * * * * * * * M U L T I P L E   R E G R E S S I O N * * * * * * * * * * * * * * * * * *

DEPENDENT VARIABLE..   VAR121   COURSE PERFORMANCE   VARIABLE LIST   1
                                                                                                        REGRESSION LIST 1

VARIABLE(S) ENTERED ON STEP NUMBER   5..   VAR218   COURSE STRESS

MULTIPLE R	0.70577	ANALYSIS OF VARIANCE	DF	SUM OF SQUARES	MEAN SQUARE	F
R SQUARE	0.49812	REGRESSION	5.	2556.32647	511.26529	16.27688
ADJUSTED R SQUARE	0.46751	RESIDUAL	82.	2575.66216	31.41051	
STANDARD ERROR	5.60451					

------------ VARIABLES IN THE EQUATION ------------   ---------- VARIABLES NOT IN THE EQUATION ----------

VARIABLE	B	BETA	STD ERROR B	F		VARIABLE	BETA IN	PARTIAL	TOLERANCE	F
VAR122	4.008354	0.58635	0.54960	53.191						
VAR201	2.433131	0.36947	0.58274	17.433						
VAR209	-3.432544	-0.26496	1.17358	8.555						
VAR211	1.082935	0.15167	0.70706	2.346						
VAR218	-1.174560	-0.08068	1.21646	0.932						
(CONSTANT)	66.19727									

MAXIMUM STEP REACHED

STATISTICS WHICH CANNOT BE COMPUTED ARE PRINTED AS ALL NINES.

* * * * * * * * * * * * * * * * * * * M U L T I P L E   R E G R E S S I O N * * * * * * * * * * * * * * * * * *

DEPENDENT VARIABLE..   VAR121   COURSE PERFORMANCE   VARIABLE LIST   1
                                                                                                        REGRESSION LIST 1

SUMMARY TABLE

VARIABLE		MULTIPLE R	R SQUARE	RSQ CHANGE	SIMPLE R	B	BETA
VAR122	STARTING GRADE POINT AVERAGE	0.54741	0.29966	0.29966	0.54741	4.008354	0.58635
VAR201	COURSE INVOLVEMENT	0.66119	0.43717	0.13751	0.38123	2.433131	0.36947
VAR209	PROTESTANT ETHIC	0.68591	0.47047	0.03331	0.05816	-3.432544	-0.26496
VAR211	COURSE JOB CHARACTERISTICS	0.70172	0.49241	0.02194	0.27139	1.082935	0.15167
VAR218	COURSE STRESS	0.70577	0.49812	0.00571	-0.13057	-1.174560	-0.08068
(CONSTANT)						66.19727	

Course characteristics (VAR211) is the next important variable, adding 2 percent more to the variance. Stress is the last variable to enter the model. The additional variance explained by stress is very little, only .006 (.498 − .492). The summary table at the end also shows the change in the R^2 or the contribution of each variable to the explained variance in performance (see RSQ change). The F values attached to the BETAs in the table, just before the summary table, indicate the significance of the influence of the independent variables. For an F to be significant with DF = (1,86), its value should be at least 3.96. Therefore, only the first three BETAs—which have F values of 53.19, 17.43, and 8.56—are significant beyond the .01 level [F value for .01 level of significance with DF = (1,86) = 6.96]. An interesting fact, though, is that belief in the protestant ethic value has a significant negative beta weight. That is, its influence on performance is negative. In other words, those with high work ethic values did not perform very well—for whatever reason.

The last two BETAs with F values of 2.35 and .93 are not significant. In other words, starting GPA, involvement in the course, and protestant ethic significantly influence student performance; the course characteristics and stress experienced do not influence performance in the course.

The answer to research question 5, part (1), based on the results of the regression analysis, is that the five independent variables explain about 50 percent of the variance in course performance. The starting grade point average is the most important of the five predictors, explaining about 30 percent of the variance with a significant beta weight of .59. The second most important predictor is course involvement, which explains an additional 14 percent of the variance, with a significant beta weight of .37. The third most important and significant predictor is the protestant ethic variable, with a beta weight of −.26. This negative beta weight indicates that the people who had high work ethic values did not perform well in the course, or that those who performed well in the course did not have high work ethic values. The other two variables—course characteristics and stress—were not significant in explaining the variance in performance.

Results of the Regression Analysis for the Dependent Variable Satisfaction

The results of the analysis regressing the five predictor variables against the criterion variable, satisfaction, are shown in Computer Output Part 7N.

Interpretation of Results

As can be seen from the results, the five independent variables explained 50 percent of the variance in satisfaction (R^2, .50462). The F value required

Computer Output Part 7N
Results of Multiple Regression Analysis with Satisfaction as the Dependent Variable

* * * * * * * * * * * * * * * * M U L T I P L E   R E G R E S S I O N * * * * * * * * * * * * * * * *

VARIABLE LIST   1
REGRESSION LIST 2

DEPENDENT VARIABLE..   VAR207   GLOBAL SATISFACTION

VARIABLE(S) ENTERED ON STEP NUMBER 1..

VAR218	COURSE STRESS
VAR122	STARTING GRADE POINT AVERAGE
VAR201	COURSE INVOLVEMENT
VAR209	PROTESTANT ETHIC
VAR211	COURSE JOB CHARACTERISTICS

MULTIPLE R	0.71037
R SQUARE	0.50462
ADJUSTED R SQUARE	0.47441
STANDARD ERROR	0.55682

ANALYSIS OF VARIANCE	DF	SUM OF SQUARES	MEAN SQUARE	F
REGRESSION	5.	25.89837	5.17967	16.70591
RESIDUAL	82.	25.42413	0.31005	

------------ VARIABLES IN THE EQUATION ------------   ----------- VARIABLES NOT IN THE EQUATION -----------

VARIABLE	B	BETA	STD ERROR B	F	VARIABLE	BETA IN	PARTIAL	TOLERANCE	F
VAR218	-0.5547513	-0.38106	0.12086	21.069					
VAR122	-0.1682804D-01	-0.02462	0.05460	0.095					
VAR201	0.2545970	0.38659	0.05790	19.337					
VAR209	0.5706014D-01	0.04404	0.11660	0.239					
VAR211	0.1374820	0.19255	0.07025	3.830					
(CONSTANT)	4.735259								

ALL VARIABLES ARE IN THE EQUATION

STATISTICS WHICH CANNOT BE COMPUTED ARE PRINTED AS ALL NINES.

* * * * * * * * * * * * * * * * M U L T I P L E   R E G R E S S I O N * * * * * * * * * * * * * * * *

VARIABLE LIST   1
REGRESSION LIST 2

DEPENDENT VARIABLE..   VAR207   GLOBAL SATISFACTION

SUMMARY TABLE

VARIABLE		MULTIPLE R	R SQUARE	RSQ CHANGE	SIMPLE R	B	BETA
VAR218	COURSE STRESS	0.49528	0.24530	0.24530	-0.49528	-0.5547513	-0.38106
VAR122	STARTING GRADE POINT AVERAGE	0.49530	0.24532	0.00003	0.01578	-0.1682804D-01	-0.02462
VAR201	COURSE INVOLVEMENT	0.68739	0.47251	0.22718	0.52555	0.2545970	0.38659
VAR209	PROTESTANT ETHIC	0.69389	0.48148	0.00897	0.31370	0.5706014D-01	0.04404
VAR211	COURSE JOB CHARACTERISTICS	0.71037	0.50462	0.02314	0.51566	0.1374820	0.19255
(CONSTANT)						4.735259	

with DF $= (5, 82)$ for significance is 2.32. The F value for this regression analysis is 16.71, which is far above the 2.32 required for $p = .05$. The results are significant at $p = .00001$. If we look at the significance of the individual beta weights, course involvement with a beta weight of .39 ($F = 19.33$; $p = .0001$), and stress with a beta weight of $-.38$ ($F = 21.07$; $p = .0001$), are both significant. Course characteristics, protestant ethic, and starting GPA, with betas of .19, .04, and $-.02$, are all not significant. Their F values are all under 3.96, which is the value required to attain significance with DF $= (1, 86)$.

In answer to the research question 5, part (2), the five variables together explained 50 percent of the variance in student satisfaction.

Review of the Analysis of Research on Research Methods

In summary, the professor who wanted to find out specific information relating to the attitudinal and behavioral responses of the students using some demographic, personality, and course characteristic variables, performed the following types of data analysis:

1. First, Cronbach's alpha and split-half reliabilities for all the measures used were tested. Those variables that did not have sufficient reliability were excluded from further analysis.

2. A feel for the data was obtained from the condescriptive routine and the Pearson correlation matrix.

3. Frequency distributions were obtained for the demographic variables.

4. Several of the hypotheses were tested, and research questions answered, by applying appropriate statistical tests and analysis. More specifically, the following were used:

    a. t Tests.

    b. χ^2 Tests.

    c. r to z Transformations.

    d. ANOVA.

    e. Stepwise and simple multiple regression analysis.

For those who would like to use the SAS program instead of the SPSS program, the Job cards and the cards necessary to set up the different procedures are illustrated as follows.

SET-UP FOR SAS PROGRAMMING

```
Col.
1

//(Same first card as for SPSS)

//▲EXEC▲SAS79

//SAS79.SYSIN▲DD▲*

DATA▲▲ADSC361▲RESEARCH;

INPUT▲VAR001-VAR126;

VAR201=(VAR003+VAR004+VAR006+VAR008+VAR011+VAR013)/6;
VAR202=(VAR005+VAR007+VAR009+VAR010+VAR012)/5;
VAR203=(VAR014+VAR018+VAR022+VAR023+VAR024+VAR025+VAR026+VAR027)/8;
VAR204=(VAR015+VAR019+VAR020+VAR021+VAR028)/5;
VAR205=(VAR017+VAR029+VAR030+VAR031)/4;
VAR206=(VAR032+VAR033+VAR034)/3;
VAR207=(VAR203+VAR204+VAR205+VAR206+VAR016)/5;
VAR209=(VAR045+VAR046+VAR047+VAR048+VAR049+VAR050+VAR051+VAR052+
    VAR053+VAR054+VAR055+VAR056+(8-VAR057)+VAR058+(8-VAR059)+
        VAR060+VAR061+VAR062+VAR063)/19;
VAR211=(VAR078+VAR079+VAR080+VAR082+VAR083)/5;
VAR214=((8-VAR087)+(8-VAR091)+VAR095+VAR099+(8-VAR103))/5;
VAR217=((8-VAR089)+VAR093+(8-VAR097)+(8-VAR101)+(8-VAR105))/5;
VAR218=(VAR106+VAR107+VAR108+VAR109+VAR110+VAR111+VAR112+VAR113+
    VAR114)/9;
VAR219=(32-(VAR115+VAR116+VAR117+VAR118))/4;
VAR220=(5-VAR119);
VAR221=(5-VAR120);
IF VAR122=0 THEN VAR122=1;
LABEL VAR122=STARTING GPA;
LABEL VAR125=GENDER;
LABEL VAR121=PERFORMANCE;
LABEL VAR124=INITIAL STAT MARKS;
LABEL VAR201=INVOLVEMENT;
LABEL VAR202=SENSE OF COMPETENCE;
LABEL VAR207=SATISFACTION;
LABEL VAR209=PROTESTANT WORK ETHIC;
LABEL VAR211=COURSE CHARACTERISTICS;
LABEL VAR214=NEED FOR ACHIEVEMENT;
LABEL VAR217=NEED FOR DOMINANCE;
LABEL VAR218=STRESS;
LABEL VAR219=SELF ESTEEM;
LABEL VAR220=GRADE ASPIRATION;
LABEL VAR221=EXPECTED GRADE;
CARDS;
        { DATA CARDS }
```

	Col. 1
<u>For Frequencies</u>:	PROC▲FREQ;
	TABLES▲VAR001▲VAR122▲VAR125▲VAR220▲VAR221;
<u>For Histograms</u>:	PROC▲CHART;
	VBAR▲VAR125▲VAR122;
<u>For Means</u>:	PROC▲MEANS;
	VAR▲VAR201▲VAR207▲VAR121;
<u>For Pearson</u> <u>Correlations</u>:	PROC▲CORR;
	VAR▲VAR201▲VAR202▲VAR207▲VAR209▲VAR211▲
	VAR214▲VAR217▲VAR218;
<u>For TTEST</u>	PROC▲TTEST;
	CLASS▲VAR125;
	VAR▲VAR121▲VAR122▲VAR124▲VAR201▲VAR202▲VAR207▲
	VAR209▲VAR211▲VAR214▲VAR217▲VAR218▲VAR219;
<u>For X^2 Test</u>:	PROC▲FREQ;
	TABLES▲VAR125*VAR220/CHISQ;
	TABLES▲VAR220*VAR221/CHISQ;
<u>For ANOVA</u>:	PROC▲ANOVA;
	CLASSES▲VAR220▲VAR221;
	MODEL▲VAR207=VAR220;
	MODEL▲VAR207=VAR221;
<u>For Multiple</u> <u>Regression Analysis</u>:	PROC▲SYSREG;
	MODEL▲VAR121=VAR201▲VAR207▲VAR211▲VAR218▲
	VAR214▲VAR209;
<u>For Stepwise Multiple</u> <u>Regression Analysis</u>:	PROC▲STEPWISE;
	MODEL▲VAR121=VAR201▲VAR207▲VAR211▲VAR218▲
	VAR214▲VAR209;
	/*
	//

SUMMARY

In this unit, we covered the procedure for analyzing data after they have been collected. By means of an example, we saw the steps necessary to get the data ready for analysis—editing, coding, categorizing, and punching data on cards. We then saw how the SPSS program is set up. Through the example of the research on research methods course, we saw various statistical analyses and tests used to examine different research questions and hypotheses. We also saw how the computer results are interpreted. The setup for an SAS program to do the same routines was also shown.

In the next unit we will learn how to write a research report after the data have been analyzed and the results interpreted.

SUPPLEMENTAL READINGS

The following topic references will guide you to seek more information.

Topic	Reference	Chapter	Page
Editing data	Clover & Balsley (1979)	8	170–171
	Emory (1980)	12	369–371
Handling blank responses	Clover & Balsley (1979)	10	236
	Emory (1980)	12	369
Statistical analysis of data	Emory (1980)	13	405–455
Hypotheses testing	Emory (1980)	13	405–454
	Kerlinger (1973)	12	198–213
	Roscoe (1975)	19, 20	170–186
Correlations	Clover & Balsley (1979)	11	251–262
	Roscoe (1975)	31	264–269
Chi-square tests	Clover & Balsley (1979)	8	178–184
	Roscoe (1975)	28–30	242–262
t Tests	Clover & Balsley (1979)	9	200–207
	Emory (1980)	13	422–424
	Roscoe (1975)	23–25	210–229

Topic	Reference	Chapter	Page
ANOVA	Clover & Balsley (1979)	9	207–211
	Emory (1980)	13	429–434
	Kerlinger (1973)	13	214–239
	Roscoe (1975)	36–41	292–361
Multiple regression	Clover & Balsley (1979)	11	274–280
	Emory (1980)	13	445–454
	Kelly, Beggs, McNeil, Eichelberger, & Lyon (1969)		
	Kerlinger (1973)	35, 36	603–658
	Kerlinger & Pedhauzer (1973)		
	McNeil, Kelly, & McNeil (1975)		
	Roscoe (1975)	42–46	362–408
Factor analysis	Cattell (1966)		
	Gorsuch (1974)		
	Rao (1965)		
Nonparametric methods	Marascuilo & McSweeney (1977)		

REFERENCES

Baker, R. L., & Schutz, R. E. (Eds.). *Instructional product research.* New York: Van Nostrand Co., 1972.

Cattell, R. B. The scree test for the number of factors. *Multivariate Behavioral Research,* 1966, *1,* 245.

Clover, V. T., & Balsley, H. L. *Business research methods* (2nd ed.). Columbus, Ohio: Grid Publishing Co., 1979.

Emory, C. W. *Business research methods* (Rev. ed.). Homewood, Ill. Richard D. Irwin, Inc., 1980.

Gorsuch, R. L. *Factor analysis.* Philadelphia: W. B. Saunders Co., 1974.

Kelly, F. J., Beggs, D. L., McNeil, K. A., Eichelberger, T., & Lyon, J. *Research design in the behavioral sciences multiple regression approach.* Carbondale: Southern Illinois University Press, 1969.

Kerlinger, F. N. *Foundations of behavioral research* (2nd ed.). New York: Holt, Rinehart and Winston, 1973.

Kerlinger, F. N., & Pedhazur, E. J. *Multiple regression in behavioral research.* New York: Holt, Rinehart and Winston, 1973.

Lazarus, R. *Psychological stress and the coping process.* New York: McGraw-Hill, 1966.

Marascuilo, L. A., & McSweeney, M. *Nonparametric and distribution-free methods for the social sciences.* Monterey, Calif.: Brooks/Cole, 1977.

McNeil, K. A., Kelly, F. J., & McNeil, J. T. *Testing research hypotheses using multiple linear regression.* Carbondale: Southern Illinois University Press, 1975.

Nie, N. H., Hull, C. H., Jenkins, J. G., Steinbrenner, K., & Bent, D. H. *Statistical Package for the Social Sciences* (Second Edition). New York: McGraw Hill, 1975.

Rao, C. R. *Linear statistical inference and its applications.* New York: John Wiley and Sons, 1965.

Roscoe, J. T. *Fundamental research statistics for the behavioral sciences* (2nd ed.). New York: Holt, Rinehart and Winston, 1975.

POINTS TO PONDER AND RESPOND TO

1. What kinds of biases do you think could be minimized or avoided during the data-analysis stage of research?

2. In the case of directional hypotheses (i.e., $\mu_1 > \mu_2$ or $\mu_1 < \mu_2$), how would we know whether the results of the *t* test obtained are significant or not?

3. When we collect data on the effects of treatment in experimental designs, which statistical test would be most appropriate to test the treatment effects?

4. What would the information STD ERR (i.e., standard error) on a computer printout in the CONDESCRIPTIVE analysis indicate?

5. From the professor's research results on the research methods course, how safe is it to conclude that the research findings are good and can be generalized to all other courses of this type? Why?

UNIT 8
THE RESEARCH REPORT

ISSUES DISCUSSED

Contents of the Research Report
- Title of the Report
- Table of Contents
- Synopsis
- The Introductory Section
- Method Section
- Results Section
- Discussion Section
- Recommendations and Implementation
- Summary
- Acknowledgments
- References
- Appendix

UNIT OBJECTIVES

After completing Unit 8 you should be able to:

1. Know what the contents of a research report should be.
2. Write a good synopsis.
3. Write a good introductory section explaining
   a. The background for the research.
   b. Preliminary data gathering.
   c. Literature review.
   d. Problem statement.
   e. Theoretical framework.
   f. Hypotheses.
   g. Details of research design.
4. Write a method section describing
   a. The population, sample, and sample characteristics.
   b. Variables and measures.
   c. Data-collection methods.
   d. Data-analytic methods to be used.
5. Write the results section, using tables where appropriate, giving
   a. A feel for the data.
   b. A correlation matrix among the primary variables of interest.
   c. Results of hypothesis testing.

6. Discuss the results, stating the generalizability of your findings and the limitations of your study.

7. Give your recommendations and suggestions for implementation in the case of applied research.

8. Write the summary and acknowledgment.

9. Give the appropriate references.

10. Include appropriate materials in the appendix.

Once the data have been analyzed and interpreted, the researcher is ready to write the research report, giving details of the study and the findings, together with suggestions and recommendations.

The research report will of course have a title, and a table of contents and a synopsis will precede the actual study report. The synopsis, referred to as an abstract in journal articles, succinctly highlights various important aspects of the study, such as the problem investigated, allowing the busy manager to get an idea of the research study and the results without having to read the full report. Any particular sections of the report that are of immediate interest can thus be reviewed by the manager before he finds the time to read the complete report.

The report will have five main parts: the introductory section, the method section, the results section, the discussion section, and—in the case of applied research—a recommendation and implementation section. A short summary of the study will follow, and the report will end with an acknowledgment to those who helped with the research. A list of references cited in the literature survey and throughout the report will follow the acknowledgment, and an appendix including items such as the organization chart of the company studied, questionnaire, and other materials considered relevant, will also be attached to the report.

Each of the above components of a research report will now be briefly explained. A copy of a student's report on an organization written as part of the requirements for a research methods course follows these explanations, and should particularly help you to understand how to document the literature survey and how to write the method section.

There are several styles of report writing each with its own format, as for example the Turabian (1971), or the APA (1974) style. Since most academic management journals follow the APA style, it is recommended that we follow the APA format. The *Publication Manual of the American Psychological Association* (1974) gives detailed instructions on how to prepare reports and manuscripts.

THE TITLE OF THE RESEARCH REPORT

The report title should succinctly describe what the study is all about. Examples of study report titles are as follows:

1. A Study of Customer Satisfaction with the Pizza Hut at Sunshine City, Illinois.
2. Factors Influencing Productivity at WORDPRO, Diamondale, Massachusetts.
3. Antecedents and Consequences of White-Collar Employees' Alienation from Work.

It should be evident that the first two titles refer to applied research projects, and that the last one refers to a basic research project.

The title page also cites the name or names of the researchers who carried out the project, their affiliation(s), and the date of the final report.

TABLE OF CONTENTS

The table of contents indicates, with page references, the important headings and subheadings of the report. A separate list of tables and figures, if any, should follow the listing of the written contents of the report.

THE SYNOPSIS

The synopsis is an account of the research study that, although very brief, should give all the important information with respect to the study in order to furnish the reader with a good overview of the problem investigated, the hypotheses tested, the data-collection methods used, the sampling design used, and the findings, recommendations, and suggestions for implementation of the recommendations. The synopsis will occupy from one to two pages.

THE INTRODUCTORY SECTION

In the case of applied research, the introductory section starts with background information about the organization studied. Among other things, this background information briefly covers pertinent details about the physical, environmental, financial, business, and human aspects of the organization. Any structural and process details that are relevant to the study will also find a place in this background section. In applied research, the next important information in the introductory section would be the details of the circumstances under which the study was done. For example, the researchers were called in by top management to study certain aspects of the organization or its work; or the research was undertaken by a team of research students who were allowed entry into the organization in order that both students and the organization might benefit from the study. Next, the gist of the unstructured and structured interviews conducted is presented in a manner that does not disclose the identity of the individuals who were interviewed. Then, using the interviews as a basis, the tentative problem arrived at, with subproblems if any, is stated. This is followed by a literature review, a more refined problem statement, a theoretical framework, and several hypotheses for testing. In sum, the introductory section thus includes the background information of the organization studied, an account of the interviews conducted, the problem statement, the literature review, the theoretical framework, and hypotheses for testing.

In the case of basic research, however, background information about the company and interview details are omitted. Instead, the introductory section for a report on basic research gives an idea of the topic that is researched, and why or how it is important to study it. The arguments would focus on the relevancy, timeliness, and appropriateness of the research in the context of current factors and trends in society and/or the organization. This is followed by a literature review, the problem statement, theoretical framework, and several hypotheses for testing if the study is analytical or predictive in nature. If, however, it is an exploratory study, several research questions (rather than hypotheses) are raised for investigation.

The end of the introductory section in a research report usually indicates the nature and type of study, the time horizon, the field setting, and the unit of analysis.

Next comes the method section.

METHOD SECTION

The method section includes all the research design issues, such as the population and sample, variables and the measures used, data-collection methods, and the data-analysis techniques to be used in the study.

Population and Sample

The population and sample for the study are described in sufficient detail to permit the reader to develop a good feel for both, and to come to her own conclusions about the validity of the results and their generalizability.

The population considered in the study should be clearly specified; for example, the population studied was blue-collar workers in the steel industry, or the board of directors of the Fortune 500 Companies, or the white-collar workers in the banking industry in Australia, Egypt, India, the United Kingdom, and the United States. The sampling design, which also includes the actual sample size used and the sample characteristics, should be fully detailed so that replications of the study are possible. The demographic characteristics of the sample include the age, educational levels, gender composition, tenure, job levels and other information of relevance to the study. Histograms of these characteristics from the frequency-distribution analysis could also be put in the appendix if considered necessary.

Variables and Measures Used

Next, the variables and the measures used in the study are detailed. That is, starting with the dependent variable, each variable is briefly defined. If the measure for the variable has been taken from another published source, the reference to the source should be given. A brief description of the validity and reliability of the measure claimed by the developer of the instrument is also given. A rigorous research study would also state the reliabilities for the particular sample in the study. If, however, the measures for the variables have been newly developed specifically for the research, then the number of items used, an example item, and the Cronbach's alpha and split-half reliabilities for the measure should be given. The validity of the measures should also be established. For your projects you should at least be able to talk about the face validity and the factorial validity. The questionnaire should be placed in the appendix with a tabulation of the items in the questionnaire that measures each of the variables in the study.

Data-Collection Methods

The data-collection methods should be discussed next. An example of such a discussion is given here:

A convenience sample of 15 organizational members representing the top, middle, and clerical levels were interviewed to surface the important variables. Next, structured interviews were held with 10 people chosen from among the first-level managers, supervisors, and clerks. This, again, was a convenience sample. After developing the theoretical framework for the study, questionnaires were developed and personally administered to 165 employees using a proportionate random sampling procedure, as explained earlier. Groups of 30 individuals were assembled in the company's conference room, and the researcher personally explained the purpose of the survey, assured anonymity, and administered the questionnaires. Respondents typically took about 15 minutes to answer the questionnaire and hand it back to the researcher.

Another example is as follows:

Questionnaires were mailed to 280 employees in the organization with a cover letter requesting that they return the completed questionnaires within 7 days in the stamped, self-addressed envelope that was enclosed with the questionnaire. Within 15 days, 148 completed questionnaires were received. At the end of the second week a reminder was sent to all of the participants to return the completed questionnaire immediately if they had not already done so. This was followed by another reminder, 10 days later. At the end of the sixth week, a total of 188 questionnaires was received—a return rate of 67 percent, which is a fairly good return rate for mail surveys. Of these, 185 questionnaires became usable for further analysis. Three had to be discarded because too many questions were left blank.

Data-Analysis Techniques

Next, the data-analytic techniques used in the data analysis are specified. Especially when new or relatively unknown techniques are used, they should be explained in detail so that the reader will be able to follow the subsequent analysis.

For your projects, you should state the types of statistical analyses and tests you propose to use for the study—for example, frequency distributions; descriptive statistics such as mean and standard deviation through use of the condescriptive command, the Pearson correlation analysis, χ^2 tests, ANOVA procedures.

Thus the method section gives all the methodological design issues of the study. Next comes the results section.

RESULTS SECTION

The results section addresses two main things: the results of the analyses and their interpretation. First, the analyses, giving a feel for the data (such as the mean, standard deviation, etc., and the Pearson correlation matrix) are presented in tabular form and briefly discussed. See Tables 1 and 2 presented later in the example study. All tables are sequentially numbered and given a heading. In Unit 7 we saw how this kind of analysis helped the professor to question the validity of the measures used. Issues of reliability and validity are usually discussed in the method section, so the goodness of the data in terms of reliability and validity would not generally be discussed in this section.

Next, the hypotheses are stated, one at a time, both in the null and in the alternate form. The appropriateness of the test used is explained, and the results of the test are then presented, using tables wherever necessary. See Table 3 in the example study. A brief interpretation of the results in the context of the hypothesis or research question then follows. The next section, the discussion section, discusses the results more fully and draws conclusions therefrom.

DISCUSSION SECTION

This section discusses the meaning of the interpretation of the results in the previous section. It details what the substantiation of the hypotheses means in terms of this research and why some of the hypotheses (if any) may not have been supported. The reasons for the nonsubstantiation of the hypotheses might be addressed through intuitive but appropriate and logical speculations about inadequacies in the sampling design, the measures, the data-collection methods, control of critical variables, respondent bias, questionnaire design, and so on. The discussion section is the place to discuss the limitations of the study. Even if all or most of the hypotheses are substantiated, the researcher should beware of making tall claims and overgeneralizing the findings of the study. Limitations of the study in terms of any of the methodological or theoretical and conceptual aspects should be stated so that the reader is aware and appreciative of the researcher's concerns for scientific rigor. Some of the methodological deficiencies are likely to pertain to inadequacies in sampling design (using convenience sample, volunteers, etc.), data-collection methods (using same-source, self-report data), measurement problems (failure to establish high reliability and/or validity), respondent and interviewer biases (moods, biases toward topics investigated, etc.), and coding and tabulation errors.

The discussion section should pull together the interpretations of the results section and give an overall picture of what the results and the interpretation mean to the study. Appropriate conclusions are drawn from the findings and presented to the reader. A sample statement from the discussion section could be as follows:

From the results of this study it is clear that the working environment plays a big part in the productivity of the workers in the steel plant in Pittsburgh. Excessive heat, fumes, stagnant water, and noise seem to impair the efficiency and the productivity of the workers in the plant. These factors have been identified in several other studies as well; these studies have already been cited. The unique finding of this study is that the noise levels affect productivity levels even more than do the toxic fumes. We can be reasonably confident about the results of this study, because it was done under tightly controlled conditions. The criticality of the noise levels is a useful finding because it is much easier to muffle noise than it is to control the toxic fumes.

The discussion section should put forth all the relevant arguments with respect to the findings, and draw conclusions and implications therefrom. If it is basic research, the discussion section will end with implications of the findings and future directions of research in the area. If it is applied research, the discussion section is followed by a recommendations and implementation section.

RECOMMENDATIONS AND IMPLEMENTATION

Based on the conclusions drawn in the discussion section, several alternatives for solving the problem, as well as a recommended solution, will find a place in this section. The pros and cons of implementing the recommendation are also discussed in sufficient detail, with cost and other implications highlighted wherever possible. How these recommendations are to be implemented should also be discussed with the reasons explained in some detail. For example, for the conclusions drawn about the working conditions in the discussion section example above, the following recommendations could be made.

Because noise seems to contribute more to low productivity than any other factor studied here, we suggest that the noise levels be reduced by at least 600 decibels. A new product called Noisuppressant has come in the market. This is a slab that is attached to the walls—wooden, brick, plaster, or any other type of wall—with a special cement. Covering the walls with this new product is preferable to the asbestos mufflers, which are believed to induce lung diseases. The cost of this material is $10 per square yard, which would amount to an expenditure of about $300,000 for this plant. We suggest that we try it in this plant now and, if the results are good, introduce it in the other plants in the Midwest as well. The worksheet in Appendix A shows how the investment will be recovered in three years through increased worker productivity, even after allowing for increased wages.

SUMMARY SECTION

The summary section highlights the research question and the answers found by doing the study, and also briefly summarizes the recommendations and the implementation. It would be less elaborate than the synopsis.

ACKNOWLEDGMENTS

An acknowledgment of the help received from others is made in the acknowledgments section. Usually, the people who allowed the researcher(s) access to the organization are thanked, as well as those who assisted in the study by collecting the questionnaires, acting as liaison persons, helping in data analysis, and so on. Each person is individually acknowledged, with mention being made of the service rendered by each. Organizational members are thanked in general for responding to the survey.

REFERENCES

Immediately after the acknowledgments, starting on a fresh page, appears a list of the references cited in the literature review and at other places in the report. The format of the references has been discussed in Unit 2 and illustrated in Table 2.1. Footnotes, if there are any in the text, are referenced either separately at the end of the report, or on the page where the footnote occurs.

APPENDIX

The appendix, which comes last, is the appropriate place for the organization chart, for newspaper clippings or other materials that substantiate what is said in the text of the report, for verbatim narration of interviews with organizational members, and for anything else that is considered useful for following the text. The appendix should also contain a copy of the questionnaire administered to the respondents, together with a table showing the location of the items in the questionnaire that tap the variables. This could be tabulated as shown in Table 8.1 and placed before the

Table 8.1

Items in the Questionnaire Tapping the Variables

Variable	Number of Items	Questionnaire Location	
		Section No.	Item Nos.
Demographics	6	1	1–6
Involvement	6	2	1–6
Satisfaction	20	2	7–13
		3	1–13
Challenge	8	2	14–18
		3	14–16
Organizational climate	10	4	1–10
Open-ended question regarding job	1	3	17
Open-ended question: General	1	4	11

questionnaire in the appendix. If there are several appendixes, they could be referenced as Appendix A, Appendix B, and so on, and appropriately labeled.

SUMMARY

This unit gives details as to the contents of a good research report. The report should have an appropriate title that gives an indication of the subject of research. A table of contents and a synopsis should precede the actual report. The report consists of five major parts: an introductory section, followed by sections on method, results, discussion, and recommendation and implementation. A summary of the study and acknowledgments follow these as the last parts of the actual report itself. A list of references and an appendix are then included. It is important to note that most of the results will be tabulated, and that the tables will be sequentially numbered and appropriately labeled in the results section.

THE STUDENT'S REPORT

Following the "Points to Ponder and Respond to" is a sample of part of a student project report, excluding the discussion section; it should help you to understand how the literature survey is documented, the methods section written, and the results section presented. Note that the student has also attached a copy of the research proposal submitted by the team to the organization at the beginning of the study. Such a research proposal helps to delineate the obligations of both parties.

SUPPLEMENTAL READINGS

For references on preparing research reports, consult the following works:

American Psychological Association. *Publication manual of the American Psychological Association,* 1974.

Clover, V. T., & Balsley, H. T. *Business research methods* (2nd ed.). Columbus, Ohio: Grid Publishing Co., 1979, Chap. 13, pp. 321–348.

Emory, C. W. *Business research methods* (Rev. ed.). Homewood, Ill.: Richard D. Irwin, Inc., 1980, Chap. 14, pp. 459–586.

Leedy, P. D. *Practical research: Planning and design.* New York: Macmillan, 1974, Chap. 11, pp. 161–178.

Murdick, R. G., & Cooper, D. R. *Business research: Concepts and guides.* Columbus, Ohio: Grid Publishing Co., 1982, Chap. 7, pp. 105–126.

Resta, P. A. *The research report.* New York: American Book Co., 1972. A self-instruction manual on scholarly research report writing.

Turabian, K. L. *A manual for writers of term papers, theses, and dissertations.* 3d ed. rev. Chicago: University of Chicago Press, 1971.

POINTS TO PONDER AND RESPOND TO

1. A good description of the sample is extremely important in any research study.

2. The limitations of the study need not necessarily be delineated because the reader will see the flaws in the study anyway.

3. The literature survey section in the report is really a waste of space.

4. A synopsis does not really give the details of the research study that would testify to its scientific quality, so it serves no useful purpose.

5. Applied research need not be as rigorous as basic research.

EXERCISE

Exercise 8.1

Critique the student report that follows. Discuss it in terms of good and bad research, suggesting what could have been done to improve the study, what aspects of the study are good, and how scientific the study is.

NATURAL SUPERMARKET:
A STUDY OF THE FACTORS
THAT ENHANCE THE ORGANIZATIONAL
COMMITMENT OF EMPLOYEES

Mike Conner
Administrative Sciences Major
Southern Illinois University
Carbondale, Illinois

Paper submitted in partial fulfillment
of the requirements for Research Methods Ad. Sc. 361

November 1980

CONTENTS

SYNOPSIS

The purpose of this research project was to investigate the organizational commitment of the employees at the Natural Supermarket store located in Rollinghills, Illinois. The dependent variable in this study was organizational commitment, and the independent variables considered were age, gender, opportunity for advancement, number of years served in the organization, and job satisfaction. Our data-collection methods comprised unstructured and structured interviews, and a 29–item questionnaire. A random sample of 40 employees was chosen for this study. The data analysis to test the several hypotheses included the use of Pearson correlations, t tests, and multiple regression analysis. The results showed that 40 percent of the variance in organizational commitment was explained by the five independent variables, and that opportunity for advancement was the most significant predictor of commitment. The women employees perceived less opportunities for advancement in the organization than the men, though there were no significant differences in the organizational commitment expressed by men and women. Job satisfaction was the second most significant variable predicting organizational commitment. As a matter of fact, organizational commitment, job satisfaction, and opportunities for advancement were significantly intercorrelated.

Several recommendations have been made to enhance the organizational commitment of employees at the Natural Supermarket. Suggestions include (1) holding meetings to clarify and explain the policies regarding promotion, (2) enhancing job satisfaction through job enrichment, and (3) instituting a simple but effective evaluation system. A phased plan for implementation of the various suggestions and a new appraisal form are discussed in detail in the report.

Our research team wishes to thank Dr. Usha Kiren, Mr. Larry Begee, and all the employees at Natural Supermarket who participated in the survey for making this research project possible.

RESEARCH PROPOSAL

Southern Illinois University
Carbondale, Illinois 62901
October 16, 1980

Mr. Larry Begee
Manager, Natural Supermarket
212 West Mauris
Rollinghills, IL 62901

Dear Mr. Begee:

Following our various interviews with you and your employees at Natural Supermarket, our team has decided on two potential areas of study within your organization: job satisfaction and organizational commitment.

The next step in our research will involve administering questionnaires to a sample of forty to fifty employees. A copy of the questionnaire will be made available to you prior to administration. We will distribute the questionnaires to the employees to be completed during their various break periods, and we will take them back personally. These questionnaires will require approximately 10 minutes for completion. This phase of our study will start on October 20, 1980, and end by October 26, 1980.

As was the case with our employee interviews, we will make sure that the normal flow of work is not obstructed by our presence and data gathering. A summary of our findings will be made available to you by January 20, 1981.

If you have any questions to ask, please contact Mike Conner of our team at 529-4758.

We wish to thank you sincerely for your cooperation and assistance in making this survey possible. We anticipate that our findings will be useful to you.

Yours truly,

Bruce McLain

Mike Conner
Bruce McLain
S.I.U. Research Project Team

INTRODUCTORY SECTION

Introduction

Organizational commitment has been the focus of many research studies because of its importance to employing organizations. With today's mobile and floating working population, it has become increasingly important for organizations to know how they can retain employees and gain their loyalty. Because organizations continually search for ways to increase employees' commitment to the organization, it was hoped that the study would offer some general insights.

More specifically, this study investigates the correlates of organizational commitment among employees in a supermarket.

Background Information of the Supermarket

Natural Supermarkets are a chain of food stores located throughout the midwestern United States. These stores are wholly owned subsidiaries of the Resson Company. There are presently four divisions located in Milwaukee, Minneapolis, New Orleans, and St. Louis (corporate headquarters).

In 1972, Natural opened a store at 212 W. Mauris in Rollinghills, and it has remained in operation for the past eight years. The store's present manager is Larry Begee, who is currently serving his third year in this position. Mr. Begee's association with Natural began eighteen years ago when he was a stockboy at the store in Belleville, Illinois. Mr. Begee was the successor to two previous managers when he was transferred to his present location from Centralia, Illinois, in 1977. He is an active supporter of the high school job program and knows most of the customers personally.

Mike Garrison is the associate manager and Ken Thompson is the assistant manager; both men are currently being trained to become future store managers.

Natural presently has a workforce of nearly 80, with college and high school students comprising the bulk of the employees. Twenty-five percent of these students hold their jobs even during the summer.

Natural's products are very similar to the lines of other supermarket chain stores. It has a full line of grocery products, a bakery department, a deli department, and a limited line of generic products. The store's income fluctuates between $30,000 and $40,000 per month, with summer being the slowest season of the year. Its organizational structure, according to Mr. Begee, is typical of most other supermarkets'.

The Unstructured and Structured Interviews

Our research team interviewed the first set of employees on September 19, 1980. Through a previous meeting with the manager, we arranged to conduct the meetings in the employees' lounge, located in the rear of the store. This particular location was chosen so as not to interfere with the normal daily workflow of employees.

Although we sensed some initial apprehension among the employees in the store, they seemed to overcome it and we were able to communicate with them in a cordial and open manner, explaining to them that this project is a part of our coursework.

During the course of our discussions, our research team attempted to surface the employees' overall impressions of the store, their fellow workers, and their respective managers and supervisors. A brief summary of the results follows, organized under three main headings. The verbatim conversations can be seen in Appendix A.

Employee Responses Regarding Their Jobs and the Store in General

During the course of our interviews, we addressed questions to the employees concerning their present job and the store. Employee reactions and responses were many and diverse.

One group expressed great pleasure over their jobs and with the entire organization. They said that their work was enjoyable and challenging, and that they found a great deal of gratification in working for Natural Supermarket. It is interesting to note that the vast majority of workers expressing these views had been employees of the company for a considerable length of time.

On the other hand, there was a group of employees who expressed very little satisfaction with their jobs or with the organization. This set of workers communicated to us that they were "there for the money, and that's all." When questioned about their attitudes concerning their job, one employee responded that she did not much care for it, whereas another worker stated that she was simply there to do a job "and that's it." These same attitudes were repeated when most other women were questioned about the Natural Supermarket as a place to work. Some of the younger male employees also expressed a similar opinion.

Employees' Impressions About Their Fellow Workers

Nearly all of the employees we talked to expressed positive attitudes toward their fellow workers. One respondent, when asked about the working relationships of the personnel, stated that it was just like a family within a store. Identical remarks were echoed by several others. However, some employees did not express this same attitude toward their fellow workers. There seemed to be an unhealthy competition for promotions and recognition, and concerns were expressed over the tensions, dishonesty, and rivalry among fellow workers. One respondent described the situation using such terms as "backstabbing" and "brownnosing."

Through subsequent structured interviews, it was gathered that the dissatisfactions among the employees revolved around the promotions within the system. Our team felt that the variables of opportunities for advancement and job satisfaction should be considered important for the research.

Employees' Reactions to Management

Opinions were decidedly split among the employees about management in general, and about the supervisors. About half the employees expressed negative attitudes toward their superiors, whereas the other half expressed more positive feelings toward their supervisors and the management of the store in general.

Those workers who communicated negative emotions cited reduction in work hours, management style, and promotional policy as a few of the underlying reasons for their negative attitude. Through more detailed discussion, we found out that women employees appeared to be very concerned that they would not be considered for promotion because of their gender. Some employees expressed dissatisfaction with management in general, citing no particular reasons for their dissatisfaction.

Of those workers who expressed more positive attitudes toward their superiors, feelings of friendship and respect for the individuals were often voiced. Moreover, this group felt that the store was better organized and run more efficiently now than in the past. Both these factors were attributed to Mr. Begee's management.

Upon concluding the interviews with the employees, our group attempted to identify the prospective variables of concern to the study. Four areas appeared to be potential topics for investigation: job satisfaction, organizational loyalty, attitudes toward promotion policies, and employee relations.

Our next phase of research was to interview Mr. Begee, the manager of Natural Supermarket.

Our discussion with Mr. Begee covered many topics and areas of concern in a relatively short period of time. He informed us that when he came to Rollinghills three years ago, the store was in a state of disarray. He worked diligently with the union and attempted to incorporate more efficient and organized methods in the store. He stated that he still works closely with the union and he runs a very efficient operation.

When questioned about his employees, Mr. Begee expressed concern over the lack of integration between departments, and the need for a general feeling of organizational commitment. Although he believed that the employees at higher levels were extremely committed, he expressed his conviction that the part-time workers lacked work commitment and were dedicated only to the extent of retaining their jobs. Mr. Begee suggested that we do our research to see how the organizational commitment of all employees in Natural Supermarket at Rollinghills can be increased.

Upon completion of our interviews with all levels of employees at Natural Supermarket, our team worked to come up with a problem statement and drew up a list of important variables that were surfaced in the interviews. In light of the fact that most employees felt very little satisfaction with their jobs and expressed no loyalty or commitment to the organization, and that Mr. Begee had stated that commitment was an area of his concern, we concluded that the variable to be studied in this research project would be organizational commitment. We also decided to examine the effects of job satisfaction, years of service, age, opportunities for advancement, and gender of the employee on the dependent variable. These five variables appeared to be important in explaining the variance in organizational commitment based on the responses of the employees in the unstructured and structured interviews described earlier.

Literature Survey

Organizational commitment has been investigated and researched for a number of years, because of its purported negative influence on turnover, and many researchers have attempted to present a good definition of the concept. Becker (1960) suggested that commitment was a form of investment one makes in the organization, whereas Dubin, Champoux, and Porter (1975) indicated that a person who is highly committed would express a strong desire to remain a member of an organization and would accept the organization's goals and directions as his own. Porter, Steers, Mowday, and Boulian (1974) defined organizational commitment as "the strength of an individual's identification with, and involvement in, a particular organization" (p. 604). More recently, Steers and Spencer (1977) attempted to define commitment to the organization as the degree to which an individual involves herself with the employing organization. Kanter (1968) identified three forms of commitment and expressed the view that it was a "process through which individual interests become attached to the carrying out of socially organized patterns of behavior which are seen as fulfilling those interests as expressing the nature and needs of the person" (p. 499). Although each of these definitions attempts to approach the topic of commitment from a slightly different viewpoint, the aspects of loyalty, conformity, and involvement are all embedded in the operational definition of the concept.

Buchanan (1974) used a questionnaire to investigate the impact of particular variables upon commitment, and to analyze its development through organizational experience. He viewed commitment as an acceptance of the organization's goals and ideals, and an attachment to the organization itself. Commitment was seen by him as consisting of three components: identification, involvement, and loyalty. Buchanan observed that little is known about the influence of certain experiences upon commitment; however, in a discussion of past research in the field, he cited the years of service, social interaction, and promotional advancement as factors influencing organizational commitment.

Buchanan studied the organizational commitment of managers over a five-year period. The results of his research indicated that initial job assignments had a direct impact on organizational commitment. Job achievement and hierarchial advancement were also seen as relevant issues.

Alutto, Hrebiniak, and Alonso (1973) studied a sample of school-teachers and nurses. In order to operationalize commitment, they examined the subjects' willingness to leave their field when jobs elsewhere offered increases in their pay scale, job freedom, work status, and personal friendships. The results of their study indicated that commitment was greatest among (1) older employees, (2) employees with more job experience, and (3) those workers who were more satisfied with their pay. Horn (1978) reported similar results on organizational commitment. When employees were asked if the community was a better place to live as a result of the company, the youngest workers agreed the least.

Steers (1977) examined hospital employees, scientists, and engineers in his study of organizational commitment. Steers, using Porter's definition of commitment (1974), examined the factors that may influence the degree of commitment an employee feels toward his particular organization. Results of his research suggested that work experience was highly associated with commitment. Six antecedent variables also had a significant association with commitment: need for achievement, group attitudes toward the organization, education, task identity, and organizational dependability.

The conclusions of Steers' research indicate that an "exchange system" underlies the degree of commitment an individual has. If the organization can fulfill the individual's needs and use the person's knowledge, skills, desires, and so forth, the chances of the individual committing herself to the organization increase. However, the research suggests that there is an inverse relationship between education and organizational commitment. It is expected that as education increases, the ability of the organization to fulfill the enhanced needs and desires decreases, resulting in a decrease in the employee's organizational commitment.

A recent study (Hrebiniak and Alutto, 1972) showed that the levels of tension associated with the job, and the number of years with the organization, were the most important variables in explaining organizational commitment. Dissatisfaction and the gender of the employee were also found to be relevant factors in explaining the variance in the levels of commitment to the organization. Hrebiniak and Alutto (1972) also suggested that married women expressed greater organizational commitment than married men.

Finally, a recent study by Stevens, Beyer, and Trice (1978) suggests that there is a strong relationship between commitment and such variables as age, organizational tenure, and job involvement. The results of this study were derived from research on a sample of 634 managers in various government organizations.

To sum up, a review of the literature suggests that organizational commitment can be best examined using age, gender, work experience, opportunities for advancement, and job satisfaction as predictors. The fact that similar variables were surfaced in our unstructured and structured interviews, reinforced our original thinking that we could use these five variables in our research to predict organizational commitment.

Problem Statement

To what extent do age, gender, job satisfaction, opportunities for advancement, and number of years served in the organization predict organizational commitment?

Theoretical Framework

The variable of primary interest to this research is the dependent variable of organizational commitment. Five independent variables are used in an attempt to explain the variance in employees' commitment to the organization. These five variables are age, opportunity for advancement, job satisfaction, years in the organization, and sex of the employee.

The greater the chances are for advancement within the organization, the higher is likely to be the level of organizational commitment expressed by the employee. When employees know that they are going to grow and prosper in the current organization, their level of commitment to stay with the organization is expected to be high. If, however, there are no opportunities for advancement perceived in the present organization, employees—especially those who want to climb up the organizational ladder—are likely to search for other jobs offering greater opportunities. Their level of commitment to stay with the present organization and get involved in its goals and activities will be low. Similarly, if employees are highly satisfied with their jobs and derive high levels of job satisfaction, they are more likely to be committed to the organization than if they are not satisfied. One usually feels obligated to be loyal and committed to the source that offers satisfaction and happiness. Also, as the period of time served in the organization increases, the amount of commitment to the organization increases. When people stay long enough with an organization, they tend to form an attachment to the place, the fellow workers, the customers, and so on, and feel reluctant to leave the place and join another institution. Their involvements in and loyalty to the existing organization would usually preclude their wanting to quit. Therefore, organizational commitment will be less among those employees who have served in the organization for the shortest period of time.

Somewhat following the lines of the preceding arguments, age also has an influence on organizational commitment. Older employees, who usually have served the organization longer, are generally more committed to the organization than their younger counterparts. This is not only because seniority carries with it some status and prestige, but also because as one advances in age, there are limited opportunities for finding a better job elsewhere. This induces more commitment and loyalty to the present organization where the employee is working. Hence, age would seem to have a positive correlation with organizational commitment. Contrary to popular opinion, female employees would be more committed to the organization than male employees, as found in Hrebiniak and Alutto's study cited earlier. This stronger commitment could be a result—especially in the case of married women—of their being dual-income family members who would thus not be unduly concerned about making more money, but would rather tend to derive greater satisfaction by doing the best possible job where they are. Thus, they may remain with the same organization for a long time. However, if the need patterns of women are high—a variable not

Figure 8.1

Schematic diagram of the theoretical framework.

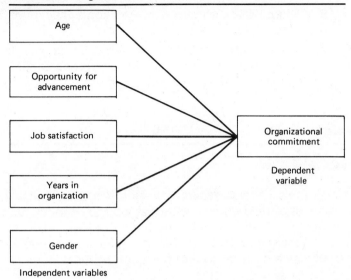

explored in the present study—they may not be as highly committed to an organization where the avenues for advancement are not open or do not exist.

On the basis of the above arguments, we theorize that there would be positive correlations between organizational commitment and each of the following variables: age, opportunities for advancement, job satisfaction, the number of years in the organization, and the gender of the employees, with women being more committed than men.

The theoretical framework is depicted in Figure 8.1.

Hypotheses

From the theoretical framework discussed above, seven hypotheses were developed for this research. They are as follows:

H_A **1.** The older an employee is, the greater will be the individual's level of commitment to the organization.

H_A **2.** If an opportunity for advancement is perceived by the employee, then there will be a greater degree of organizational commitment.

H_A **3.** There will be a positive correlation between organizational commitment and the number of years served in the organization.

H_A **4.** Females will have greater organizational commitment than males.

H_A **5.** The perceived opportunities for promotion will be greater among male employees than among female employees.

H_A **6.** There will be a positive correlation between job satisfaction and organizational commitment.

H_A **7.** The five independent variables will significantly explain a high percentage of the variance in the organizational commitment of employees at Natural Supermarket.

The Research Design Details

Type of Study

The purpose of this research project was to establish the relationships between the independent variables of age, gender, opportunity for advancement, job satisfaction, and number of years served in the organization, and the dependent variable of organizational commitment; thus, this project was a correlational rather than a causal study.

Nature of Study

Because this research project attempted to analyze the relationships between the dependent and independent variables, this study was analytical in nature.

Study Setting

This is a field study because it examined attitudes and behaviors of people in their natural work environment. Variables were neither controlled nor manipulated, and no artificial setting was created for the study.

Time Horizon

The data for this research were collected over a two-month period. Because no previous research had been done by the team on this organization, nor was any subsequent extension of the research contemplated, the study is cross-sectional in nature.

Unit of Analysis

Because the researchers were interested in ascertaining the degree of organizational commitment of Natural employees, the unit of analysis for this project was each individual employee.

METHOD SECTION

Population and Sample

The population for the study comprised employees in the various departments within the Rollinghills, Illinois, Natural Supermarket store. Natural
currently has a workforce of 80 employees. Structured and unstructured
interviews were conducted using a convenience sample of 15 employees
each time, to surface potential areas for investigation. A questionnaire
consisting of 29 items was later administered to a representative sample of
40 employees selected through random sampling.

Data Collection Methods

The questionnaires were administered on the premises on a Thursday
evening and a Saturday afternoon, because practically all the employees
report to work on these two days. Our research team assured the employees that their responses would be anonymous and confidential, and the
respondents completed the questionnaires in the back room within 10 to
15 minutes.

Sample Characteristics

Females comprised 53 percent of the sample and 47 percent were males.
The mean age of the respondents was 26. Fifty-five percent of the respondents were not married. The mean pay of the respondents was between
$5.00 and $5.99 per hour, and the mean length of service of the employees
in the organization was two to four years. All had at least a high school
education, 10 percent had a bachelor's degree, and 20 percent were in
college.

Variables and Measures

The 29–item questionnaire tapped nine personal information items: age,
gender, education, marital status, number of children, tenure, number of
other organizations worked for, job status, and pay. These were measured
by single items. Opportunity for advancement, job satisfaction, and organizational commitment were measured through multiple items on a five-
point Likert-type scale as described below.

Opportunity for Advancement

This variable was tapped through five items that measured employees' perceived scope for advancement, management's willingness to promote efficient workers, and general overall norms for promotion in the organization. A sample item is "The opportunities to get promoted in this organization are very good." The Cronbach's alpha for these items was .84. The items had factorial validity.

Job Satisfaction

In an attempt to operationalize the definition of job satisfaction, the concept was divided into three related dimensions: satisfaction with work, satisfaction with supervision, and satisfaction with co-workers. These three dimensions were each tapped through two questions. The six questions that measured job satisfaction had Cronbach's alpha of .76. All of the items appeared to have face validity.

Organizational Commitment

Steers and Spencer (1977) have defined organizational commitment as the individual's degree of identification with the employing organization. Buchanan (1974) defined commitment as an individual's attachment to an organization's goals and ideals. Because the reliability and validity of the measures used in these reports has been established, eight items were randomly drawn from the two sources in order to measure the concept for this research project. The Cronbach's alpha of these eight items was .89 for this sample.

Data Analysis Methods

Frequency distributions, correlations, and means, standard deviations, and other statistics were obtained by the Frequencies, Pearson Corr, and Condescriptive commands. The hypotheses were tested through the correlations obtained, *t* tests, and simple multiple regression analysis.

RESULTS

Feel for the Data

The mean, standard deviation, and the variance of the three variables of organizational commitment, job satisfaction, and perceived opportunity for advancement are as in Table 1. As can be seen from the table, all three

Table 1

Means, Standard Deviations, and Variances of the Three Multiple Item Variables in the Natural Sample[a]

Variable[b]	Mean	Standard Deviation	Variance
Organizational commitment	2.88	.64	.41
Satisfaction	2.69	.64	.41
Opportunity for advancement	2.77	.78	.62

[a] $n = 40$.
[b] The means for the three variables rest on a five-point scale, with 1 denoting very high, and 5 denoting very low on the variables.

variables are a little to the left on the five-point scale, denoting average commitment, satisfaction, and opportunity for advancement. All three have very little variance. However, the maximum and minimum on each of the variables are such that there is sufficient indication that the responses ranged through all points on the scales.

The Pearson correlation matrix of the eight variables investigated in this study is shown in Table 2. As can be seen, two of the variables are correlated over .59. The intercorrelations among organizational commit-

Table 2

Pearson Correlation Matrix for the Natural Supermarket Sample[a]

	Organizational commitment	Job satisfaction	Opportunities for advancement	Tenure	Pay	Age	Sex	Education
Organizational commitment	1.0							
Job satisfaction	.56[c]	1.0						
Opportunities for advancement	.60[c]	.51[b]	1.0					
Tenure	−.17	.09	.15	1.0				
Pay	−.35[c]	−.12	−.04	.73[c]	1.0			
Age	−.31[b]	−.21	−.20	.55[c]	.48[c]			
Gender[d]	−.19	−.13	−.39[c]	.06	.04	−.20	1.0	
Education	.01	.11	.05	.22	.18	.07	−.10	1.0

[a] $n = 40$.
[b] $p \le .05$.
[c] $p \le .01$.
[d] Females, 1; males, 2.

ment, job satisfaction, and opportunities for advancement were greater than .5.

Hypotheses Testing

Hypothesis 1

H_0: There is no relationship between age and organizational commitment.

H_A: The greater the age of an employee, the greater will be the level of commitment to the organization.

The Pearson correlation results showed a correlation coefficient of $-.31$, significant at the $p = .04$ level. Remembering that 1 on the five-point scale meant high commitment and 5 signified low commitment, we find that, as hypothesized, age and organizational commitment are significantly correlated. Thus, this hypothesis was substantiated.

Hypothesis 2

H_0: There is no relationship between perceived opportunity for advancement and the extent of organizational commitment of employees.

H_A: If a good opportunity of advancement is perceived, then there will be a greater degree of organizational commitment.

A significant correlation of .60 was found at the $p = .0001$ level (see Pearson correlation matrix). Thus the null hypothesis was rejected.

Hypothesis 3

H_0: There is no relationship between tenure and organizational commitment.

H_A: There will be a positive correlation between organizational commitment and the number of years served by employees in the organization.

No significant correlation was found between tenure and organizational commitment ($r = -.17; p = .14$). Thus the alternate hypothesis was not substantiated.

Hypothesis 4

H_0: There will be no gender differences in the organizational commitment felt by the employees.

H_A: Females will have greater organizational commitment than males.

No significant mean differences in the organizational commitment of men and women were found through the use of a t-test analysis ($t = .37$; $p = .25$). Thus this hypothesis was also not substantiated.

Hypothesis 5

H_0: There will be no mean differences in the perceived opportunities for promotion among male and female employees in the organization.

H_A: The opportunities for promotion will be perceived to be greater by the male employees.

A t test showed significant differences between the mean score of 2.5 for males and that for females of 3.7 ($t = 3.6$; $p = .001$). Thus this hypothesis was substantiated. Women perceived themselves as having fewer opportunities for advancement in the organization. (A higher score indicates fewer opportunities.)

Hypothesis 6

H_0: There will be no relationship between job satisfaction and organizational commitment.

H_A: There will be a positive correlation between job satisfaction and organizational commitment.

The correlation between job satisfaction and organizational commitment is significant ($r = .56$; $p = .0001$), as can be seen from the Pearson correlation matrix. Thus the null hypothesis was rejected.

Hypothesis 7

H_0: The five independent variables in the theoretical framework will not significantly explain the variance in the organizational commitment of the employees.

H_A: The five independent variables of age, tenure, gender, job satisfaction, and opportunities for advancement will significantly explain the variance in the organizational commitment of the employees.

The results of the multiple regression analysis, regressing the five independent variables against organizational commitment is shown in Table 3. As can be seen, the five variables together significantly explained 40 percent of the variance in organizational commitment ($R^2 = .402$; $F = 29.86$; $p = .0001$). The beta values of both job satisfaction and opportunities for advancement were significant. Thus, the hypothesis that the five predictors would significantly explain the variance in organizational commitment was substantiated.

Table 3

Results of the Multiple Regression Analysis Regressing the Five Independent Variables Against Organizational Commitment

Predictors	Beta	F
Age	.09	.32
Tenure	.08	.27
Gender	.07	.25
Job satisfaction	.38	18.2[a]
Opportunities for advancement	.57	27.4[a]

$R^2 = .402$
$F = 29.86$[a]
$DF = 5,34$

[a]$p < .001$.

In summary, four of the seven hypotheses were substantiated, and three were not. The research question as to how organizational commitment can be enhanced has been answered by the results of the data analyses. Job satisfaction and perceived opportunities for advancement significantly influence organizational commitment, and hence by increasing these two, organizational commitment of members can be increased.

CONCLUDING NOTE

Within a short period of time you have been introduced to a fairly sophisticated practical approach to understanding, designing, and conducting research for managing results through people in organizations. The preceding eight units were not intended to make expert researchers of you, but we hope they have heightened your awareness of the value and usefulness of scientific research for organizational problem solving. We expect that your level of sophistication as consumers of research has been considerably enhanced and that you will now be more discriminating in accepting research findings, whether they pertain to published research or research conducted in your own organization. We also hope that with the greater knowledge and grasp of research that you currently have, you will, as managers, be able to deal with researchers and consultants more effectively, and examine and comment on their reports more intelligently and scientifically. In the immediate present, we believe you will be able to use the knowledge and skills you have gained through this book profitably in writing term papers or project reports for other courses, especially in the management area. Constantly applying the library research skills, conceptualizing the relationships among the variables in any situation in a logical manner, analyzing data by computer, and interpreting and discussing the results of research will help keep the newly learned skills alive, which will come in handy in solving problems in the managerial context in the future.

It may be helpful once again to highlight some of the important points covered in this book that will be particularly useful to you in managing situations:

1. Developing a sensitivity for, and being able to identify, important variables operating in a particular situation.

2. Being able to gather information quickly by asking the appropriate questions, of appropriate sources of information, and in an unbiased manner.

3. Locating and being able to extract relevant information from published sources.

4. Being able to conceptualize clearly the logical relationships among variables in any given situation.

5. Becoming sensitive to sources of biases in both published articles and project reports given to you by consultants and researchers, and thus becoming more discriminating and sophisticated consumers of research.

Research is a useful problem-solving tool. It is an important area in which professional managers of the complex organizations of today and tomorrow need increasingly to acquire knowledge. We hope that this book will in some measure help you to achieve this goal.

GLOSSARY OF TERMS

Accuracy The extent of absence of bias in the sample; reflects the degree to which underestimation or overestimation of the population characteristics are present or absent in the sample chosen.

Alternate Hypothesis The educated conjecture that sets the parameters that one expects to find. This alternate hypothesis is tested in order either to accept or to reject the null.

Ambiguous Questions Questions that are not clearly worded and that respondents may interpret in many ways.

Analytical Study A study that tries to explain why or how certain variables influence the dependent variable of interest to the researcher.

Applied Research Research conducted in a work setting with the specific intention of solving an existing problem in the situation.

Area Sampling Cluster sampling within a specified area or region; a probability sampling design.

Attitudinal Factors People's feelings, dispositions, and reactions to factors in the work environment such as the work itself, the co-workers, or supervision.

Basic Research Research conducted to generate knowledge and understanding of phenomena in the work setting that would add to the existing body of knowledge about organizations and management theory.

Behavioral Factors Actual behaviors exhibited by employees on the job such as being late, working hard, remaining absent, or quitting work.

Bias Any error that can creep into the data, introduced through the researcher, the respondent, or the measuring instrument.

Bibliography A systematic alphabetical listing of authors, referencing the titles of their works that are of relevance to the study, and where they can be located.

Broad Problem Area The entire situation in which one senses a possible need for research and problem solving.

Causal Analysis Analysis done to detect cause→effect relationships between two variables.

Causal Study A research study conducted to establish cause→effect relationships among variables.

Classification Data Personal information or demographic details of the respondents such as age, marital status, educational level.

Closed Questions Questions with a clearly delineated set of alternatives that confine the respondents' choice to selecting from among the given alternatives.

Cluster Sampling A probability sampling design in which the sample comprises groups or chunks of elements with intragroup heterogeneity and intergroup homogeneity.

Comparative Study A study conducted by collecting data from several settings or organizations.

Complex Probability Sampling Several probability sampling designs (such as systematic and stratified random), which offer an alternative to the cumbersome, simple random sampling design.

Concurrent Validity Established through empirical validity in a situation where a variable considered to provide a direct measure of the expected behavior (criterion variable) is simultaneously measured along with the independent variable and the two are significantly correlated, as theorized.

Congruent Validity Establishes the goodness of a measure based on the correlations between one test and another, both of which have been established as a measure of the same attribute.

Construct Validity Testifies to how well the results obtained from the use of the measure, fit the theories around which the test was designed.

Content Validity Establishes the representative sampling of a whole set of items that measures a concept, and reflects how well the dimensions and elements of the concept have been delineated.

Contextual Factors Factors relating to the organization being studied such as the background and environment of the organization, including the origin and purpose of the company, size, resources, financial position, and the like.

Contrived Setting An artificially created or "lab" environment in which research is conducted.

Control Group The group that is not exposed to any treatment in an experiment.

Controlled Variable Any exogenous or extraneous variable that could contaminate the cause→effect relationship, but the effects of which can be controlled by the researcher in an experiment through the process either of matching or of randomization.

Convenience Sampling A nonprobability sampling design in which information or data for the research are gathered from members of the population who are conveniently accessible to the researcher.

Convergent Validity A congruence test established when two different instruments measuring the same concept are highly correlated.

Correlational Analysis Analysis done to trace the mutual influence of variables on one another.

Correlational Study A research study conducted to identify the important factors associated with the variables of interest.

Criterion-Related Validity The establishment of the validity of an instrument that measures a concept, by correlating the scores on the concept as measured by the instrument with a criterion or dependent variable.

Criterion Variable The main variable that poses the problem for a study (i.e., the variable of primary interest to the researcher—the dependent variable).

Cross-Sectional Study A research study for which data are gathered just once (maybe stretching over a period of days, weeks, or months), to answer the research question.

Deduction The process of arriving at conclusions based on the interpretation of the meaning of the results of data analysis.

Dependent Variable *See* Criterion Variable.

Descriptive Study A research study that describes the variables in a situation that are of interest to the researcher.

Directional Hypothesis An educated conjecture as to the direction of the relationship between two variables; it could be stated in terms of positive or negative, or more or less relationships.

Discriminant Validity Established when two measures tapping two opposite or two different concepts are negatively correlated, thus distinguishing the two measures.

Disproportionate Stratified Random Sampling A probability sampling design that involves a procedure in which the number of sample subjects chosen from each stratum is not directly proportionate to the total number of elements in the respective strata.

Double-Barreled Question Refers to the improper framing of a single question that should be posed as two or more separate questions, so that the respondent can give clear and unambiguous answers to each of the questions.

Double Sampling A probability sampling design that involves the process of collecting information from a set of subjects twice, such as using a sample to collect preliminary information, and later using a subsample of the primary sample for more information.

Dynamic Panels Consist of a changing composition of members who serve as the sample subjects for a research study conducted over an extended period of time.

Editing Data The process of going over the data and ensuring that they are complete and acceptable for the data analysis.

Efficiency in Sampling Attained when the sampling design chosen either results in a cost reduction to the researcher or offers greater precision in terms of sample size.

Element   A single member of the population.

Empirical Validity   Attests to the goodness of the measuring instrument by pragmatically establishing the theorized correlations between two concepts through the actual data collected.

Endogenous Variables   Variables or factors that have a bearing on the cause→effect relationship that the researcher is interested in investigating.

Exogenous Variables   Variables or factors in which the researcher is not interested, but that may contaminate or confound the cause→effect relationships under investigation.

Experimental Design   A study design in which the researcher imposes some artificial constraints in the setting, manipulates the independent variable to establish cause→effect relationships, or both.

Experimental Group   The group that is exposed to a treatment in an experimental design.

Explanatory Variable   *See* Endogenous Variables.

Exploratory Study   A research study in areas where very little prior knowledge or information is available on the subject under investigation.

External Consultants   Research experts outside the organization who are hired to research specific problems and find solutions.

External Validity   The extent of generalizability of the results of a causal study to other field settings.

Extraneous Variable   *See* Exogenous Variables.

Face-to-Face Interview   The information-gathering situation in which the interviewer asks the interviewee the information needed for the research when both meet in person for the purpose.

Face Validity   A form of content validity examining whether the test item, on the face of it, reads as if it is measuring what it is supposed to measure.

Factorial Validity   Indicates, through the use of factor-analytic techniques, whether a test is a pure measure of some specific factor or dimension.

Field Experiment   An experiment done to detect cause→effect relationships in the natural environment in which events normally occur.

Field Study   A study conducted in the natural environment of the organizational setting, with a minimal amount of researcher interference with the normal flow of events in the situation.

Fundamental Research   *See* Basic Research.

Funneling Technique The questioning technique that consists of initially asking general and broad questions of respondents, and gradually narrowing the focus until the questions center on more specific themes.

Generalizability The extent of applicability of the research findings in one setting, to other settings.

Halo Effect The respondents' tendency to continue responding to all the questions at one end of the scale.

History Effects Factors that might unexpectedly occur while the experiment is in progress that would contaminate the cause→effect relationships and thus threaten the internal validity of the experimental results.

Hypothesis An educated conjecture about the logically developed relationship between two or more variables, expressed in the form of testable statements.

Hypothetico-Deductive Method of Research The seven-step process of observing, preliminary data gathering, theorizing, hypothesizing, further more focused data collection, data analysis, and interpreting the meaning of results.

Independent Variable A variable that influences the dependent or criterion variable and accounts for or explains the variance in the dependent variable.

Instrumentation Effects The threat to internal validity in experimental designs caused by changes in the measuring instrument between the pretest and the posttest.

Interitem Consistency Reliability A test of the consistency of responses to all the items of a measure, thus establishing the fact that all the items hang together as a set, to measure the concept.

Internal Consistency Homogeneity of the items in the measure that tap a construct.

Internal Consultants Research experts within the organization who are utilized to investigate and find solutions to the organization's problems.

Internal Validity of Experiments The extent of precision and confidence in establishing cause→effect relationships in experimental designs.

Interrater Reliability The consistency of the judgment of several raters on how they see a phenomenon or interpret the responses of subjects.

Interval Scale A multipoint scale that taps the differences, the order, and the equality of the magnitude of the differences in the responses on the scale.

Intervening Variable   A variable that surfaces as a function of the independent variable, and helps in conceptualizing and explaining the influence of the independent variable on the dependent variable.

Interviewing   A data-collection method in which the researcher asks for information verbally from the respondents.

Judgment Sampling   A purposive, nonprobability sampling design in which the sample subject is chosen on the basis of the individual's ability to provide the type of special information needed by the researcher.

Lab Experiment   An experimental design set up in an artificially contrived setting where controls and manipulations are introduced to establish cause→effect relationships among variables of interest to the researcher.

Leading Questions   Questions phrased in such a manner as to lead the respondent to give the responses that the researcher would like to obtain.

Literature Review   The documentation of a comprehensive review of the published work from secondary sources of data in the areas of specific interest to the researcher.

Literature Survey   *See* Literature Review.

Loaded Questions   Questions that would elicit highly biased, emotional responses from the subjects.

Logical Validity   Includes content validity and construct validity, both of which are derived from logical reasoning and deciding whether the measures conform to accepted logic or logical themes.

Longitudinal Study   A research study for which data are gathered at several points in time to answer a research question.

Manipulation   The way the researcher exposes the independent variable to the subjects, to determine cause→effect relationships in experimental design.

Matching   A method of controlling for exogenous variables, in which the experimental and control groups are "matched" or evenly spread on the variables that are expected to confound the cause→effect relationships investigated by the researcher, thus deliberately spreading the contaminating factors equally across all groups.

Maturation Effects   The threat to internal validity that is a function of the biological, psychological, and other processes operating within the respondents as a result of the passage of time.

Moderating Variable   A variable upon which the relationship between two other variables is contingent. That is, if the moderating variable is present (or absent), the theorized relationship between two variables will hold good—not otherwise.

Mortality The loss of research subjects as experiments are in progress, which confounds the cause→effect relationships.

Motivational Research A particular data-gathering technique directed toward surfacing information, ideas, and thoughts that are not easily verbalized, or that remain unconscious in the respondents.

Multistage Cluster Sampling A probability sampling design that could be described as a stratified sampling of clusters.

Nominal Scale A scale that categorizes individuals or objects into mutually exclusive and collectively exhaustive groups, and gives basic, categorical information on the variable of interest.

Noncontrived Setting Research conducted in the natural environment where events normally occur (i.e., the field setting).

Nondirectional Hypothesis An educated conjecture of some kind of relationship between two variables, the directionality of which cannot be guessed.

Nonparticipant Observer A researcher who collects observational data without becoming an integral part of the organizational system.

Nonprobability Sampling A sampling design in which the elements in the population do not have a known or predetermined chance of being selected as sample subjects.

Null Hypothesis The conjecture that sets the parameters that one expects not to find.

Objectivity Interpreting the results on the basis of the facts emanating from the data analysis, as opposed to subjective or emotional biases.

Observational Survey The gathering of data by observing people or events either in the lab setting or in the natural environment, and recording the information.

One-Shot-Study *See* Cross-Sectional Study.

Open-Ended Questions Questions that enable the respondent to give answers in a free-flowing format without restricting his range of choices to alternatives suggested by the researcher.

Operational Definition Defining a construct in measurable terms by reducing it from its level of abstraction through the delineation of its dimensions and elements such that the behavioral components of the construct or concepts lend themselves to measurement.

Ordinal Scale A scale that not only categorizes the qualitative differences in the variable of interest, but also allows for the rank ordering of these categories in some meaningful way.

Panel Studies Studies conducted over a period of time to determine the effects of certain changes made in a situation by using a panel or group of subjects as the sample base.

Parallel-Form Reliability   Reliability that is established when responses to two comparable sets of measures tapping the same construct are highly correlated.

Parsimony   Is gained by efficiently explaining the variance in the dependent variable of interest through the use of a smaller, rather than a greater number of independent variables.

Participant-Observer   A researcher who collects observational data by herself becoming a member of the system from which data are collected.

Population   The entire group of people, events, or things that the researcher desires to investigate.

Population Frame   A listing of all the elements in the population from which the sample is drawn.

Posttest   A test given to the subjects to measure the dependent variable of interest to the researcher after exposing them to a treatment.

Precision   The closeness of the estimated sample characteristics to the population characteristics; determined by the extent of the variability of the sampling distribution of the sample mean.

Predictive Study   A study that goes beyond analyzing the relationships among the variables in a particular situation, to predicting the relationships among some critical variables in other similar situations.

Predictive Validity   Validity that is established in a situation in which a variable considered to produce a direct measure of the expected behavior (criterion variable) occurs at a point in time that is later than when the independent variable is introduced and measured, and the two measures are significantly correlated as theorized.

Predictor Variable   *See* Independent Variable.

Pretest   A test given to the subjects to measure the dependent variable of interest to the researcher before exposing them to a treatment.

Primary Data   Data collected from the problem situation firsthand, in order to analyze them and find solutions to the problem being researched.

Probability Sampling   The sampling design in which the elements in the population have some known chance or probability of being selected as sample subjects.

Problem Definition   A precise, succinct statement of the question or issue that is to be investigated, with the objective of finding answers and solutions to the problem.

Problem Statement   *See* Problem Definition.

Proportionate Stratified Random Sampling   A probability sampling design in which the number of sample subjects drawn from each stratum is proportionate to the total number of elements in the respective strata.

Purposiveness in Research The situation in which research is focused on solving a well-identified and defined problem, rather than aimlessly looking for answers to vague questions.

Purposive Sampling A nonprobability sampling design in which the required information is gathered from special or specific targets or groups of people on some rational basis.

Questionnaire A preformulated written set of questions to which the respondent records his answers, usually within rather closely delineated alternatives.

Quota Sampling A form of purposive sampling in which a predetermined proportion of people is sampled from different groups of interest to the researcher, on a logical but convenient basis.

Randomization The process of controlling for the exogenous variables by randomly assigning members among the various experimental and control groups such that the confounding variables are randomly distributed across all groups.

Ratio Scale A scale that has an absolute zero origin, and hence indicates not only the magnitude of the differences but also the proportion of the differences.

Recall-Dependent Questions Questions that elicit from the respondents information that involves recalling experiences from the past that may be hazy in their memory.

Reliability The accuracy of the measuring instrument, determined by establishing its consistency and stability.

Replicability The extent to which similar results can be obtained when identical research is conducted at different times or in different organizational settings.

Representativeness of the Sample The extent to which the sample that is selected possesses the same characteristics as the population from which it is taken.

Research An organized, systematic, data-based, critical, scientific inquiry or investigation into a specific problem, undertaken with the objective of finding answers or solutions to it.

Restricted Probability Designs *See* Complex Probability Sampling.

Rigor The theoretical and methodological precision adhered to in conducting research.

Sample A subset or subgroup of the population.

Sample Size The actual number of subjects chosen as sample to represent the population characteristics.

Sampling The process of selecting items from the population so that the sample characteristics can be generalized to the population, and involves both design choice and sample size decisions.

Scale A tool or mechanism by which individuals are distinguished on the variables of interest in some meaningful way.

Scientific Investigation A step-by-step, logical, organized, and rigorous effort to solve problems.

Secondary Data Data that have already been gathered by researchers, data published in statistical and other journals, and information available from any published or unpublished source available either within or outside the organization—all of which the researcher might find useful.

Selection Effects The threat to internal validity that is a function of improper or unmatched selection of subjects for the experimental and control groups.

Simple Random Sampling A probability sampling design in which every single element in the population has a known and equal chance of being selected as a subject.

Simulation A model-building technique for assessing the possible effects of changes that might be introduced in a system.

Social Desirability The respondents' need to give socially or culturally acceptable responses to the questions posed by the researcher even if they are not true.

Solomon Four-Group Design The experimental design that sets up two experimental groups and two control groups, giving one experimental group and one control group both the pretest and posttest, and giving the other experimental group and control group only the posttest.

Split-Half Reliability The correlation coefficient between one half of the items measuring a concept and the other half of the items measuring the same concept.

Stability of a Measure The ability of the measure to repeat the same results over time with low vulnerability to changes in the situation.

Static Panels Consist of the same group of people serving as the sample subjects over an extended period of time for a research study.

Statistical Regression The threat to internal validity that results when various groups in the study have been selected on the basis of their extreme (very high or very low) scores on some important variables.

Stratified Random Sampling A probability sampling design that first divides the population into meaningful, nonoverlapping subsets, and then randomly chooses the subjects from each subset.

Structural Variables Factors related to the form and design of the organization such as the roles and positions, communication channels, control systems, reward systems, and span of control.

Structured Interviews Interviews conducted by the researcher with a predetermined list of questions to be asked of the interviewer.

Structured Observational Studies   Studies in which the researcher observes and notes down specific activities and behaviors that have been clearly delineated as important factors to the research before the commencement of the study.

Subject   A single member of the sample.

Synopsis   A brief summary of the research study.

Systematic Sampling   A probability sampling design that involves the choosing of every *n*th element in the population for the sample.

Telephone Interview   The information-gathering method by which the interviewer asks the interviewee over the telephone for the information needed for the research, instead of during a personal meeting.

Test-Retest Reliability   A way of establishing the stability of the measuring instrument by correlating the scores obtained by administering the instrument to the same set of respondents at two different points in time.

Testability   The ability to subject the data collected to appropriate statistical tests in order to substantiate or reject the hypotheses developed in the research study.

Testing Effects   The distorting effects on the experimental results (the posttest scores) caused by the respondents having been sensitized to the posttest through the pretest.

Theoretical Framework   A logically developed, described, and elaborated network of associations among variables of interest to the research study.

Treatment   The manipulation of the independent variable in experimental designs so as to determine its effects on some dependent variable of interest to the researcher.

Unbiased Questions   Questions posed in a way so as to elicit the least response bias. This can be ensured by following the principles of wording and measurement, and by taking care not to emphasize certain key words, not making inappropriate suggestions to the interviewee, not inflecting the voice, and so on.

Uncontrolled Variable   Any exogenous or extraneous variable that confounds the cause→effect relationship in experimental designs, the effects of which cannot be controlled by the researcher.

Unit of Analysis   The level of aggregation of the data that are collected for analysis, in order to answer the research question.

Unobtrusive Measures   Measures obtained not through the cooperation of the subjects themselves, but through the gathering of data from sources other than people, such as examining birth and death records or counting the number of cigarette butts in the ashtray.

Unrestricted Probability Sampling   *See* Simple Random Sampling.

Unstructured Interviews Interviews conducted with the primary purpose of surfacing some important preliminary issues relevant to the problem situation, without the researchers having a planned or predetermined sequence of questions.

Unstructured Observational Studies Studies in which the researcher observes and makes notes of almost all of the activities and behaviors that occur in the situation without predetermining what particular variables will be of specific interest to the study.

Validity Proof as to whether the instrument, technique, or process used to measure a concept does indeed measure the intended concept.

Variable Anything that can take on differing or varying values.

ANSWERS TO EXERCISES

EXERCISE 3.1

The dependent variable is organizational commitment because it is the primary variable of interest to the applied researcher, who wants to increase the commitment of the members in the bank.

EXERCISE 3.2

The dependent variable is communication because the production manager is interested in knowing why workers are reluctant to communicate with him.

EXERCISE 3.3

Variable	Label	Reason
Production	Dependent variable	Main variable of interest
Supervision	Independent variable	⎰ Help to explain the vari-
Training	Independent variable	⎱ ance in production

Explanation

Production is the dependent variable because the manager seems to be interested in raising the level of production of workers. That is, the manager wants to explain the variance in production levels through the two variables according to her initial hunches. Supervision and training are the two independent variables, which, in the manager's opinion, are likely to explain the variance in the production level that is the dependent variable.

Diagram

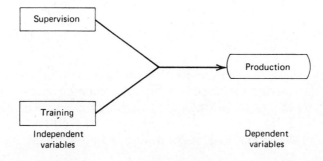

EXERCISE 3.4

Variable	Label	Reason
Job satisfaction	Dependent variable	Variable of primary interest
Pay	Independent variable	⎰ Influence job satisfaction
Fringe benefits	Independent variable	⎱ and explain the variance in it

Explanation

Job satisfaction, the dependent variable, is of primary interest to the consultant, who speculates that the variables of pay and fringe benefits actually decrease it. Pay and fringe benefits are the independent variables because they are, in this case, expected to influence job satisfaction in a negative way. That is, as pay and fringe benefits go up, job satisfaction is expected to go down. The variance in job satisfaction would thus be explained by pay and fringe benefits.

Diagram

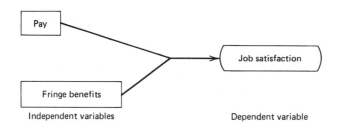

Independent variables   Dependent variable

EXERCISE 3.5

Variable	Label
Productivity	Dependent variable
Off-the-job classroom training	Independent variable
Age	Moderating variable

Explanation

The main variable of interest to the manager is productivity—the dependent variable—the variance in which is expected to be explained by the independent variable, off-the-job classroom training. The more off-the-job training given to the workers, the greater the productivity. However, only those who are under fifty years of age would increase their productivity with increased off-the-job training. This will not be true for those who are over fifty years of age. Thus age is the moderating variable.

Diagram

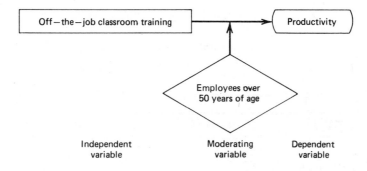

| Independent variable | Moderating variable | Dependent variable |

EXERCISE 3.6

Variable	Label
Pub visits	Dependent variable
Interaction	Independent variable
Gender	Moderating variable

Explanation

The dependent variable is visits to the pub, the variance in which can be accounted for by the independent variable, interaction among the workers. The more job-related interactions of the workers, the more their inclination to stay together after the work hours and go to the pub for a drink. However, this relationship between interaction and visits to the pub does not hold true for *all* the workers; it is true only for the male workers. The female workers, no matter how much they interact—and they interact just as much as the men do—do not tend to stay after work and join the men for a drink at the local pub. Thus gender moderates the relationship between interaction and going to the pub for a drink.

Diagram

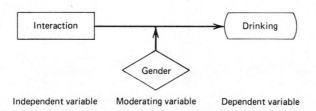

Independent variable   Moderating variable   Dependent variable

EXERCISE 3.7

Situation 1

Motivation to Work as an *Independent* Variable

The performance of employees is influenced by their motivation to work.

Situation 2

Motivation to Work as an *Intervening* Variable

Employees perform better when they are given challenging jobs, because such jobs tend to motivate them to work.

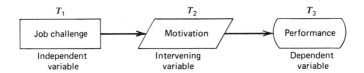

Situation 3

Motivation to Work as a *Moderating* Variable

The performance of employees with low levels of motivation to work will not improve despite increases in job challenge.

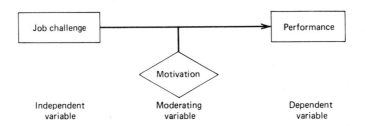

EXERCISE 3.8

Variable	Label
Life satisfaction	Dependent variable
Multiple roles	Independent variable
Stress	Intervening variable
Self-concept	Moderating variable

Explanation

Life satisfaction is the dependent variable, which is of primary interest, and attempts are made to explain the variance in life satisfaction through several factors. Life satisfaction is directly influenced by multiple roles, the independent variable. The greater the number of roles taken on by dual-career family members, the lesser their experienced satisfactions in life. This relationship is clarified by noting that stress is experienced because dual-career family members take on multiple roles, which, in turn, lowers the levels of satisfaction in their lives. In other words, stress is a function of taking on the multiple roles, and this intervening variable helps us to see how multiple roles influence life satisfaction. Although this relationship among multiple roles, stress, and life satisfaction generally holds true, it is not true for *all* dual-career family members. Those who have a high self-concept do not derive lower levels of satisfaction, even though they take on multiple roles, and may even feel stressed by it. Only those who do not have a high self-concept experience lower levels of life satisfaction when they take on multiple roles, and feel stressed because of it.

Diagram

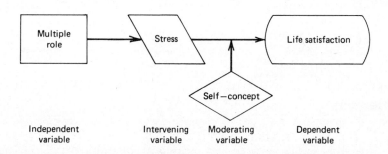

EXERCISE 3.9

Variable	Label
Morale	Dependent variable
Working conditions	Independent variable
Pay scale	Independent variable
Vacation benefits	Independent variable
Side income	Moderating variable
Happiness	Intervening variable

Explanation

The independent variables of improved working conditions, better pay, and vacation benefits influence the dependent variable of morale. When these three independent variables are high in a work situation, then morale is also high. However, increased pay will not increase the morale of all workers. Only those who do not have good side incomes will experience greater happiness (the intervening variable) when their pay is increased, and consequently also higher morale. For others, the relationship between pay and morale will not hold good. The intervening variable, happiness, is a function of high pay (for those without side incomes). It clarifies the relationship between pay and morale.

Diagram

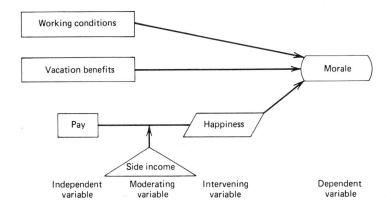

Problem Statement

Will improving the working conditions and increasing pay scales and vacation benefits improve the morale of all employees?

EXERCISE 3.10

Problem Statement

How can the job satisfaction and family satisfaction of both spouses in dual-career families be increased?

Theoretical Framework

The family counselor is interested in finding ways to increase both the job satisfaction and family satisfaction of dual-career family members. Therefore, both job satisfaction and family satisfaction are dependent variables. There are four independent variables in this situation, two of them influencing job satisfaction and two influencing family satisfaction. The two independent variables that help explain the variance in job satisfaction are job involvement and discretionary time spent on job-related activities. This relationship between the two independent variables and job satisfaction is, however, moderated by the gender of the spouse. In other words, only male members in dual-career families (i.e., husbands) derive greater job satisfaction when their job involvement increases and they spend more of their discretionary time in job-related matters. The reason for this may be that because men are the traditional breadwinners, their identity is tied to the work setting; thus the more ego-involved they become in their jobs, the more satisfactions they derive from the job setting. Likewise, the more discretionary time they spend on job-related activities, the more job satisfaction they derive, because they identify so closely with their role of careerpersons and breadwinners. It also seems logical that the more time they spend on job-related activities, the more they are going to be ego-involved in their jobs, and the more the job involvement, the greater the probability of their spending more time on job-related activities. Thus there is a relationship between the two independent variables themselves, each influencing the other.

This relationship between the two independent variables and the dependent variable, however, does not hold true for wives in dual-career families. This is because wives have traditionally been homemakers, and their taking on the career roles does not absolve them of their family responsibilities and domestic work. This dual role and responsibility might restrict the satisfactions they derive from the job, and even when they get more job-involved and invest more discretionary time in job-related matters, their job satisfaction may not be enhanced. Thus, the relationship among job involvement, discretionary time, and job satisfaction might hold good for men but not for women.

The dependent variable of family satisfaction is influenced by the two independent variables of couples: (1) spending more time in each other's company, and (2) helping each other in planning family activities. This is understandable, because any satisfaction derived in the family situation or setting is a function of the harmonious and meaningful interactions among the family members. The more time spent together, and the more the joint and harmonious planning of family activities, the greater will be the family satisfactions enjoyed by both spouses in dual-career families.

Diagram

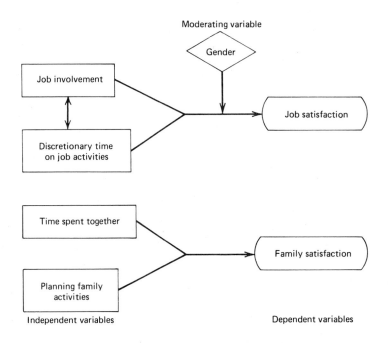

EXERCISE 3.12

1. H_0: There is no relationship between working conditions and the morale of employees.

H_A: If working conditions are improved, then the morale of the employees will be improved.

2. H_0: There is no relationship between vacation benefits and employees' morale.

H_A: Better vacation benefits will improve employees' morale.

3. H_0: There is no difference in the relationship between pay and happiness among those who have side incomes and those who do not.

H_A: Only those who do not have side incomes will become happier if their pay is increased.

4. H_0:　There is no relationship between happiness and morale.
   H_A:　Happiness and morale are positively correlated.

5. H_0:　Working conditions, vacation benefits, and pay have no influence on the morale of employees.
   H_A:　Working conditions, vacation benefits, and pay all have positive influences on morale.

EXERCISE 3.14

1. This would be a *causal study* because the operator wants to prove to the supervisor that the fumes are causing operators to be low in their efficiency. In other words, the machine tool operator is trying to establish the fact that fumes *cause* low efficiency in workers.

2. This is an *analytical study* because the machine tool operator wants to establish that fumes cause low efficiency and convince her workshop supervisor through such analysis.

3. This would be a *field experiment* because though it would be designed in the natural environment where the work naturally is done, the amount of fumes will have to be manipulated while other factors such as atmospheric pressure may have to be controlled. Because the experimental design would be set up in the natural environment of the workers, this will be a *field experiment.*

4. The unit of analysis would be the *individual operators.* The data will be collected with respect to each operator and then the conclusion will be made as to whether the operators are less efficient because of the fumes emitted in the workshop.

5. This would be a *longitudinal* study because data will be gathered at more than one point in time. First, the efficiency of the operators would be assessed at a given rate of fume emission. Then the fumes emitted would be manipulated to varying degrees, and at each manipulation the efficiency of the workers would again be assessed to confirm that the high rate of fume emission causes a drop in operators' efficiency.

EXERCISE 5.1*

Ten questions that would measure stress are as follows:

1. To what extent do you feel anxious and nervous?

2. How often do you feel unduly pressured by the events that are happening in your life?

3. How often are you confused by the situation surrounding you?

4. How frequently have you had headaches and/or stomach upsets during the past four weeks?

5. How often do you feel that the demands on you are overwhelming?

6. How often has your blood pressure shot up during the past six months?

7. How well do you sleep at night?

8. Do you ever feel that you are going to have a nervous breakdown?

9. Are you troubled by your hands sweating so that you feel damp and clammy?

10. Do you wake up rested in the morning?

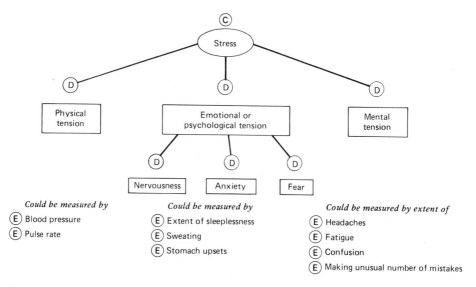

*D = dimensions and E = elements of the concept (C) of stress.

EXERCISE 5.2*

Twelve items to measure the concept of enriched jobs are as follows:

1. To what extent do you find your job challenging?

2. To what extent does your job use all the skills and knowledge you possess?

3. To what extent does your job permit you to do a task from beginning to end instead of only doing fragmented pieces of the task?

4. How repetitive are your duties?

5. How much opportunity do you have to do a job from beginning to end?

6. To what extent do you find out how well you are doing on the job as you are working?

7. How meaningful is the work you do in the sense of it making a contribution to society?

8. To what extent do you feel you are doing something worthwhile on your job?

9. How good do you feel about the challenges that your job offers?

10. How much are you left on your own to do your work?

11. How much opportunity do you have to do a number of different things?

12. How significant to others is the work you do?

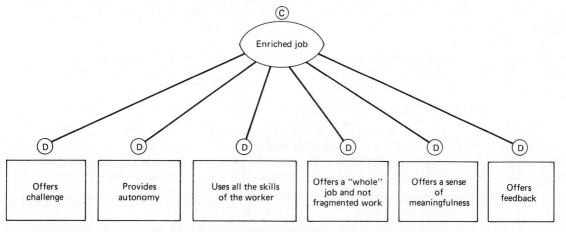

*D = dimensions and E = elements of the concept (C) of enriched jobs.

EXERCISE 5.3

Two variables that lend themselves to nominal scaling, along with mutually exclusive and collectively exhaustive categories, are as follows:

Types of Employees in a Computer Firm

☐ Accounts clerk   ☐ Systems analyst
☐ Machine operator   ☐ Supervisor
☐ Mechanic   ☐ Manager
          ☐ Other (specify)

**Types of Departments
in a Research Laboratory**

☐ Mathematics department

☐ Physics department

☐ Chemistry department

☐ Statistics department

☐ Computer sciences department

☐ Operations research department

☐ Other (specify)

EXERCISE 5.4

The following is an ordinal scale for consumer preferences for different brands of beer.

> Rank the following brands of beer in the order of your preference. In the boxes provided next to each brand name, write the number that denotes your ranking. That is, write 1 next to your favorite brand, 2 next to the next favorite one, and so on, until each brand name has a number. If you do not drink beer at all, put a check mark (√) in the last box.

☐ Budweiser   ☐ Olympia

☐ Coors   ☐ Pabst

☐ Michelob   ☐ Strohs

☐ Miller   ☐ Do not drink beer at all

EXERCISE 5.5

Three variables that could be tapped on an interval scale are morale, enthusiasm, and level of activity.

EXERCISE 5.6

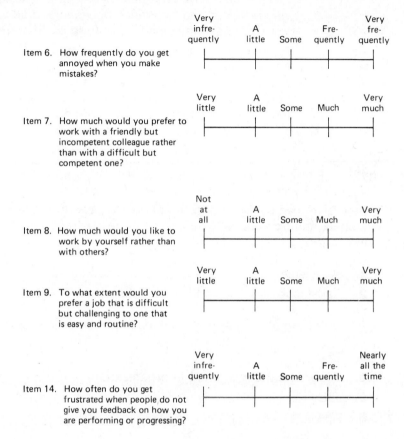

Item 6. How frequently do you get annoyed when you make mistakes?

Very infrequently — A little — Some — Frequently — Very frequently

Item 7. How much would you prefer to work with a friendly but incompetent colleague rather than with a difficult but competent one?

Very little — A little — Some — Much — Very much

Item 8. How much would you like to work by yourself rather than with others?

Not at all — A little — Some — Much — Very much

Item 9. To what extent would you prefer a job that is difficult but challenging to one that is easy and routine?

Very little — A little — Some — Much — Very much

Item 14. How often do you get frustrated when people do not give you feedback on how you are performing or progressing?

Very infrequently — A little — Some — Frequently — Nearly all the time

EXERCISE 5.7

Scale	Variable and Explanation
Nominal	Buyers of a product can be nominally grouped under three categories: those who like the product and buy, those who are indifferent to the product and buy, and those who do not like the product, yet buy it anyway.
Ordinal	Customer rank ordering of preferences for various name brands of jeans.
Interval	Extent of appeal of a particular advertisement to customers on a five point scale ranging from very little to very much. Here customers are split into five groups, they are ranked

from those who like very little to those who like very much, there is also an assessment of the *extent* of the appeal, and we know that the difference between two adjacent points in the scale have the same magnitude of difference.

Ratio | Percentage of sales increase of a product. There is an absolute zero origin (when there is no additional sale made at all during a particular year, the sales increase is zero), and a 10 percent increase in sales is twice as much as a 5 percent increase. Thus this scale has both a zero origin and a measure of proportion. Hence, it is a ratio scale.

EXERCISE 5.8

Before we can design a questionnaire, we need to list the variables to be tapped, and operationally define the more abstract concepts. The following variables are mentioned in the study:

1. Involvement (or the other end of the continuum, alienation).
2. Satisfaction with work life (i.e., satisfaction at the workplace).

The following demographic variables might be of interest to the study:

3. Sex.
4. Tenure (number of years in organization).
5. Job level.
6. Age.
7. Education.

These demographic variables are chosen because they might have an influence on the involvement (or alienation) of the employees, their level of satisfaction, and the relationship between the two.

Operational Definition of Involvement

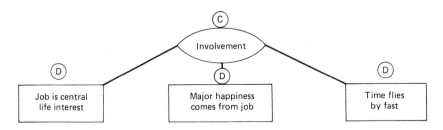

Low involvement can be considered as alienation.

Items that measure involvement are as follows:

1. The major happiness of my life comes from my job.
2. Time at work flies by quickly.
3. Working here is a drag.
4. Most things in life are more important than work.
5. I live, eat, and breathe my job.
6. My work is not the most important part of my life.

Operational Definition of Satisfaction

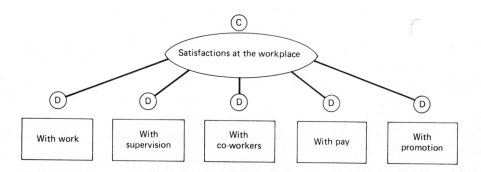

Questions that tap satisfaction at the workplace are as follows:

To what extent would you agree with the following statements?

1. My work is fascinating.
2. My work gives me a sense of accomplishment.
3. My supervisor praises good work.
4. My supervisor is not very capable.
5. My co-workers are very stimulating.
6. I get a lot of cooperation at the workplace.
7. My pay is barely adequate to take care of my expenses.
8. People can live comfortably with their pay in this organization.
9. The opportunities for advancement are very good here.
10. The promotion policies here are very unfair.

QUESTIONNAIRE

Serakan Company, Inc.

1606 E. Mars
Osio, IL 67160
December 4, 1983

Dear Employee,

As the president of your company, I am interested in conducting a minisurvey on your reactions to working in this organization. The responses you give might give me an indication of any changes that may be necessary for offering you a better quality of worklife. Your honest and straightforward answers will help me to help you. I do not need your names—only your truthful answers. Any suggestions from you will be most welcome.

Thank you for your cooperation.

Yours truly,

Anita Krish

Anita Krish, President

Personal Data

Department in which you are working: _____

┌───┐
│ Please check the boxes most appropriate for the items below. │
└───┘

Age (years)

☐ Under 25
☐ 25–35
☐ 36–45
☐ 46–55
☐ Over 55

Education

☐ High school
☐ Some college
☐ Bachelor's degree
☐ Master's degree
☐ Doctoral degree

Sex

☐ M
☐ F

Job Level

☐ Manager
☐ Supervisor
☐ Clerk
☐ Secretary
☐ Technician
☐ Other (specify)

Number of Years in this Organization

☐ Less than 1
☐ 1–3
☐ 4–8
☐ 9–15
☐ Over 15

Here are some questions that ask you to tell us how you experience your worklife in general. Please circle the appropriate number on the scales below.

To what extent would you agree with the following statements, on a scale of 1 to 7, one denoting very low agreement, and 7 denoting very high agreement.

		Very Low						Very High
1.	The major happiness of my life comes from my job.	1	2	3	4	5	6	7
2.	Time at work flies by quickly.	1	2	3	4	5	6	7
3.	Working here is a drag.	1	2	3	4	5	6	7
4.	Most things in life are more important than work.	1	2	3	4	5	6	7
5.	I live, eat, and breathe my job.	1	2	3	4	5	6	7
6.	My work is not the most important part of my life.	1	2	3	4	5	6	7
7.	My work is fascinating.	1	2	3	4	5	6	7
8.	My work gives me a sense of accomplishment.	1	2	3	4	5	6	7
9.	My supervisor praises good work.	1	2	3	4	5	6	7
10.	My supervisor is not very capable.	1	2	3	4	5	6	7
11.	My co-workers are very stimulating.	1	2	3	4	5	6	7
12.	I get a lot of cooperation at the workplace.	1	2	3	4	5	6	7
13.	My pay is barely adequate to take care of my expenses.	1	2	3	4	5	6	7
14.	People can live comfortably with their pay in this organization.	1	2	3	4	5	6	7
15.	The opportunities for advancement are very good here.	1	2	3	4	5	6	7
16.	The promotion policies here are very unfair.	1	2	3	4	5	6	7

In the space provided below, please make any comments that you may like to, regarding any aspect of the work or organization. Your suggestions for improvement will be very much appreciated.

Thank you!

APPENDIX
STATISTICAL TABLES

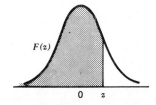

Table I

Cumulative Normal Probabilities

z	F(z)	z	F(z)	z	F(z)	z	F(z)
.00	.5000000	.36	.6405764	.72	.7642375	1.08	.8599289
.01	.5039894	.37	.6443088	.73	.7673049	1.09	.8621434
.02	.5079783	.38	.6480273	.74	.7703500	1.10	.8643339
.03	.5119665	.39	.6517317	.75	.7733726	1.11	.8665005
.04	.5159534	.40	.6554217	.76	.7763727	1.12	.8686431
.05	.5199388	.41	.6590970	.77	.7793501	1.13	.8707619
.06	.5239222	.42	.6627573	.78	.7823046	1.14	.8728568
.07	.5279032	.43	.6664022	.79	.7852361	1.15	.8749281
.08	.5318814	.44	.6700314	.80	.7881446	1.16	.8769756
.09	.5358564	.45	.6736448	.81	.7910299	1.17	.8789995
.10	.5398278	.46	.6772419	.82	.7938919	1.18	.8809999
.11	.5437953	.47	.6808225	.83	.7967306	1.19	.8829768
.12	.5477584	.48	.6843863	.84	.7995458	1.20	.8849303
.13	.5517168	.49	.6879331	.85	.8023375	1.21	.8868606
.14	.5556700	.50	.6914625	.86	.8051055	1.22	.8887676
.15	.5596177	.51	.6949743	.87	.8078498	1.23	.8906514
.16	.5635595	.52	.6984682	.88	.8105703	1.24	.8925123
.17	.5674949	.53	.7019440	.89	.8132671	1.25	.8943502
.18	.5714237	.54	.7054015	.90	.8159399	1.26	.8961653
.19	.5753454	.55	.7088403	.91	.8185887	1.27	.8979577
.20	.5792597	.56	.7122603	.92	.8212136	1.28	.8997274
.21	.5831662	.57	.7156612	.93	.8238145	1.29	.9014747
.22	.5870604	.58	.7190427	.94	.8263912	1.30	.9031995
.23	.5909541	.59	.7224047	.95	.8289439	1.31	.9049021
.24	.5948349	.60	.7257469	.96	.8314724	1.32	.9065825
.25	.5987063	.61	.7290691	.97	.8339768	1.33	.9082409
.26	.6025681	.62	.7323711	.98	.8364569	1.34	.9098773
.27	.6064199	.63	.7356527	.99	.8389129	1.35	.9114920
.28	.6102612	.64	.7389137	1.00	.8413447	1.36	.9130850
.29	.6140919	.65	.7421539	1.01	.8437524	1.37	.9146565
.30	.6179114	.66	.7453731	1.02	.8461358	1.38	.9162067
.31	.6217195	.67	.7485711	1.03	.8484950	1.39	.9177356
.32	.6255158	.68	.7517478	1.04	.8508300	1.40	.9192433
.33	.6293000	.69	.7549029	1.05	.8531409	1.41	.9207302
.34	.6330717	.70	.7580363	1.06	.8554277	1.42	.9221962
.35	.6368307	.71	.7611479	1.07	.8576903	1.43	.9236415

Table I (*Continued*)

z	F(z)	z	F(z)	z	F(z)	z	F(z)
1.44	.9250663	1.77	.9616364	2.10	.9821356	2.43	.9924506
1.45	.9264707	1.78	.9624620	2.11	.9825708	2.44	.9926564
1.46	.9278550	1.79	.9632730	2.12	.9829970	2.45	.9928572
1.47	.9292191	1.80	.9640697	2.13	.9834142	2.46	.9930531
1.48	.9305634	1.81	.9648521	2.14	.9838226	2.47	.9932443
1.49	.9318879	1.82	.9656205	2.15	.9842224	2.48	.9934309
1.50	.9331928	1.83	.9663750	2.16	.9846137	2.49	.9936128
1.51	.9344783	1.84	.9671159	2.17	.9849966	2.50	.9937903
1.52	.9357445	1.85	.9678432	2.18	.9853713	2.51	.9939634
1.53	.9369916	1.86	.9685572	2.19	.9857379	2.52	.9941323
1.54	.9382198	1.87	.9692581	2.20	.9860966	2.53	.9942969
1.55	.9394292	1.88	.9699460	2.21	.9864474	2.54	.9944574
1.56	.9406201	1.89	.9706210	2.22	.9867906	2.55	.9946139
1.57	.9417924	1.90	.9712834	2.23	.9871263	2.56	.9947664
1.58	.9429466	1.91	.9719334	2.24	.9874545	2.57	.9949151
1.59	.9440826	1.92	.9725711	2.25	.9877755	2.58	.9950600
1.60	.9452007	1.93	.9731966	2.26	.9880894	2.59	.9952012
1.61	.9463011	1.94	.9738102	2.27	.9883962	2.60	.9953388
1.62	.9473839	1.95	.9744119	2.28	.9886962	2.70	.9965330
1.63	.9484493	1.96	.9750021	2.29	.9889893	2.80	.9974449
1.64	.9494974	1.97	.9755808	2.30	.9892759	2.90	.9981342
1.65	.9505285	1.98	.9761482	2.31	.9895559	3.00	.9986501
1.66	.9515428	1.99	.9767045	2.32	.9898296	3.20	.9993129
1.67	.9525403	2.00	.9772499	2.33	.9900969	3.40	.9996631
1.68	.9535213	2.01	.9777844	2.34	.9903581	3.60	.9998409
1.69	.9544860	2.02	.9783083	2.35	.9906133	3.80	.9999277
1.70	.9554345	2.03	.9788217	2.36	.9908625	4.00	.9999683
1.71	.9563671	2.04	.9793248	2.37	.9911060	4.50	.9999966
1.72	.9572838	2.05	.9798178	2.38	.9913437	5.00	.9999997
1.73	.9581849	2.06	.9803007	2.39	.9915758	5.50	.9999999
1.74	.9590705	2.07	.9807738	2.40	.9918025		
1.75	.9599408	2.08	.9812372	2.41	.9920237		
1.76	.9607961	2.09	.9816911	2.42	.9922397		

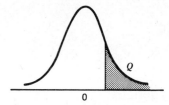

Table II

Upper Percentage Points of the *t* Distribution

v	Q = 0.4 2Q = 0.8	0.25 0.5	0.1 0.2	0.05 0.1	0.025 0.05	0.01 0.02	0.005 0.01	0.001 0.002
1	0.325	1.000	3.078	6.314	12.706	31.821	63.657	318.31
2	.289	0.816	1.886	2.920	4.303	6.965	9.925	22.326
3	.277	.765	1.638	2.353	3.182	4.541	5.841	10.213
4	.271	.741	1.533	2.132	2.776	3.747	4.604	7.173
5	0.267	0.727	1.476	2.015	2.571	3.365	4.032	5.893
6	.265	.718	1.440	1.943	2.447	3.143	3.707	5.208
7	.263	.711	1.415	1.895	2.365	2.998	3.499	4.785
8	.262	.706	1.397	1.860	2.306	2.896	3.355	4.501
9	.261	.703	1.383	1.833	2.262	2.821	3.250	4.297
10	0.260	0.700	1.372	1.812	2.228	2.764	3.169	4.144
11	.260	.697	1.363	1.796	2.201	2.718	3.106	4.025
12	.259	.695	1.356	1.782	2.179	2.681	3.055	3.930
13	.259	.694	1.350	1.771	2.160	2.650	3.012	3.852
14	.258	.692	1.345	1.761	2.145	2.624	2.977	3.787
15	0.258	0.691	1.341	1.753	2.131	2.602	2.947	3.733
16	.258	.690	1.337	1.746	2.120	2.583	2.921	3.686
17	.257	.689	1.333	1.740	2.110	2.567	2.898	3.646
18	.257	.688	1.330	1.734	2.101	2.552	2.878	3.610
19	.257	.688	1.328	1.729	2.093	2.539	2.861	3.579
20	0.257	0.687	1.325	1.725	2.086	2.528	2.845	3.552
21	.257	.686	1.323	1.721	2.080	2.518	2.831	3.527
22	.256	.686	1.321	1.717	2.074	2.508	2.819	3.505
23	.256	.685	1.319	1.714	2.069	2.500	2.807	3.485
24	.256	.685	1.318	1.711	2.064	2.492	2.797	3.467
25	0.256	0.684	1.316	1.708	2.060	2.485	2.787	3.450
26	.256	.684	1.315	1.706	2.056	2.479	2.779	3.435
27	.256	.684	1.314	1.703	2.052	2.473	2.771	3.421
28	.256	.683	1.313	1.701	2.048	2.467	2.763	3.408
29	.256	.683	1.311	1.699	2.045	2.462	2.756	3.396
30	0.256	0.683	1.310	1.697	2.042	2.457	2.750	3.385
40	.255	.681	1.303	1.684	2.021	2.423	2.704	3.307
60	.254	.679	1.296	1.671	2.000	2.390	2.660	3.232
120	.254	.677	1.289	1.658	1.980	2.358	2.617	3.160
∞	.253	.674	1.282	1.645	1.960	2.326	2.576	3.090

This table is condensed from Table 12 of the *Biometrika Tables for Statisticians*, Vol. 1 (1st ed.), edited by E. S. Pearson and H. O. Hartley. Reproduced with the kind permission of E. S. Pearson and the trustees of *Biometrika*.

Table III
Upper Percentage Points of the χ^2 Distribution

Q\ν	0.995	0.990	0.975	0.950	0.900	0.750	0.500
1	$392704 \cdot 10^{-10}$	$157088 \cdot 10^{-9}$	$982069 \cdot 10^{-9}$	$393214 \cdot 10^{-8}$	0.0157908	0.1015308	0.454937
2	0.0100251	0.0201007	0.0506356	0.102587	0.210720	0.575364	1.38629
3	0.0717212	0.114832	0.215795	0.351846	0.584375	1.212534	2.36597
4	0.206990	0.297110	0.484419	0.710721	1.063623	1.92255	3.35670
5	0.411740	0.554300	0.831211	1.145476	1.61031	2.67460	4.35146
6	0.675727	0.872085	1.237347	1.63539	2.20413	3.45460	5.34812
7	0.989265	1.239043	1.68987	2.16735	2.83311	4.25485	6.34581
8	1.344419	1.646482	2.17973	2.73264	3.48954	5.07064	7.34412
9	1.734926	2.087912	2.70039	3.32511	4.16816	5.89883	8.34283
10	2.15585	2.55821	3.24697	3.94030	4.86518	6.73720	9.34182
11	2.60321	3.05347	3.81575	4.57481	5.57779	7.58412	10.3410
12	3.07382	3.57056	4.40379	5.22603	6.30380	8.43842	11.3403
13	3.56503	4.10691	5.00874	5.89186	7.04150	9.29906	12.3398
14	4.07468	4.66043	5.62872	6.57063	7.78953	10.1653	13.3393
15	4.60094	5.22935	6.26214	7.26094	8.54675	11.0365	14.3389
16	5.14224	5.81221	6.90766	7.96164	9.31223	11.9122	15.3385
17	5.69724	6.40776	7.56418	8.67176	10.0852	12.7919	16.3381
18	6.26481	7.01491	8.23075	9.39046	10.8649	13.6753	17.3379
19	6.84398	7.63273	8.90655	10.1170	11.6509	14.5620	18.3376
20	7.43386	8.26040	9.59083	10.8508	12.4426	15.4518	19.3374
21	8.03366	8.89720	10.28293	11.5913	13.2396	16.3444	20.3372
22	8.64272	9.54249	10.9823	12.3380	14.0415	17.2396	21.3370
23	9.26042	10.19567	11.6885	13.0905	14.8479	18.1373	22.3369
24	9.88623	10.8564	12.4011	13.8484	15.6587	19.0372	23.3367
25	10.5197	11.5240	13.1197	14.6114	16.4734	19.9393	24.3366
26	11.1603	12.1981	13.8439	15.3791	17.2919	20.8434	25.3364
27	11.8076	12.8786	14.5733	16.1513	18.1138	21.7494	26.3363
28	12.4613	13.5648	15.3079	16.9279	18.9392	22.6572	27.3363
29	13.1211	14.2565	16.0471	17.7083	19.7677	23.5666	28.3362
30	13.7867	14.9535	16.7908	18.4926	20.5992	24.4776	29.3360
40	20.7065	22.1643	24.4331	26.5093	29.0505	33.6603	39.3354
50	27.9907	29.7067	32.3574	34.7642	37.6886	42.9421	49.3349
60	35.5346	37.4848	40.4817	43.1879	46.4589	52.2938	59.3347
70	43.2752	45.4418	48.7576	51.7393	55.3290	61.6983	69.3344
80	51.1720	53.5400	57.1532	60.3915	64.2778	71.1445	79.3343
90	59.1963	61.7541	65.6466	69.1260	73.2912	80.6247	89.3342
100	67.3276	70.0648	74.2219	77.9295	82.3581	90.1332	99.3341
z_Q	-2.5758	-2.3263	-1.9600	-1.6449	-1.2816	-0.6745	0.0000

Table III (*Continued*)

v \ Q	0.250	0.100	0.050	0.025	0.010	0.005	0.001
1	1.32330	2.70554	3.84146	5.02389	6.63490	7.87944	10.828
2	2.77259	4.60517	5.99147	7.37776	9.21034	10.5966	13.816
3	4.10835	6.25139	7.81473	9.34840	11.3449	12.8381	16.266
4	5.38527	7.77944	9.48773	11.1433	13.2767	14.8602	18.467
5	6.62568	9.23635	11.0705	12.8325	15.0863	16.7496	20.515
6	7.84080	10.6446	12.5916	14.4494	16.8119	18.5476	22.458
7	9.03715	12.0170	14.0671	16.0128	18.4753	20.2777	24.322
8	10.2188	13.3616	15.5073	17.5346	20.0902	21.9550	26.125
9	11.3887	14.6837	16.9190	19.0228	21.6660	23.5893	27.877
10	12.5489	15.9871	18.3070	20.4831	23.2093	25.1882	29.588
11	13.7007	17.2750	19.6751	21.9200	24.7250	26.7569	31.264
12	14.8454	18.5494	21.0261	23.3367	26.2170	28.2995	32.909
13	15.9839	19.8119	22.3621	24.7356	27.6883	29.8194	34.528
14	17.1170	21.0642	23.6848	26.1190	29.1413	31.3193	36.123
15	18.2451	22.3072	24.9958	27.4884	30.5779	32.8013	37.697
16	19.3688	23.5418	26.2962	28.8454	31.9999	34.2672	39.252
17	20.4887	24.7690	27.5871	30.1910	33.4087	35.7185	40.790
18	21.6049	25.9894	28.8693	31.5264	34.8053	37.1564	42.312
19	22.7178	27.2036	30.1435	32.8523	36.1908	38.5822	43.820
20	23.8277	28.4120	31.4104	34.1696	37.5662	39.9968	45.315
21	24.9348	29.6151	32.6705	35.4789	38.9321	41.4010	46.797
22	26.0393	30.8133	33.9244	36.7807	40.2894	42.7956	48.268
23	27.1413	32.0069	35.1725	38.0757	41.6384	44.1813	49.728
24	28.2412	33.1963	36.4151	39.3641	42.9798	45.5585	51.179
25	29.3389	34.3816	37.6525	40.6465	44.3141	46.9278	52.620
26	30.4345	35.5631	38.8852	41.9232	45.6417	48.2899	54.052
27	31.5284	36.7412	40.1133	43.1944	46.9630	49.6449	55.476
28	32.6205	37.9159	41.3372	44.4607	48.2782	50.9933	56.892
29	33.7109	39.0875	42.5569	45.7222	49.5879	52.3356	58.302
30	34.7998	40.2560	43.7729	46.9792	50.8922	53.6720	59.703
40	45.6160	51.8050	55.7585	59.3417	63.6907	66.7659	73.402
50	56.3336	63.1671	67.5048	71.4202	76.1539	79.4900	86.661
60	66.9814	74.3970	79.0819	83.2976	88.3794	91.9517	99.607
70	77.5766	85.5271	90.5312	95.0231	100.425	104.215	112.317
80	88.1303	96.5782	101.879	106.629	112.329	116.321	124.839
90	98.6499	107.565	113.145	118.136	124.116	128.299	137.208
100	109.141	118.498	124.342	129.561	135.807	140.169	149.449
z_Q	+0.6745	+1.2816	+1.6449	+1.9600	+2.3263	+2.5758	+3.0902

Table IV
Percentage Points of the F Distribution: Upper 5% Points

v_2 \ v_1	1	2	3	4	5	6	7	8	9	10	12	15	20	24	30	40	60	120	∞
1	161.4	199.5	215.7	224.6	230.2	234.0	236.8	238.9	240.5	241.9	243.9	245.9	248.0	249.1	250.1	251.1	252.2	253.3	243.3
2	18.51	19.00	19.16	19.25	19.30	19.33	19.35	19.37	19.38	19.40	19.41	19.43	19.45	19.45	19.46	19.47	19.48	19.49	19.50
3	10.13	9.55	9.28	9.12	9.01	8.94	8.89	8.85	8.81	8.79	8.74	8.70	8.66	8.64	8.62	8.59	8.57	8.55	8.53
4	7.71	6.94	6.59	6.39	6.26	6.16	6.09	6.04	6.00	5.96	5.91	5.86	5.80	5.77	5.75	5.72	5.69	5.66	5.63
5	6.61	5.79	5.41	5.19	5.05	4.95	4.88	4.82	4.77	4.74	4.68	4.62	4.56	4.53	4.50	4.46	4.43	4.40	4.36
6	5.99	5.14	4.76	4.53	4.39	4.28	4.21	4.15	4.10	4.06	4.00	3.94	3.87	3.84	3.81	3.77	3.74	3.70	3.67
7	5.59	4.74	4.35	4.12	3.97	3.87	3.79	3.73	3.68	3.64	3.57	3.51	3.44	3.41	3.38	3.34	3.30	3.27	3.23
8	5.32	4.46	4.07	3.84	3.69	3.58	3.50	3.44	3.39	3.35	3.28	3.22	3.15	3.12	3.08	3.04	3.01	2.97	2.93
9	5.12	4.26	3.86	3.63	3.48	3.37	3.29	3.23	3.18	3.14	3.07	3.01	2.94	2.90	2.86	2.83	2.79	2.75	2.71
10	4.96	4.10	3.71	3.48	3.33	3.22	3.14	3.07	3.02	2.98	2.91	2.85	2.77	2.74	2.70	2.66	2.62	2.58	2.54
11	4.84	3.98	3.59	3.36	3.20	3.09	3.01	2.95	2.90	2.85	2.79	2.72	2.65	2.61	2.57	2.53	2.49	2.45	2.40
12	4.75	3.89	3.49	3.26	3.11	3.00	2.91	2.85	2.80	2.75	2.69	2.62	2.54	2.51	2.47	2.43	2.38	2.34	2.30
13	4.67	3.81	3.41	3.18	3.03	2.92	2.83	2.77	2.71	2.67	2.60	2.53	2.46	2.42	2.38	2.34	2.30	2.25	2.21
14	4.60	3.74	3.34	3.11	2.96	2.85	2.76	2.70	2.65	2.60	2.53	2.46	2.39	2.35	2.31	2.27	2.22	2.18	2.13
15	4.54	3.68	3.29	3.06	2.90	2.79	2.71	2.64	2.59	2.54	2.48	2.40	2.33	2.29	2.25	2.20	2.16	2.11	2.07
16	4.49	3.63	3.24	3.01	2.85	2.74	2.66	2.59	2.54	2.49	2.42	2.35	2.28	2.24	2.19	2.15	2.11	2.06	2.01
17	4.45	3.59	3.20	2.96	2.81	2.70	2.61	2.55	2.49	2.45	2.38	2.31	2.23	2.19	2.15	2.10	2.06	2.01	1.96
18	4.41	3.55	3.16	2.93	2.77	2.66	2.58	2.51	2.46	2.41	2.34	2.27	2.19	2.15	2.11	2.06	2.02	1.97	1.92
19	4.38	3.52	3.13	2.90	2.74	2.63	2.54	2.48	2.42	2.38	2.31	2.23	2.16	2.11	2.07	2.03	1.98	1.93	1.88
20	4.35	3.49	3.10	2.87	2.71	2.60	2.51	2.45	2.39	2.35	2.28	2.20	2.12	2.08	2.04	1.99	1.95	1.90	1.84
21	4.32	3.47	3.07	2.84	2.68	2.57	2.49	2.42	2.37	2.32	2.25	2.18	2.10	2.05	2.01	1.96	1.92	1.87	1.81
22	4.30	3.44	3.05	2.82	2.66	2.55	2.46	2.40	2.34	2.30	2.23	2.15	2.07	2.03	1.98	1.94	1.89	1.84	1.78
23	4.28	3.42	3.03	2.80	2.64	2.53	2.44	2.37	2.32	2.27	2.20	2.13	2.05	2.01	1.96	1.91	1.86	1.81	1.76
24	4.26	3.40	3.01	2.78	2.62	2.51	2.42	2.36	2.30	2.25	2.18	2.11	2.03	1.98	1.94	1.89	1.84	1.79	1.73
25	4.24	3.39	2.99	2.76	2.60	2.49	2.40	2.34	2.28	2.24	2.16	2.09	2.01	1.96	1.92	1.87	1.82	1.77	1.71
26	4.23	3.37	2.98	2.74	2.59	2.47	2.39	2.32	2.27	2.22	2.15	2.07	1.99	1.95	1.90	1.85	1.80	1.75	1.69
27	4.21	3.35	2.96	2.73	2.57	2.46	2.37	2.31	2.25	2.20	2.13	2.06	1.97	1.93	1.88	1.84	1.79	1.73	1.67
28	4.20	3.34	2.95	2.71	2.56	2.45	2.36	2.29	2.24	2.19	2.12	2.04	1.96	1.91	1.87	1.82	1.77	1.71	1.65
29	4.18	3.33	2.93	2.70	2.55	2.43	2.35	2.28	2.22	2.18	2.10	2.03	1.94	1.90	1.85	1.81	1.75	1.70	1.64
30	4.17	3.32	2.92	2.69	2.53	2.42	2.33	2.27	2.21	2.16	2.09	2.01	1.93	1.89	1.84	1.79	1.74	1.68	1.62
40	4.08	3.23	2.84	2.61	2.45	2.34	2.25	2.18	2.12	2.08	2.00	1.92	1.84	1.79	1.74	1.69	1.64	1.58	1.51
60	4.00	3.15	2.76	2.53	2.37	2.25	2.17	2.10	2.04	1.99	1.92	1.84	1.75	1.70	1.65	1.59	1.53	1.47	1.39
120	3.92	3.07	2.68	2.45	2.29	2.17	2.09	2.02	1.96	1.91	1.83	1.75	1.66	1.61	1.55	1.50	1.43	1.35	1.25
∞	3.84	3.00	2.60	2.37	2.21	2.10	2.01	1.94	1.88	1.83	1.75	1.67	1.57	1.52	1.46	1.39	1.32	1.22	1.00

Table IV (Continued)

Upper 2.5% Points

v_2 \ v_1	1	2	3	4	5	6	7	8	9	10	12	15	20	24	30	40	60	120	∞
1	647.8	799.5	864.2	899.6	921.8	937.1	948.2	956.7	963.3	968.6	976.7	984.9	993.1	997.2	1001	1006	1010	1014	1018
2	38.51	39.00	39.17	39.25	39.30	39.33	39.36	39.37	39.39	39.40	39.41	39.43	39.45	39.46	39.46	39.47	39.48	39.49	39.50
3	17.44	16.04	15.44	15.10	14.88	14.73	14.62	14.54	14.47	14.42	14.34	14.25	14.17	14.12	14.08	14.04	13.99	13.95	13.90
4	12.22	10.65	9.98	9.60	9.36	9.20	9.07	8.98	8.90	8.84	8.75	8.66	8.56	8.51	8.46	8.41	8.36	8.31	8.26
5	10.01	8.43	7.76	7.39	7.15	6.98	6.85	6.76	6.68	6.62	6.52	6.43	6.33	6.28	6.23	6.18	6.12	6.07	6.02
6	8.81	7.26	6.60	6.23	5.99	5.82	5.70	5.60	5.52	5.46	5.37	5.27	5.17	5.12	5.07	5.01	4.96	4.90	4.85
7	8.07	6.54	5.89	5.52	5.29	5.21	4.99	4.90	4.82	4.76	4.67	4.57	4.47	4.42	4.36	4.31	4.25	4.20	4.14
8	7.57	6.06	5.42	5.05	4.82	4.65	4.53	4.43	4.36	4.30	4.20	4.10	4.00	3.95	3.89	3.84	3.78	3.73	3.67
9	7.21	5.71	5.08	4.72	4.48	4.32	4.20	4.10	4.03	3.96	3.87	3.77	3.67	3.61	3.56	3.51	3.45	3.39	3.33
10	6.94	5.46	4.83	4.47	4.24	4.07	3.95	3.85	3.78	3.72	3.62	3.52	3.42	3.37	3.31	3.26	3.20	3.14	3.08
11	6.72	5.26	4.63	4.28	4.04	3.88	3.76	3.66	3.59	3.53	3.43	3.33	3.23	3.17	3.12	3.06	3.00	2.94	2.88
12	6.55	5.10	4.47	4.12	3.89	3.73	3.61	3.51	3.44	3.37	3.28	3.18	3.07	3.02	2.96	2.91	2.85	2.79	2.72
13	6.41	4.97	4.35	4.00	3.77	3.60	3.48	3.39	3.31	3.25	3.15	3.05	2.95	2.89	2.84	2.78	2.72	2.66	2.60
14	6.30	4.86	4.24	3.89	3.66	3.50	3.38	3.29	3.21	3.15	3.05	2.95	2.84	2.79	2.73	2.67	2.61	2.55	2.49
15	6.20	4.77	4.15	3.80	3.58	3.41	3.29	3.20	3.12	3.06	2.96	2.86	2.76	2.70	2.64	2.59	2.52	2.46	2.40
16	6.12	4.69	4.08	3.73	3.50	3.34	3.22	3.12	3.05	2.99	2.89	2.79	2.68	2.63	2.57	2.51	2.45	2.38	2.32
17	6.04	4.62	4.01	3.66	3.44	3.28	3.16	3.06	2.98	2.92	2.82	2.72	2.62	2.56	2.50	2.44	2.38	2.32	2.25
18	5.98	4.56	3.95	3.61	3.38	3.22	3.10	3.01	2.93	2.87	2.77	2.67	2.56	2.50	2.44	2.38	2.32	2.26	2.19
19	5.92	4.51	3.90	3.56	3.33	3.17	3.05	2.96	2.88	2.82	2.72	2.62	2.51	2.45	2.39	2.33	2.27	2.20	2.13
20	5.87	4.46	3.86	3.51	3.29	3.13	3.01	2.91	2.84	2.77	2.68	2.57	2.46	2.41	2.35	2.29	2.22	2.16	2.09
21	5.83	4.42	3.82	3.48	3.25	3.09	2.97	2.87	2.80	2.73	2.64	2.53	2.42	2.37	2.31	2.25	2.18	2.11	2.04
22	5.79	4.38	3.78	3.44	3.22	3.05	2.93	2.84	2.76	2.70	2.60	2.50	2.39	2.33	2.27	2.21	2.14	2.08	2.00
23	5.75	4.35	3.75	3.41	3.18	3.02	2.90	2.81	2.73	2.67	2.57	2.47	2.36	2.30	2.24	2.18	2.11	2.04	1.97
24	5.72	4.32	3.72	3.38	3.15	2.99	2.87	2.78	2.70	2.64	2.54	2.44	2.33	2.27	2.21	2.15	2.08	2.01	1.94
25	5.69	4.29	3.69	3.35	3.13	2.97	2.85	2.75	2.68	2.61	2.51	2.41	2.30	2.24	2.18	2.12	2.05	1.98	1.91
26	5.66	4.27	3.67	3.33	3.10	2.94	2.82	2.73	2.65	2.59	2.49	2.39	2.28	2.22	2.16	2.09	2.03	1.95	1.88
27	5.63	4.24	3.65	3.31	3.08	2.92	2.80	2.71	2.63	2.57	2.47	2.36	2.25	2.19	2.13	2.07	2.00	1.93	1.85
28	5.61	4.22	3.63	3.29	3.06	2.90	2.78	2.69	2.61	2.55	2.45	2.34	2.23	2.17	2.11	2.05	1.98	1.91	1.83
29	5.59	4.20	3.61	3.27	3.04	2.88	2.76	2.67	2.59	2.53	2.43	2.32	2.21	2.15	2.09	2.03	1.96	1.89	1.81
30	5.57	4.18	3.59	3.25	3.03	2.87	2.75	2.65	2.57	2.51	2.41	2.31	2.20	2.14	2.07	2.01	1.94	1.87	1.79
40	5.42	4.05	3.46	3.13	2.90	2.74	2.62	2.53	2.45	2.39	2.29	2.18	2.07	2.01	1.94	1.88	1.80	1.72	1.64
60	5.29	3.93	3.34	3.01	2.79	2.63	2.51	2.41	2.33	2.27	2.17	2.06	1.94	1.88	1.82	1.74	1.67	1.58	1.48
120	5.15	3.80	3.23	2.89	2.67	2.52	2.39	2.30	2.22	2.16	2.05	1.94	1.82	1.76	1.69	1.61	1.53	1.43	1.31
∞	5.02	3.69	3.12	2.79	2.57	2.41	2.29	2.19	2.11	2.05	1.94	1.83	1.71	1.64	1.57	1.48	1.39	1.27	1.00

Table IV (Continued)
Upper 1% Points

ν₂＼ν₁	1	2	3	4	5	6	7	8	9	10	12	15	20	24	30	40	60	120	∞
1	4052	4999.5	5403	5625	5764	5859	5928	5982	6022	6056	6106	6157	6209	6235	6261	6287	6313	6339	6366
2	98.50	99.00	99.17	99.25	99.30	99.33	99.36	99.37	99.39	99.40	99.42	99.43	99.45	99.46	99.47	99.47	99.48	99.49	99.50
3	34.12	30.82	29.46	28.71	28.24	27.91	27.67	27.49	27.35	27.23	27.05	26.87	26.69	26.60	26.50	26.41	26.32	26.22	26.13
4	21.20	18.00	16.69	15.98	15.52	15.21	14.98	14.80	14.66	14.55	14.37	14.20	14.02	13.93	13.84	13.75	13.65	13.56	13.46
5	16.26	13.27	12.06	11.39	10.97	10.67	10.46	10.29	10.16	10.05	9.89	9.72	9.55	9.47	9.38	9.29	9.20	9.11	9.06
6	13.75	10.92	9.78	9.15	8.75	8.47	8.26	8.10	7.98	7.87	7.72	7.56	7.40	7.31	7.23	7.14	7.06	6.97	6.88
7	12.25	9.55	8.45	7.85	7.46	7.19	6.99	6.84	6.72	6.62	6.47	6.31	6.16	6.07	5.99	5.91	5.82	5.74	5.65
8	11.26	8.65	7.59	7.01	6.63	6.37	6.18	6.03	5.91	5.81	5.67	5.52	5.36	5.28	5.20	5.12	5.03	4.95	4.86
9	10.56	8.02	6.99	6.42	6.06	5.80	5.61	5.47	5.35	5.26	5.11	4.96	4.81	4.73	4.65	4.57	4.48	4.40	4.31
10	10.04	7.56	6.55	5.99	5.64	5.39	5.20	5.06	4.94	4.85	4.71	4.56	4.41	4.33	4.25	4.17	4.08	4.00	3.91
11	9.65	7.21	6.22	5.67	5.32	5.07	4.89	4.74	4.63	4.54	4.40	4.25	4.10	4.02	3.94	3.86	3.78	3.69	3.60
12	9.33	6.93	5.95	5.41	5.06	4.82	4.64	4.50	4.39	4.30	4.16	4.01	3.86	3.78	3.70	3.62	3.54	3.45	3.36
13	9.07	6.70	5.74	5.21	4.86	4.62	4.44	4.30	4.19	4.10	3.96	3.82	3.66	3.59	3.51	3.43	3.34	3.25	3.17
14	8.86	6.51	5.56	5.04	4.69	4.46	4.28	4.14	4.03	3.94	3.80	3.66	3.51	3.43	3.35	3.27	3.18	3.09	3.00
15	8.68	6.36	5.42	4.89	4.56	4.32	4.14	4.00	3.89	3.80	3.67	3.52	3.37	3.29	3.21	3.13	3.05	2.96	2.87
16	8.53	6.23	5.29	4.77	4.44	4.20	4.03	3.89	3.78	3.69	3.55	3.41	3.26	3.18	3.10	3.02	2.93	2.84	2.75
17	8.40	6.11	5.18	4.67	4.34	4.10	3.93	3.79	3.68	3.59	3.46	3.31	3.16	3.08	3.00	2.92	2.83	2.75	2.65
18	8.29	6.01	5.09	4.58	4.25	4.01	3.84	3.71	3.60	3.51	3.37	3.23	3.08	3.00	2.92	2.84	2.75	2.66	2.57
19	8.18	5.93	5.01	4.50	4.17	3.94	3.77	3.63	3.52	3.43	3.30	3.15	3.00	2.92	2.84	2.76	2.67	2.58	2.49
20	8.10	5.85	4.94	4.43	4.10	3.87	3.70	3.56	3.46	3.37	3.23	3.09	2.94	2.86	2.78	2.69	2.61	2.52	2.42
21	8.02	5.78	4.87	4.37	4.04	3.81	3.64	3.51	3.40	3.31	3.17	3.03	2.88	2.80	2.72	2.64	2.55	2.46	2.36
22	7.95	5.72	4.82	4.31	3.99	3.76	3.59	3.45	3.35	3.26	3.12	2.98	2.83	2.75	2.67	2.58	2.50	2.40	2.31
23	7.88	5.66	4.76	4.26	3.94	3.71	3.54	3.41	3.30	3.21	3.07	2.93	2.78	2.70	2.62	2.54	2.45	2.35	2.26
24	7.82	5.61	4.72	4.22	3.90	3.67	3.50	3.36	3.26	3.17	3.03	2.89	2.74	2.66	2.58	2.49	2.40	2.31	2.21
25	7.77	5.57	4.68	4.18	3.85	3.63	3.46	3.32	3.22	3.13	2.99	2.85	2.70	2.62	2.54	2.45	2.36	2.27	2.17
26	7.72	5.53	4.64	4.14	3.82	3.59	3.42	3.29	3.18	3.09	2.96	2.81	2.66	2.58	2.50	2.42	2.33	2.23	2.13
27	7.68	5.49	4.60	4.11	3.78	3.56	3.39	3.26	3.15	3.06	2.93	2.78	2.63	2.55	2.47	2.38	2.29	2.20	2.10
28	7.64	5.45	4.57	4.07	3.75	3.53	3.36	3.23	3.12	3.03	2.90	2.75	2.60	2.52	2.44	2.35	2.26	2.17	2.06
29	7.60	5.42	4.54	4.04	3.73	3.50	3.33	3.20	3.09	3.00	2.87	2.73	2.57	2.49	2.41	2.33	2.23	2.14	2.03
30	7.56	5.39	4.51	4.02	3.70	3.47	3.30	3.17	3.07	2.98	2.84	2.70	2.55	2.47	2.39	2.30	2.21	2.11	2.01
40	7.31	5.18	4.31	3.83	3.51	3.29	3.12	2.99	2.89	2.80	2.66	2.52	2.37	2.29	2.20	2.11	2.02	1.92	1.80
60	7.08	4.98	4.13	3.65	3.34	3.12	2.95	2.82	2.72	2.63	2.50	2.35	2.20	2.12	2.03	1.94	1.84	1.73	1.60
120	6.85	4.79	3.95	3.48	3.17	2.96	2.79	2.66	2.56	2.47	2.34	2.19	2.03	1.95	1.86	1.76	1.66	1.53	1.38
∞	6.63	4.61	3.78	3.32	3.02	2.80	2.64	2.51	2.41	2.32	2.18	2.04	1.88	1.79	1.70	1.59	1.47	1.32	1.00

INDEX